Vegetarianism

Vegetarianism
A Way of Life

Dudley Giehl

Foreword by

Isaac Bashevis Singer

BARNES & NOBLE BOOKS
A DIVISION OF HARPER & ROW, PUBLISHERS
New York, Cambridge, Hagerstown,
Philadelphia, San Francisco, London,
Mexico City, São Paulo, Sydney

Grateful acknowledgment is made for permission to reprint: Chart on pages 18 and 19, from "Nutritional Studies of Vegetarians" by Mervyn G. Hardinge, M.D., Hulda Crooks, and Frederick J. Stare, M.D. Reprinted by permission from *Journal of the American Dietetic Association*, Vol. 48: 27, 1966. Copyright 1966 by The American Dietetic Association.

Chart on page 35, from "The Role of Nutritional Factors in the Prevention of Coronary Heart Disease" by William E. Connor and Sonja L. Connor. Reprinted from *Preventive Medicine*, Vol. 1, Academic Press, 1972, p. 52.

Chart on page 36, from "Diet and the Epidemology of Coronary Heart Disease" by Ancel Keys. Reprinted from the *Journal of the American Medical Association*, Vol. 164, No. 17 (August 24, 1957), p. 1916. Copyright 1957, American Medical Association.

Chart on page 37, from "Serum-Cholesterol, Diet, and Coronary Heart-Disease: An Inter-Racial Survey in the Cape Peninsula" by B. Bronte-Stewart, Ancel Keys, J. F. Brock. Reprinted from *Lancet*, November 26, 1955, p. 1105.

Figure on page 74, from *Vegetable Protein Meat Extenders and Analogues* by Zbigniew Duda, FAO of UN, 1974, p. 5. Reprinted by permission of the Food and Agriculture Organization of the United Nations.

First BARNES & NOBLE BOOKS edition published 1981.

ISBN: 0-06-464045-0   (previously ISBN: 0-06-011504-1)

81 82 83 84 85 10 9 8 7 6 5 4 3 2 1

Contents

v

Foreword

by

Isaac Bashevis Singer

Even though the number of people who commit suicide is quite small, there are few people who have never thought about suicide at one time or another. The same is true about vegetarianism. We find very few people who have never thought that killing animals is actually murder, founded on the premise that might is right. This is true today and it was also true in ancient times as Dudley Giehl shows in his work *Vegetarianism, A Way of Life*. Ovid, Plutarch, Porphyry, and in later generations, Byron and Shelley and still later, Bernard Shaw and Edward Fitzgerald were all interested in this question—I will call it the eternal question: What gives man the right to kill an animal, often torture it, so that he can fill his belly with its flesh? We know now, as we have always known instinctively, that animals can suffer as much as human beings. Their emotions and their sensitivity are often stronger than those of a human being. Various philosophers and religious leaders tried to convince their disciples and followers that animals are nothing more than machines without a soul, without feelings. However, anyone who has ever lived with an animal—be it a dog, a bird, or even a mouse—knows that this theory is a brazen lie, invented to justify cruelty.

The only justification for killing animals is the fact that man can keep a knife or an ax in his hands and is shrewd enough and selfish enough to do slaughter for what he thinks is his own good. The

Old Testament has many passages where the passion for meat is considered to be evil. According to the Bible, it was only a compromise with so-called human nature that God has allowed people to eat meat. I'm often astonished when I read about highly sensitive poets, preachers of morality, humanists, and do-gooders of all kinds who found pleasure in hunting—chasing after some poor, weak hare or fox and teaching dogs to do likewise. I often read of people who say that when they retire they will go fishing. They say this with an understanding that from then on they won't do any damage to anybody. An epoch of charity and tranquillity will begin in their life. It never occurs to them for a moment that innocent beings will suffer and die from this innocent little sport.

Dudley Giehl seems to have the same feelings as I do because not only is he a vegetarian but he has devoted his life to arousing people's consciences in this matter—to tell them again and again that by eating the flesh of animals, by hunting, they are committing murder all the time. All their nice talk about humanism, a better tomorrow, a beautiful future, has no meaning at all as long as they kill to eat or kill for pleasure. It is true that there is no evidence whatsoever that nature or even God is against the killing of animals. But is there any evidence that nature is against killing human beings? The earth receives all kinds of blood. It does not discriminate.

I, personally, am very pessimistic about the hope that humanity's disregard for animals will end soon. I'm sometimes afraid that we are approaching an epoch where the hunting of human beings may become a sport. But it is good that there are some people who express a deep protest against the killing and torturing of the helpless, playing with their fear of death, enjoying their misery. Even if God or nature sides with the killers, the vegetarian is saying: I protest the ways of God and man. We may admire God's wisdom but we are not obliged to praise what seems to us His lack of mercy. It may be that somewhere the Almighty has an answer for what He is doing. It may be that one day we will grasp His answer. But as long as we don't understand it, we shouldn't agree and we shouldn't flatter Him.

I do not fool myself in thinking that Mr. Giehl's book will bring about an end to human cruelty, but at least it will stir some minds. And, as a vegetarian, I'm grateful to him for doing this so well. I personally believe that as long as human beings will go on shedding the blood of animals, there will never be any peace. There is only one little step from killing animals to creating gas chambers à la Hitler and concentration camps à la Stalin—all such deeds are done in the name of "social justice." There will be no justice as long as man will stand with a knife or with a gun and destroy those who are weaker than he is. In the name of myriads of oxen, cows, chickens, pigs, fish and other animals, I say, "Thank you, Mr. Giehl. Let people know they are not so good as they think they are and that they deserve many of the misfortunes that come upon them for being so cold-bloodedly indifferent to all of us."

ISAAC BASHEVIS SINGER

Introduction

The subject of vegetarianism has attracted much attention in recent years. Unfortunately, the general public has been exposed to a great deal of misinformation on its various aspects.

Some writers have cited quirky vegetarian diets which are clearly inadequate as proof that vegetarians are undernourished. Either through malice or ignorance, these writers fail to note that poor eating habits, and not vegetarianism per se, are the cause of malnutrition in the cases they have presented. If a particular individual or group of individuals follows a vegetarian diet which is deficient in one or more nutrients, the emphasis of the study should be on the deficient nutrients and not on vegetarian diets in general, simply because the malnourished subject happens to be a vegetarian. In a case study done on flesh eaters who develop scurvy, the emphasis will be placed on their inadequate intake of vitamin C and not on the fact that they happen to be flesh eaters. Very simply, flesh foods contain no nutrients that cannot be obtained from non-flesh-food sources.

In addition to misleading reports on the nutritional aspects of vegetarian diets, many books and articles which deal with vegetarianism as a lifestyle are highly misleading. Many articles have referred to the macrobiotic diet as vegetarian when, in fact, many persons who follow that diet eat fish and are therefore not really vegetarians. Some writers' knowledge of vegetarianism is evidently based on interviews they have had with a few individual vegetarians or a particular group of individuals who follow this diet. In discussing the vegan diet, one writer comments: "Food is eaten in its whole, unprocessed, natural raw state." This writer later remarks: "Alcohol, tea, coffee, soft drinks, tobacco, and vitamins are taboo." This characterization of veganism as a sect which includes abstinence from alcohol, tobacco, and cooked food among its tenets is quite ridiculous. Indeed, the only thing that all vegans have in common is their abstinence from all types of animal foods, including dairy products and eggs as well as meat. Otherwise, their dietary and other personal habits are quite diverse. A considerable number of vegans do, in fact, smoke tobacco and drink alcohol.

Aside from the vegetarian stereotypes that are presented by ill-informed writers, stereotypical images of vegetarians are also presented by vegetarian writers who dogmatically postulate that vegetarianism is somehow necessarily connected to a particular lifestyle. Porphyry (232?–304?) explicitly states that his lengthy treatise on vegetarianism is addressed to the intelligentsia. He does not feel that the common people would be swayed by his arguments, which deal largely with vegetarianism as an ethical issue. The contemporary writer Hans Holzer includes abstinence from alcoholic beverages and tobacco among "vegetarian guidelines" that are listed in his book, *The Vegetarian Way of Life*.

It is really quite silly to create a stereotype of vegetarians, since there are many different reasons why people have adopted this diet, e.g., for reasons of health, ethics, religion, ecology, economics. Moreover, even among those who are motivated to abstain from flesh food for any of the aforementioned reasons, there are highly diverse personalities. Jack Lucas, a member of the Science Council of the International Vegetarian Union, views vegetarianism and the need to develop nuclear power as pressing ecological issues. In his book *Our Polluted Food* Lucas advocates both vegetarianism and nuclear power, connecting these issues to various problems associated with industrial and agricultural pollution. There are, however, many vegetarians concerned with ecological issues who have spoken out against nuclear power. Indeed, articles opposing nuclear power have appeared in American and British vegetarian journals. There are many vegetarians who belong to the "Clamshell Alliance," a U.S. antinuclear group noted for their civil-disobedience tactics. Many individuals are deeply committed to vegetarianism as an ethical issue out of a respect for all animals. However, it is certainly not possible to stereotype the ethical philosophy of these vegetarians, since their position on other ethical issues is quite diverse. India's freedom was won through the effective passive-resistance campaign led by Mohandas Gandhi. However, the notion that ethically motivated vegetarians are all pacifists like Tolstoy and Gandhi is quickly dispelled by citing Air Chief Marshal Hugh Dowding, commander of the British Royal Air Force during World War II. Air Chief Marshal Dowding is best known for winning the crucial Battle of Britain, in which his vastly outnumbered R.A.F. pilots repulsed the major offensive launched by Germany's Luftwaffe.

The politics of vegetarians runs the gamut of political ideologies. Vegetarians as a whole do not even hold similar views on various issues relating to food and nutrition. Some have adopted ascetic eating habits while others who are true gourmets take great pride in their ability to prepare all sorts of elaborate, savory vegetarian concoctions. Some do not use any kind of spices, while others, particularly those in India, relish heavily spiced dishes. Some vegetarians use eggs and dairy products. Some abstain from eggs but use dairy products. Some abstain from all animal products, including honey. Some drink alcoholic beverages while others are strict teetotalers. Some are connoisseurs of fine coffee while others characterize this beverage as a poison. Some use only bottled spring water or distilled water because fluoride is added to most municipal water reservoirs. Some eat only organically grown foods. Some have a penchant for so-called "junk foods" like pastries, pretzels, and potato chips, which have little nutritional value.

These are only a few of the many items that can be cited to illustrate the point that vegetarians are a highly diverse group of individuals. Indeed, the only thing that vegetarians as a whole have in common is their practice of abstaining from the flesh of animals.

This book covers a wide range of issues on vegetarianism. Some of these, such as health, have a profound effect on our daily lives. Some issues, such as ethics, are philosophical in nature. Others, such as esoteric religious concepts, are strictly academic in nature but are, nonetheless, interesting from a historical standpoint.

I have used more numbered bibliographic notes than may seem necessary. This was done in order to direct the reader to background material on various issues discussed, in addition to citing sources for quotes and information of a somewhat controversial nature that one might ordinarily wish to read in its original context.

Vegetarianism

1

The Three Basic
Vegetarian Diets

There are three basic vegetarian diets: the lacto-ovo, lacto, and vegan. The lacto-ovo diet includes the use of eggs and dairy products—*lacto* referring to dairy and *ovo* referring to eggs. People classified as lacto vegetarians use dairy products but, unlike their lacto-ovo counterparts, they do not use eggs or any foodstuffs made with eggs. Vegans do not use eggs, dairy products, or any foodstuffs prepared with eggs or dairy products. Many vegans also do not use honey. In addition to eliminating all types of animal foodstuffs from their diet, a considerable number of vegans also avoid using nonfood animal products, e.g., leather, fur, wool, etc. These practices are based on an ethical philosophy that it is wrong to kill animals or to exploit them in any way.

THE LACTO-OVO DIET

Most vegetarian gourmets favor the lacto-ovo diet over the lacto vegetarian or vegan diets simply because it allows for greater variety in the types of dishes one might wish to make. Eggs and/or dairy products are important ingredients in such popular items as pancakes, soufflés and pastries. Aside from their frequent use in such concoctions, dairy products and eggs in themselves offer lacto-ovo vegetarians much variety. Eggs can be prepared several different ways, e.g., scrambled, fried, poached, hard-boiled. Milk is processed in many different ways to produce a wide variety of items, including yogurt, ice cream, butter, and cheese. Indeed, the scope of this variety may be noted in the fact that there are more than 400 different types of cheeses.

Aside from the question of variety, there are certain health advantages in adopting the lacto-ovo diet. Both dairy products and eggs are a source of complete protein, since sufficient amounts of all the essential amino acids are found in either of these foods.* While it is possible for vegans to fulfill their nutritional requirement for complete protein by combining different types of plant protein foods, it is simply more convenient to obtain one's complete protein from eggs and dairy products. It should be noted, however, that certain dairy products, such as butter, are very poor sources of protein. Also, while fluid whole milk contains all the essential amino acids, its protein content is relatively low. The best sources of complete protein for lacto-ovo vegetarians would be cheese and eggs. Aside from their high protein content, both eggs and cheese are recognized as excellent protein foods as measured in terms of "net protein utilization." Net protein utilization represents the "digestibility" as well as the biological value of a given protein food. Digestibility denotes the proportion of a food's protein (measured by its nitrogen constituent) which is absorbed from the intestine. The term "biological value" refers to the amount of protein (measured by its nitrogen constituent) which is retained in the body after being absorbed from the intestine.† In terms of net protein utilization, eggs are considered to be the most nearly perfect protein food.

In addition to being a good source of complete protein, eggs and several types of dairy products are good sources of vitamin B_{12}. One's need for this vitamin is adequately fulfilled in a lacto-ovo vegetarian diet. Vitamin B_{12} is not present to any significant extent in foods of plant origin. It should also be noted that a considerable amount of B_{12} is destroyed in the processing of certain dairy products, such as evaporated milk and yogurt. Consequently, these foods are poor sources of vitamin B_{12}.

The most serious health objection to the lacto-ovo diet is that it is undesirably high in dietary cholesterol notwithstanding the fact that lacto-ovo vegetarians generally have significantly lower serum

---

* See Chapter 2, "The Protein Myth," pp. 17–20.
† Methodology for measuring "digestibility," "biological value," and "net protein utilization" can be found in *Hawk's Physiological Chemistry*, 14th ed., pp. 858–59.

cholesterol levels than flesh eaters. The yolks of eggs are the single greatest source of dietary cholesterol.

The apparent relationship between cholesterol intake and heart disease has naturally been a major cause of concern to egg producers. In an attempt to counter this adverse publicity, U.S. egg producers established a group which called itself the National Commission on Egg Nutrition to promote their product. This commission's report, which appeared in ads and booklets, declared: "There is absolutely no scientific evidence that eating eggs, even in quantity, will increase the risk of a heart attack." The American Heart Association and four public-interest-law groups asked the Federal Trade Commission to prohibit this "false, deceptive and misleading advertising."[1] More than a year after the injunction against the egg commission's deceptive advertising campaign was sought, a Federal Trade Commission judge ruled against the egg industry. In his 101-page decision, Judge Ernest G. Barnes ruled that statements made by the so-called National Commission on Egg Nutrition in its ads were "false, misleading, deceptive and unfair." He further declared: "There exists a substantial body of competent and reliable scientific evidence that eating eggs increases the risk of heart attacks or heart disease . . . this evidence is systematic, consistent, strong and congruent."[2]

Most Europeans and Americans, upon deciding to become vegetarians, adopt the lacto-ovo vegetarian diet. There are two basic reasons for this: (1) Many people are quite unfamiliar with the vegan diet. (2) Even those who fully intend to take up the more restrictive lacto vegetarian or vegan diet, find that the transition is made easier by first adopting the lacto-ovo vegetarian diet on a temporary basis. Many of these people have stated that giving up meat was relatively easy but that to break the habit of using eggs and especially dairy products required a great deal of will power. Indeed, there are many lacto-ovo vegetarians who view the vegan diet as an ideal lifestyle which they would like to adopt at some future period.

THE LACTO DIET

Eliminating eggs from one's diet is certainly helpful in maintaining desirable serum cholesterol levels—a major concern to most Americans since heart disease is a leading cause of death in the United

States. Notwithstanding the fact that the protein one obtains from eggs is superior to the quality of protein obtained from any type of dairy product, milk has been referred to as nature's most perfect food. Indeed, milk and many products made from milk contain protein, fat, and carbohydrates. Milk is also a rich source of calcium and phosphorus. However, milk is hardly a perfect food. It is a poor source of iron and contains essentially no vitamin C. Moreover, most grains, including cereal products, are better sources of vitamin B_1 than milk. Curiously enough, milk is often cited as a good source of vitamin D. Actually, milk in its natural state is a poor source of vitamin D. It is fortified with vitamin D, as required by law in the United States and many western European countries. Some countries, such as France, prohibit the fortification of milk with vitamin D.

While milk and various types of milk products are basically good, wholesome foods, the human need for these foods has been grossly exaggerated by the dairy industry. In recent U.S. congressional hearings on nutrition education, it was pointed out that the National Dairy Council's recommendation to drink three or more glasses of milk each day is hardly in accord with good nutritional practices. Specifically, it was noted that the Dairy Council's recommended daily calcium intake was far in excess of the recommendations set by leading scientific groups, such as the World Health Organization and the National Academy of Sciences.[3] The Federal Trade Commission was particularly displeased with a series of commercials, sponsored by the California Milk Producers' Advisory Board, which represented milk as an essential food and suggested that milk drinking was a possible means of preventing colds. In one commercial the "Dear Abby" columnist stated: "I very seldom have a cold . . . and I think I probably can attribute that to the fact I have been a milk drinker all my life." In another commercial, a well-known Olympic swimming champion asserted: "I think milk is something your body really needs." The Federal Trade Commission's complaint against the California Milk Producers' Advisory Board, filed in a Washington, D.C., federal district court on April 10, 1974, notes that milk is not an essential food, that "not everyone can consume large or unlimited quantities without any adverse health effects . . . ," and that statements to the contrary are "false and misleading." People who suffer from heart disease and "milk intolerant" persons would certainly be among those whose health would be adversely affected by heavy milk consumption.

A significant portion of the world's population is not able to digest milk properly after early childhood because of a lactase deficiency. Lactase is an enzyme (present in the intestine) which facilitates the digestion of milk by splitting lactose (a disaccharide) into glucose and galactose, which are then absorbed and metabolized in the tissues. While all newborn mammals have considerably high levels of lactase, this enzyme disappears at some period during childhood in all species except the human being and the domesticated cat. The continued presence of lactase in human beings after childhood has been generally attributed to an evolutionary change. Indeed, the lactase enzyme is commonly found in adult populations of ethnic groups that have a long tradition of using the milk of domesticated animals throughout their life, e.g., European Caucasians and the people of India. Conversely, a considerable segment of ethnic populations which do not have a long tradition of milk drinking (e.g., Asians, Arabs, native Indians of North and South America, and Africans) are not able to digest milk properly because the lactase enzyme is not present in their intestinal tract after childhood. The incidence of lactase deficiency among the U.S. black population is estimated to be 70 percent.[4] The incidence of lactase deficiency among the Caucasian population in the United States is believed to be as high as 15 percent.[5] The lactase-deficiency phenomenon is commonly referred to as "milk intolerance." People who are "milk intolerant" may experience bloating, abdominal gas, cramps, and diarrhea when they drink milk. The dairy industry's advertising campaign slogan "You never outgrow your need for milk" is most absurd in view of the large number of adult Americans who are milk intolerant.

THE VEGAN DIET

Vegans regard cow's milk as an unnatural food since it was intended (by Nature) to be nourishment for calves—not people. No animal in its natural state continues to use its own mother's milk, let alone the milk of another species, after infancy. While some may view this fact simply as a philosophical issue, the use of cow's milk by human beings does present certain health problems. The U.S.

Department of Agriculture Yearbook of 1959 notes: "An important difference between cow's milk formulas and human milk lies in the fact that while the milk of a healthy mother is always fresh and free from bacteria, any artificial formula must be heat-treated to destroy harmful organisms." The brucella organism, in particular, can be transmitted to humans from the milk of infected cows, causing undulant fever.

Bovine disease has been kept under control by the extensive use of antibiotics. However, this extensive use of antibiotics by dairy farmers has led to other problems. Some people are particularly sensitive to the antibiotic residues contained in milk.[6] While this problem affects only a small segment of the population, an increase in the prevalence of antibiotic-resistant bacteria is a most serious problem, which looms over all those who use animal products. Many dairy farmers do not even heed the USDA guidelines for the amount of antibiotic residue allowed in milk. Levels in excess of these guidelines were found in 15 percent of the dairy cows tested by the Food Safety and Quality Service agency of the USDA.[7] A more detailed discussion of the use of antibiotics by livestock owners and the ramifications of this practice are presented in Chapter 4, "The Meat Industry, the Consumer, and the Law."

The vegan diet contains no cholesterol since cholesterol is present only in animal foods. Moreover, whereas most animal foods, including dairy products and eggs, are high in saturated fats, there are relatively few foodstuffs of plant origin which contain saturated fats. Since the vegan diet is generally low in saturated fats and high in fats of the polyunsaturated type, vegans have serum cholesterol levels which are substantially lower than those of lacto or lacto-ovo vegetarians:

> A comparison of the respective adult male and female groups shows that the pure vegetarians have a polyunsaturated:saturated fatty acid ratio approximately five and four times that of the nonvegetarians and three and a half times that of the lacto-ovo vegetarians. It would thus appear that the type of fat consumed is more important than the total fat intake and that as the polyunsaturated:saturated fatty acid ratio increases, the level of serum cholesterol decreases.[8]

An examination of the apparent relationship between heart disease and the consumption of foods high in cholesterol and saturated fats

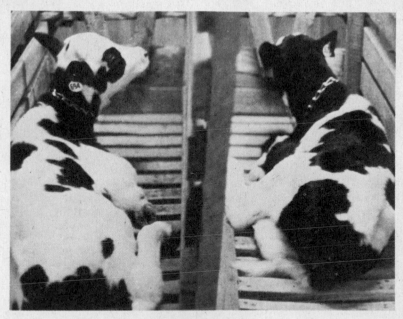

Veal calves, like these on a farm in Connecticut, spend their entire lives confined to small stalls. (Photo courtesy of the Humane Society of the United States)

is presented in Chapter 3, "Anatomy, Diet, and Disease."

Notwithstanding the fact that vegans often refer to the health advantages associated with their diet, the vast majority of vegans make a commitment to abstain from animal foods primarily for ethical reasons. Some newborn calves are only allowed to nurse for 2 or 3 days before they are separated from their dam. Others are not allowed to nurse at all, being taken away from their dam soon after birth. Filial devotion is viewed as a mawkish sentiment, which would interfere with a dairy farmer's profits.

It is particularly significant to note that the dairy industry has strong ties with the meat industry. The slaughter of calves for veal is certainly among the more sordid aspects of dairying. Milch cows must periodically be made pregnant in order to maintain lactation. The average dairy cow gives birth to four or five calves during her lifetime. The male offspring of milch cows are almost invariably slaughtered for veal. They are useless to the dairy farmer, since they are not milk producers, and since they come from a dairy strain, it is not practical to raise them as beef cattle. Some veal calves are slaughtered within a month after they are born. The meat that is produced from these animals (referred to as "bob" or "bobby veal") is often marketed as a canned or frozen convenience food and is used for breaded cutlets and patties. Because it is so tender, this type of veal is commonly used in baby foods. Much of the veal cuts that are highly prized by gourmands come from calves that spend their entire life (13 to 15 weeks) confined to stalls that measure 2 feet wide by 4½ feet long and 3½ feet high. They are not fed grains nor are they afforded the comfort of straw bedding, since grains and straw are sources of iron. The calf's enforced iron-deficient diet and its lack of exercise results in an anemic condition which makes for a whiter, more tender veal.

In addition to male calves, a substantial number of the dairy cows themselves are killed for their meat. This fact is cited by Glenn Lake, president of the National Milk Producers Federation. In his testimony at a U.S. congressional hearing on the Beef Research and Consumer Information Act, Mr. Lake commented: "While some may not view this legislation as affecting dairy producers, it must be borne in mind that the dairy farmer is a substantial producer of beef and, in many sections of the Nation, local beef production is centered largely in the dairy herds of the region." He further notes: "Dairy cows make up almost 20 percent of the Nation's cow herd. A substantial portion of the beef marketed today originates on the dairy farms of the country. The value of this beef and the cost of producing it and maintaining our cow herd, of course, is of vital concern to every dairyman."[9] The practicality of slaughtering a portion of one's dairy herd for meat is noted by Alfred Franklin in his testimony at U.S. congressional hearings on the Dairy Herd Reduction Act of 1978: "As any dairyman will tell you a good price for dairy beef will do several things—one, it will increase yearly cash flow without raising production cost or debt; secondly, it will reduce herd size and decrease family labor and business pressures; and thirdly, it will reduce the amount of milk forced upon the market. Now I ask you, isn't this just what we are all aiming for?"[10] It is estimated that about 30 percent of the beef produced in the United States comes from dairy cattle.[11] A full 80 percent of the beef produced in England is derived from that country's dairy industry.[12]

Chickens are cramped together in small cages as a space-saving measure. Production efficiency is more important than the chickens' comfort. These creatures are viewed simply as egg-producing machines. (Photo courtesy of the Humane Society of the United States)

The use of eggs, like dairy products, involves the destruction of innocent animals. When Leghorns used for egg production are bred to augment the laying stock, the male offspring are immediately destroyed since they serve no useful purpose. The male chicks are returned to the incubator, where they suffocate, or they might simply be thrown into empty boxes on top of one another and left to die.[13] Laying hens are subjected to various forms of cruelty. They are confined to a large poultry house with thousands of other birds. The chickens in many of these large-scale "factory farm" operations never actually see the light of day. Artificial light, referred to as "stimulighting," beams overhead for 17 hours a day to stimulate laying. These birds are so crowded together in their cages that they are not able to spread their wings and are barely able to turn around. Another source of discomfort is the metal grating on the bottom of the cage, which often causes injury to the hens' feet. The incredible stress of this environment gives rise to fighting and even cannibalism. Consequently, it is a common practice to cut off a portion of a hen's beak when it is one or two weeks old in order to diminish the chances of injury caused by pecking. This debeaking process is done again when the beak grows back in another three to five months. Egg farmers do little to ameliorate stressful, overcrowded conditions—the basic cause of fighting as well as disease in large egg-producing operations.

Mortality among laying hens on a single egg farm may run as high as 15 percent annually.[14] A study conducted by the Poultry Science Department of Cornell University examined the mortality rate among laying hens as related to the degree of overcrowding. Three groups of layers were kept for a period of three years in cages which measured 12 by 18 inches. In one group where there were three laying hens to a cage, the mortality rate was 9.6 percent. In another group where there were four layers to a cage, the mortality was 16.4 percent. A mortality rate of 23 percent was reported in the group where five layers were confined to this 12-by-18-inch cage. The researchers who made this study reported that it was more practical to keep 4 layers instead of 3 in a cage of this size despite the higher mortality rate because the profits realized by the greater number of eggs produced and lower overall production costs are simply greater than the monetary losses incurred from the increased number of hens which die as a result of this overcrowding.[15] A New Jersey man who operates a farm that has 80,000 laying hens allots 9 hens to a cage which measures 18 by 24 inches. While conceding that the hens are crowded, he dismisses this cruelty, citing compelling economic considerations: "But sometimes you have to do things to get the most out of your stock."[16]

There are laws in the United States and Great Britain which stipulate that animals confined to cages should be given enough space to allow sufficient freedom of movement to insure the animal's comfort. However, these anti-cruelty laws regarding caged animals do not apply to animals that are raised for food, since this would place too great an economic burden on livestock farmers, particularly those involved in the poultry business.[17] In addition to the government's sanction of the cruelty which factory farming entails, even officials of so-called humane organizations condone these practices. Com-

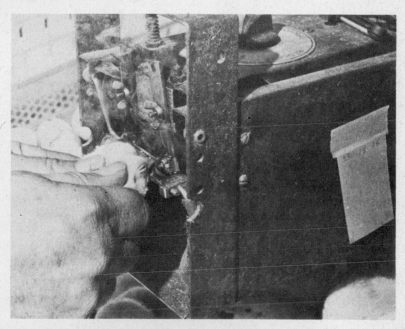

Chickens' beaks are clipped in order to control cannibalism which results from the stress of overcrowding. (Photo courtesy of the Humane Society of the United States)

menting on this issue, a speaker for the American Humane Association stated: "We do have to meet food demands, and mass farming techniques may be the only way to do it."[18]

No hen actually lives long enough to die of old age. When a laying hen is no longer able to produce enough eggs to warrant the expense of keeping her, she is used for meat. Some lacto-ovo vegetarians purchase eggs that come only from "free-range" hens in the belief that the use of this product does not involve cruelty. These uncaged hens are certainly better off than those which are crowded in cages on factory farms. However, "free-range" hens, like their caged counterparts, are killed to be used for meat when their egg production falls off. One small egg-producer, who takes good care of the free-range laying hens on his farm during the period in which they are productive, comments: "We try not to get attached to any of the birds. All of them will be meat eventually. . ."[19]

NUTRITIONAL ISSUES

While some nutritionists have cited important health advantages to be derived from adopting the vegan diet, others have expressed serious reservations about the adequacy of this diet. Critics of veganism are particularly concerned that a diet derived solely from plant foods may be deficient in vitamin B_{12}, vitamin D, calcium, and quality protein. These fears, while often exaggerated, are not entirely without foundation. Some of the vegans in a study conducted by Drs. Mervyn Hardinge and Fredrick Stare were found to have intakes of riboflavin (B_2), calcium, and protein that were somewhat below the dietary allowances for these nutrients set by the Food and Nutrition Board of the National Academy of Sciences. It is significant to note, however, that the standard set by the Food and Nutrition Board is not a minimum standard—these guidelines allow for a wide margin of safety.

CALCIUM

Vegans obtain their calcium from foods such as sesame seeds, kelp, almonds, soybeans, filberts, parsley, brazil nuts, chickpeas, white beans, dried figs, sunflower seeds, and molasses. Vegans can adequately fulfill their calcium requirements by using such foods. Many vegans have calcium intakes that are somewhat lower than the amounts recommended by the Food and Nutrition Board. Some scientists feel that these recommended calcium requirements are set much too high. D. M. Hegsted, a nutrition professor at the Harvard School of Public Health, has criticized the dubious testing procedures used by the Food and Nutrition Board to determine calcium requirements: "Nearly all the evidence upon which the allowances are based has been collected by the balance technic. There is now no reason to believe that these measurements bear any relation to calcium requirements of adults."[20] Professor Hegsted further notes that numerous calcium studies conducted with rats are highly misleading because the calcium requirement for these animals is "tremendous" compared to human calcium needs.[21]

Aside from simply measuring calcium intake, various factors which affect the utilization of calcium in the body should be taken into

CALCIUM — *sesame seeds, kelp, almonds*
soybeans
filberts, sunflower seed
THE VEGAN DIET 13

consideration. An adequate supply of vitamin D is necessary for calcium absorption. Actually, it is possible to satisfy one's requirement for vitamin D exclusively from exposure to the ultraviolet rays of the sun,[22] which synthesize vitamin D from a precursor (7-dehydrocholesterol) in the skin.[23] Although persons living in temperate climates would be exposed to this ultraviolet radiation only during the summer months, it is significant to note that vitamin D can be stored in one's body for relatively long periods of time. Consequently, the Food and Nutrition Board of the National Academy of Sciences sets no minimum recommended limit for dietary sources of vitamin D for adults. However, a daily minimum of 400 units is set for children and pregnant or lactating women.[24] Vegan children and vegan women who are pregnant or lactating should make sure that their diet contains adequate amounts of vitamin D. Vegans may obtain vitamin D in the form of fortified foods, particularly soy milk, soy margarine, and cereals.

While vitamin D is necessary for calcium absorption, phytic acid appears to inhibit the absorption of this mineral. Phytic acid is found mainly in whole-grain foods. Since vegans tend to use relatively large amounts of such foods, the issue of phytates is sometimes raised in regard to the question of calcium deficiency. Actually, the adverse qualities of phytates have been exaggerated by some nutritionists. It appears that one quickly adapts to a diet high in phytates. After a brief period of transition, there is a normal absorption of calcium.[25] Moreover, the body adapts to high and low levels of calcium intake. There is actually a greater efficiency in calcium absorption when calcium intake is lowered.[26]

VITAMIN B₁₂

The one essential nutrient that cannot be obtained from a vegan diet is vitamin B_{12}, which is available only in animal foods. Lacto-ovo and lacto vegetarians obtain their B_{12} from the eggs, and/or dairy products that they use. Ruminant animals possess the ability to manufacture vitamin B_{12} themselves through fermentations by microflora in their digestive tracts. It appears that certain types of algae possess the ability to manufacture vitamin B_{12} themselves also. It has, therefore, been suggested that such algae could be grown and harvested as a vegetable source of this vitamin.[27] It has also been suggested that human beings might be able to satisfy their need for B_{12} by using certain foods which have undergone a fermentive process. Nutritionist U. D. Register theorizes that the widespread use of soy sauce and other such fermented foods in the Orient may account for the fact that B_{12} deficiencies are relatively uncommon among Oriental vegans.[28] While reports of possible vegetable sources of B_{12} are interesting, they are, nevertheless, inconclusive in regard to the central question of whether or not it is actually practical or even possible to satisfy one's B_{12} requirement exclusively with plant foods.

Vitamin B_{12} can be produced by a fermentive process which involves the actions of microorganisms. Vitamin B_{12} manufactured in this manner is acceptable to most vegans, who take this supplement as a tablet or through foods which have been fortified with it. Foods such as soy milk and cereals are frequently fortified with various nutrients, including vitamin B_{12}. Although it is important for vegans to use B_{12} supplements, the actual requirement for this vitamin is often overstated. Figures on recommended daily allowances are particularly misleading in view of the fact that the body stores considerable amounts of this vitamin. Most people have storage levels sufficient to maintain adequate serum B_{12} levels for up to five years.[29]

The regulation of B_{12} in the body as well as the effect of low serum B_{12} levels varies considerably from one individual to another. One clinical study conducted with 26 vegans cited four subjects with normal serum B_{12} levels who had lived exclusively on plant foods without taking B_{12} supplements for periods of 13 years and longer.[30] There are various theories on how some people are capable of adjusting to the absence of B_{12} in their diet. Unfortunately, this is a subject which is still not clearly understood. It should suffice to note that researchers like Ernest Lester Smith and Frey Ellis who have made extensive studies of B_{12}, stress that it is most unwise for vegans to go without taking some form of B_{12} supplements. Citing the objections that some vegans might raise in regard to using a B_{12} supplement, Smith notes: "Vegans who take it need have no fear that they are compromising their principles. Its production involves no animal product at any stage, nor can it be regarded as a 'drug'; it is on the contrary a micro-nutrient essential to the health of every living creature."[31]

RIBOFLAVIN (VITAMIN B₂)

In a clinical study of vegans, lacto-ovo vegetarians, and meat eaters conducted by Drs. Hardinge and Stare, it was noted that the mean intake of riboflavin was lower in the vegan group than in that of the other two groups.[32] It was reported that a few of the vegan subjects used in this study had riboflavin intakes that were somewhat below the allowances recommended by the Food and Nutrition Board. Similarly, other researchers have reported that some of their vegan subjects had riboflavin intakes below recommended allowances set for this nutrient.

Although it appears that vegans generally have a lower riboflavin intake than either lacto-ovo or lacto vegetarians, there is no indication that vegans do not get an adequate supply of this vitamin. Actually, most vegans appear to have riboflavin intakes which are in accord with the recommended allowances. Several different plant foods are good sources of riboflavin, including wheat germ, almonds, cashews, chestnuts, soybeans, kidney beans, lima beans, split peas, and lentils. In fact, brewers yeast is the richest source of riboflavin available.

PROTEIN

Some people feel that it would be difficult to obtain adequate protein from a vegan diet since no single plant food contains all the essential amino acids. Vegans combine different types of plant protein foods (e.g., grains and legumes) to compensate for this deficiency. Although it is obviously more convenient to obtain one's protein from a single food such as cheese or eggs, it is nevertheless a relatively simple procedure to put together meals which contain complete protein. A more detailed discussion of the adequacy of protein obtained from plant foods is presented in Chapter 2, "The Protein Myth."

2

The Protein Myth

> One farmer says to me, "You cannot live on
> vegetable food solely, for it furnishes nothing
> to make bones with;" and so he religiously de-
> votes a part of his day to supplying his system
> with the raw material of bones; walking all the
> while he talks behind his oxen, which, with vege-
> table-made bones, jerk him and his lumbering
> plow along in spite of every obstacle. Some
> things are really necessaries of life in some cir-
> cles, the most helpless and diseased, which in
> others are luxuries merely, and in others still
> are entirely unknown.
>
> HENRY DAVID THOREAU

More flesh food is consumed in the United States per capita than
in any other country in the world. Meat has always been regarded
by the American public as a quality protein food aside from its
value as a status symbol. What acounts for this American prepossession
with protein, particularly meat protein? There are three common
fallacies regarding protein: (1) there are no good sources of protein
other than flesh foods; (2) one should eat a lot of protein for optimum
health; if some is good, more is better; and (3) protein is a good
energy-giving food.

Fallacy 1. There are no good sources of protein other than flesh food.

Protein, to be sure, is a necessary food element. The body needs
protein for growth and tissue repair. A fully grown person uses
protein primarialy for tissue repair. There are many non-meat sources

16

of protein, including grains (corn, millet, wheat, oats, rice, barley, etc.), legumes (lentils, peas, garbanzos, soybeans, kidney beans, black beans, white beans, mung beans, etc.), brewer's yeast, seeds (sunflower, sesame, pumpkin, etc.), dairy products (milk, cheese, yogurt, etc.), eggs, and a large variety of nuts, including nut butters. It should be noted, however, that not all of these foods are sources of complete protein.

Protein is composed of 22 different amino acids. All but 8 of these amino acids can be synthesized by the body itself. Those which cannot be synthesized in the body and must be obtained from protein foods are referred to as "essential amino acids." Eggs, as well as most dairy products, contain all eight essential amino acids and are therefore good sources of complete protein. There is no single plant food that contains adequate quantities of all the essential amino acids. Consequently, unlike their lacto-ovo and lacto vegetarian counterparts, vegans are not able to satisfy their need for complete protein with any single food item. However, vegans can obtain complete protein by a simple method of food combining.

Meals can be made up of two different types of vegetable protein foods which jointly contain all the essential amino acids. For instance, legumes are a good source of the essential amino acids lysine and isoleucine but are deficient in tryptophan and methionine, two other essential amino acids. Conversely, grains are a good source of tryptophan and methionine but are deficient in lysine and isoleucine. It is therefore possible to compensate for the respective essential-amino-acid deficiencies that characterize each of these protein food classes by simply combining some type of grain with some type of legume in a single meal. Many meals that are made up of legume and grain combinations are actually quite common, including "Spanish rice" (rice with kidney beans), pasta con lenticchie (pasta with lentils), a casserole of peas and brown rice, peanut butter on whole-grain bread, and tahini or hummus on whole-wheat pita bread. Also, one can prepare a complete-protein meal by serving some type of whole grain bread with any type of legume soup, e.g., lentil, split pea, bean.

People in various cultures have traditionally relied on plant foods to provide most or all of their protein needs. A report by the Committee on Nutritional Misinformation of the National Academy of Sciences notes: "The worldwide practice of combining cereals and le-

Protein in Vegetarian Diets[1]

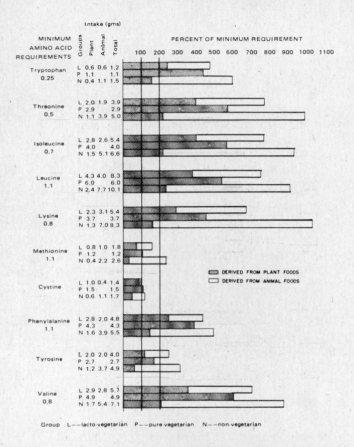

Actual intake and percent of minimum daily requirement of essential amino acids in diets of vegetarian and nonvegetarian adult men.

gumes in the food of man and farm animals provides evidence of the supplementary effect of one plant food on another. If this mixing of plant protein foods is done judiciously, combinations of lower-quality protein foods can give mixtures of about the same nutritional value as high-quality animal protein foods."[2] Some nutritionists are still skeptical about the adequacy of vegan diets in respect to complete protein. They often point to vegans who, either through choice or

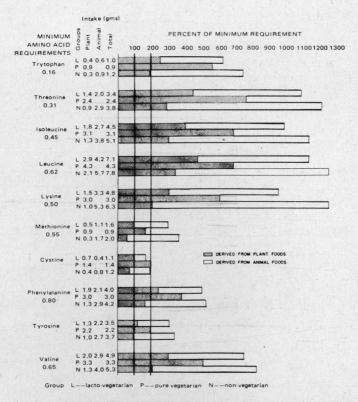

Actual intake and percent of minimum daily requirement of essential
amino acids in diets of vegetarian and nonvegetarian adult women.

circumstances beyond their control, live on very restricted diets. In
one such misleading report, the nutritional status of two African
tribes was studied. One tribe consumed meat, milk, and blood, in
addition to maize, millet, plantains, and yams. The diet of the vegetarian tribe consisted of only the aforementioned non-animal products.
The study calls attention to the fact that the people of the meat-
eating tribe were taller, had less anemia, and were in better general
health than the members of the vegetarian tribe. The researchers
concluded that animal protein was responsible for the better health

of the former tribe, completely ignoring the fact that the diet of the vegetarian tribe was considerably restricted by virtue of the environment and their economic status. Their diet contained little protein of any sort and this fact—not the lack of meat per se—resulted in nutritional deficiencies.[3]

A report published in the *American Journal of Clinical Nutrition* notes that some of the misinformation on human protein requirements can be traced to the misleading practice of using rats as subjects in protein studies:

> Although there is a high correlation between the biological values obtained with adult human beings and growing rats, specific differences do exist. For example, the requirement of lysine is higher for the young rat. Also on a comparable basis the human subject can meet minimum requirements with less food nitrogen than the rat. By using the nitrogen balance method in human subjects, investigators have shown that the minimum requirement of protein is essentially the same on diets containing all plant foods or those containing animal products, indicating a similar quality of protein.[4]

This report further notes: "Although a high correlation exists between the biological values obtained with human subjects and growing rats, the protein requirements for rats are greater than for human subjects."[5]

A clinical study conducted with lacto-ovo vegetarians, vegans, and flesh eaters, found that the flesh eaters had the highest intake of all the essential amino acids. The lacto-ovo vegetarians had higher intakes of most essential amino acids than their vegan counterparts. However, the researchers who conducted this study duly reported: "When the minimum essential amino acid requirements for men and women are prorated for adolescents and pregnant women to meet their higher recommended protein allowances, each group exceeded twice its requirement for every essential amino acid and surpassed this amount by large margins for most of them."[6]

Fallacy 2. One should eat a lot of protein for optimum health; if some is good, more is better.

In a study comparing the total protein, albumin, and globulin levels of vegetarians and flesheaters, Drs. Mervyn Hardinge and Fredrick Stare reported: "It is of interest that despite the lower protein intakes of the vegetarian groups there was no lowering of the serum protein values even among the 'pure' vegetarian groups who had utilized a relatively lower all-plant diet an average of 9 to 16 years. Since the protein intake of all the vegetarian groups was almost equal to or exceeded the National Research Council's recommended allowances, it appears that above a certain level of dietary protein intake, whether of plant or animal origin, the level of serum protein concentration is not measurably affected."[7]

Excessive intakes of protein serve no useful purpose for proper body maintenance since protein is not stored in the body. The nitrogen portion of the amino acids not used by the body is converted into urea in the liver and then goes to the kidneys to be processed further. Since excess protein is converted to waste, the kidneys of flesheaters must deal with significantly more nitrogenous wastes than would be found in the kidneys of vegetarians.*

Fallacy 3. Protein is a good energy-giving food.

Carbohydrates are much superior to protein for providing energy. Protein is drawn upon as a source of energy when there is not an adequate amount of carbohydrates and fats in one's diet. Protein is also used as a source of energy by the body when there is an excess of protein. However, this is an expensive and inefficient source of energy.†

A person will, indeed, become weak from a diet that is deficient in protein. However, it should not therefore be assumed that eating large quantities of protein will make one stronger. Tests conducted by Dr. Irving Fisher of Yale University demonstrated that vegetarians could perform twice as well as meat eaters when put through a series of endurance tests. Dr. Fisher then took his meat-eating subjects and reduced their protein intake by 20 percent. When they were retested with these same exercises, their endurance efficiency actually increased 33 percent. Animals noted for their great strength and endurance, like the ox, the horse, the elephant, and the gorilla, are all vegetarians. It should also be noted that these animals are much larger than the human species and yet are able to find food from plant sources to supply all their protein needs.

* See Chapter 3, "Anatomy, Diet, and Disease," pp. 29–30.
† See Chapter 6, "Diet and Economy," p. 75.

CONCLUSION

Many people are now beginning to recognize the value of vegetable protein. The meat industry itself has seen the handwriting on the wall. Meat-packing companies have invested in "textured vegetable protein" products. These processed foods look and taste very much like meat but contain only vegetable substances. Packaged meats that contain up to 30 percent extenders are gradually winning acceptance. Miles Laboratories, a major producer of textured vegetable protein products, even purchased a two-page, full-color ad in *The National Provisioner,* a trade magazine of the meat industry. The ad noted that their product is ". . . very high in protein, low in calories and low in saturated fats."[8]

The shift to vegetable protein by most of the world's people is inevitable. The only question that remains is exactly how long this will take. At some future period, historians will relate how generations of people from many of the world's most powerful nations obtained their protein from dead animals.

3

Anatomy, Diet, and Disease

Ah! how unlike the man of times to come
Of half that live the butcher and the tomb;
Who, foe to Nature, hears the gen'ral groan,
Murders their species, and betrays his own.
But just disease to luxury succeeds,
And ev'ry death its own avenger breeds;
The Fury-passions from that blood began,
And turn'd on Man a fiercer savage, Man.

ALEXANDER POPE

ARE HUMAN BEINGS "NATURALLY" A FLESH-EATING SPECIES?

The controversy as to whether or not *Homo sapiens* should be classified as a flesh-eating species centers on the definition of the word "natural." Some assert that it is "unnatural" for human beings to eat flesh since the human anatomy is ill suited to utilizing dead animals as a source of food. Others maintain that the practice of flesh eating can be traced back to prehistoric hominids and that a considerable segment of the human race has, throughout the course of history, used flesh as a food. This is, indeed, true. Nonetheless, it should be noted that a significant portion of the human race throughout history either did not eat meat at all or ate it only on rare occasions. Furthermore, if we are to equate the term "natural"

23

with primitivism, particularly in reference to the eating habits of prehistoric hominids, we must then recognize cannibalism as a "natural" practice since it is known that the early hominids ate members of their own species as well as other animals.

There are many people who dislike the term "flesh eater." They prefer to disassociate themselves from rapacious carnivores. They contend that human beings are neither carnivores nor herbivores but are rather omnivores, i.e., we were "naturally" endowed with the ability to use both plant and animal foods. The word "omnivorous" is derived from the Latin words "omnis" (all) and "vorare" (to devour). Devouring all, that is, indiscriminate feeding, may be an accurate description of the human omnivore's eating habits but it is hardly a flattering one. Moreover, despite the claim that flesh foods are required by human beings as part of a so-called "balanced diet," it has been amply demonstrated that meat contains no essential nutrients that cannot be otherwise obtained from plant sources.

Plutarch was among the first writers who referred to anatomical differences between human beings and the flesh-eating animal species, citing our inadequacies as predators:

> We declare, then, that it is absurd for them to say that the practice of flesh-eating is based on Nature. For that man is not naturally carnivorous is, in the first place, obvious from the structure of his body. A man's frame is in no way similar to those creatures who were made for flesh-eating; he has no hooked beak or sharp nails or jagged teeth, no strong stomach or warmth of vital fluids able to digest and assimilate a heavy diet of flesh. It is from this very fact, the evenness of our teeth, the smallness of our mouth, the softness of our tongues, our possession of vital fluids too inert to digest meat that Nature disavows our eating of flesh. If you declare that you are naturally designed for such a diet, then first kill for yourself what you want to eat. Do it, however, only through your own resources, unaided by cleaver or cudgel or any kind or axe.[1]

Nearly 2,000 years after Plutarch wrote this essay, the relevance of his anatomical comparisons is supported by contemporary studies in physiology.

HUMAN NATURE: THE MEANS TO
HUNT/THE WILL TO KILL

The human hand is better suited to harvesting fruits and vegetables than to killing prey. Our fingers, similar to those of the apes, enable us to pick from trees, bushes, and vines a wide variety of plant foods. The dexterity of our hands, especially the opposable thumb, combined with our intelligence, resulted in our ability to create an organized system of planting and harvesting—agriculture.

Despite ingenious devices such as duck calls, decoys, and high-powered rifles, the prowess of the human hunter still cannot match the biological advantages with which the true carnivore is naturally endowed. The human being must substitute telescopic lenses for the keen sight of the true carnivorous animals, which are able to spot their prey even in the darkness of night. The human hunter also lacks the keen sense of smell that a true carnivore possesses. Instead of seeking prey by smell human predators will often lure their victims to them with such enticements as duck calls or decoys. Even after birds are shot from the air these human predators have great difficulty finding their fallen prey. The task is, therefore, often left to the hunting dog, whose keen sense of smell will lead it to its master's prize. The carnivores are quadrupeds. They possess not only the necessary speed to overtake their prey but they also have sharp, retractable claws which enables them to pull their victims to the ground and hold them fast. Shelley sarcastically commented: "A Mandarin of the first class, with nails two inches long, would probably find them alone inefficient to hold even a hare."[2] One might then argue that being a highly evolved, intelligent species we have even from prehistoric times used weapons such as knives or the bow and arrow to kill our prey. Does the invention and use of such weapons conform to one's conception of obtaining food by our "natural" abilities? If so, we should then classify napalm, poison gas, the atomic bomb and all other weapons of war as "natural," since they are also the products of human intelligence.

Aside from the matter of natural abilities, does the human species at large have the instinct to kill? Many of our present-day human hunters consider killing a "sport." However, even this perversion can hardly be explained as the "killer instinct" that is a necessary part of survival for the natural carnivore. Shelley, in his essay "A Vindication of Natural Diet," elaborates on the question of whether or not we, as human beings, truly possess the instinct to kill. He forthrightly asserts that flesh is an unnatural food for the human species and offers a challenge to those who would contradict the merits of his argument:

> Let the advocate of animal food force himself to a decisive experiment on its fitness, and as Plutarch recommends, tear a living lamb with his teeth and, plunging his head into its vitals, slake his thirst with the steaming blood; when fresh from the deed of horror let him revert to the irresistible instincts of nature that rise in judgment against it, and say, Nature formed me for such work as this. Then, and then only, would he be consistent.[3]

Shelley, it seems, failed to reckon with the fact that *Homo sapiens* are a highly rational species and, as such, possess the uncanny ability to rationalize behavior which might be viewed as inconsistent.

EATING FOR ENERGY

Unlike carnivores who obtain their energy from protein, the non-flesh-eating animals use carbohydrates to supply most of their daily energy requirements. Carbohydrates make up a major portion of the human diet. In fact, even people on a meat-based diet obtain more that half of their total daily calories from carbohydrates. Human beings rely on protein for energy when their carbohydrate intake is insufficient to supply this need. Normally, a person's intake of carbohydrates is more than sufficient to meet energy requirements. The carbohydrates which are not immediately used for fuel are either converted into fat or stored by the liver and muscles in the form of glycogen. Thus, the liver and muscles contain a readily available source of energy that is necessary for a normal active life.

ANATOMY OF THE MOUTH

The sharp, pointed teeth of carnivorous animals are particularly well suited for tearing flesh but inefficient for dealing with most types of plant foods. Moreover, their jaws work in a straight up and down motion. The large set of molar teeth found in non-flesh-eating animals are well-suited to the kind of grinding that is necessary for proper mastication of carbohydrate foods. The non-flesh-eating animal's facility for grinding foods is also evidenced by the relatively free movement of the lower jaw, which is capable of moving laterally, backward and forward, and up and down.

Proponents of the theory that *Homo sapiens* should be classified as omnivores note that human beings do, in fact, possess a modified form of canine teeth. However, it is significant to note that these so-called "canine teeth" are even more prominent in animals that traditionally never eat flesh, e.g., apes, camels, and the male musk deer. It should also be noted that the shape and length as well as the hardness of these so-called canine teeth can hardly be compared to those of true carnivorous animals. A principal factor determining the hardness of teeth is the phosphate of magnesia content. Human teeth usually contain 1½ percent phosphate of magnesia whereas the teeth of carnivores are composed of nearly 5 percent of this substance. It is for this reason they are able to break through the bones of their prey, enabling them to reach the nutritious marrow. While most vegetarian species content themselves with plant foods, the flesh-eating human beings prefer to defy their nature. They will never require the kind of teeth possessed by true carnivores as long as they have meat tenderizers and steak knives. Indeed, if necessity is truly the "mother of invention," flesh-eating humankind have greater need for her than for "mother nature."

PRODUCTION AND ELIMINATION OF WASTES

Carnivorous animals are better equipped than human beings to deal with the type of waste products created by flesh foods. Waste is created by either (1) the digestive process or (2) the process of metabolism.

DIGESTIVE WASTE

Digestive waste consists of residues from various digestive juices, bacteria, and undigestible material such as cellulose. The term "digestibility" is used to describe the extent to which various foods are digested. Plant protein has a lower digestibility than animal protein since human beings have no enzyme to digest cellulose; the principal constituent of plant fiber. The cellulose component of plant foods is, therefore, not broken down and absorbed but is simply passed out of the body in an undigested state. This would appear to be an inefficient use of a food component. However, while cellulose is not used as a source of nourishment per se, its presence in the diet serves to stimulate peristaltic action. The high-fiber diet produces large, soft colonic content, which is easily passed through the bowel. The high-fiber content of certain plant foods has long been recognized as a factor in the prevention of constipation. Moreover, there is much evidence to indicate that conditions often associated with constipation, such as diverticulosis and hiatus hernia, are related to insufficient dietary fiber.[4]

A vegetarian diet will usually contain significantly greater quantities of fiber than a meat-based diet. Notwithstanding their use of dairy products and eggs, lacto-ovo vegetarians tend to consume greater amounts of high-fiber vegetables than those who use flesh foods. One study which compared the dietary fiber intake of meat eaters, lacto-ovo vegetarians, and vegans found that the lacto-ovo vegetarians consumed twice as much fiber as the meat-eating subjects. The dietary fiber intake for the vegan subjects was predictably greater than that for either of the other two groups. The fiber intake of the vegans was, in fact, nearly two times greater than that of their lacto-ovo counterparts.[5]

METABOLIC WASTE

"Metabolism" is a term used to describe the sum total of the ongoing physiological processes of anabolism and catabolism that take place in every cell of our body. "Anabolism" refers to all the body processes of a constructive (building up) nature, such as the utilization of elements from various foodstuffs that have been digested, absorbed and carried to various parts of the body. "Catabolism" refers to the destructive (breaking down) process, such as the combustion of chemical compounds for the release of energy. Waste products destined for eventual elimination from the body are created as a result of the catabolism process. The end products of protein catabolism must undergo more extensive processing than the waste created by carbohydrates or fats. Oxidation of fats and carbohydrates in their pure form creates only water and carbon dioxide. In addition to these substances, the oxidation of protein also produces nitrogen waste. Unlike fats or carbohydrates, protein is not stored in the body for future use. If more protein is consumed than is needed for its basic function (tissue repair), the excess amino acids (protein constituents) are converted to fuel uses. The nitrogen portion of these amino acids becomes waste. It is, therefore, evident that a high-protein diet necessarily produces excessive waste, especially nitrogenous waste.

In addition to the waste created as a result of excessive protein intake, meat in itself contains its own waste products. When an animal is slaughtered, its metabolic process ceases. The cells can no longer receive their necessary nutriments nor are they able to pass off their waste products. Therefore, by eating meat we are taking into our own bodies the waste products contained in the animal's body. It should be apparent that by eating flesh we are doing more than simply taking additional waste into our systems. Aside from the issue of quantity, these wastes are of a more pernicious nature than those created as part of our own metabolism. The animal, after all, is now dead.

The waste products created by flesh foods are retained in the human body for a substantially longer period of time than in the body of any of the carnivorous species. The alimentary canals of non-flesh-eating animals range from 12 (in primates) to 30 (in sheep) times the length of their bodies. However, the carnivorous animals possess alimentary canals which are only three times the length of their bodies.

THE KIDNEYS

The kidneys extract waste products from the blood as it passes through them by way of a filtering action. These wastes are dissolved in water and excreted in their final form as urine. Commenting on the additional strain placed on our kidneys as a result of this added waste, Dr. John Harvey Kellogg notes: "Comparative analyses of the urine of low protein feeders and those who take an ordinary mixed diet show that even moderate meat-eaters require of their kidneys three times the amount of work in elimination of nitrogenous wastes that is demanded of the kidneys of flesh abstainers. While the kidneys are young they are usually able to bear this extra burden so that no evidence of injury appears; but as they become worn with advancing age they become unable to do their work efficiently."[6]

One of the more recent weight-reducing diet fads is the low-carbohydrate, high-protein diet, which usually consists largely of flesh foods. The people who adopt this diet are usually advised to drink large quantities of water, since fluids, as previously explained, are vital to the kidneys' ability to process waste. It is, therefore, necessary to drink significantly greater quantities of water so that the kidneys can process the additional amounts of this matter created by such a diet. Dr. Robert Atkins, one of the leading proponents of this dietary program, has been severely criticized by various medical organizations, including the American Medical Association. It has been noted that the extensive use of flesh food prescribed in this diet will create an excess of uric acid. Dr. Atkins himself conceded this point, stating: "I admit that kidney stones are a conceivable complication resulting from increased uric acid."[7] The A.M.A. has expressed strong concern that adoption of the "Atkins Diet" can cause kidney failure in persons already suffering from renal problems.

Persons who are afflicted with chronic kidney disorders are often treated by a dialysis machine. This device assists the kidneys in their function of removing waste materials from the blood. It is particularly interesting to note that persons who require kidney dialysis can significantly extend the periods of time between their treatments by eliminating flesh foods from their diet.

THE COLON

Waste is stored in the colon before it is finally eliminated from the body. Essentially no digestion occurs in the colon. Various digestive juices that serve to detoxify pathogens during digestion are not present in the colon; there are only residues of these secretions. Consequently, the warmth, moisture, and lack of antiseptic agents makes the colon an ideal environment for harmful bacteria to breed. The amount of time that waste remains in the colon is substantially longer for human beings than for carnivorous animals because of the difference in the lengths of their respective colons. The short colon of the carnivore is better suited to deal with the waste created by a flesh diet than the longer, more complex colon of *Homo sapiens.*

It is widely believed that there is a relationship between meat consumption and cancer of the colon. Epidemiological studies show that the incidence of colon cancer is significantly higher among populations where meat consumption is high than among those populations where flesh foods comprise a relatively small portion of the total caloric intake.[8]

A group of English researchers who conducted studies comparing the fecal flora of subjects from different countries found that there was a greater concentration of bile acids and a significantly higher ratio of anaerobes/aerobes in the fecal flora of persons in countries where there is a high incidence of colon cancer (U.S., England, Scotland) than in those people who lived in countries where the incidence of colon cancer is low (Uganda, Japan, India). A group of English subjects in Uganda who maintained traditional "Western" eating habits were found to have fecal flora virtually the same as that of the English subjects who lived in England.[9] A study conducted by researchers at the American Health Foundation demonstrated that the fecal flora of Americans on a typical "Western-type diet" contained a significantly higher concentration of neutral sterols, bile acids, and anaerobic bacteria than that of American vegetarians.[10] In another study, it was demonstrated that the fecal excretion of neutral sterols and bile acids decreased significantly when volunteers on a high-fat, high-meat diet were put on a vegetarian diet.[11]

It has been hypothesized that the degradation of certain steroids by anaerobic bacteria creates carcinogenic substances, the most notable being deoxycholic acid.[12] Thus, the etiological relationship between meat eating and colon cancer is based on evidence that, compared to diets which include little or no meat, the so-called mixed or Western-type diet generates greater quantities of steroids and anaerobic bacteria which metabolize these steroids, creating greater quantities of certain steroid metabolites which are known to possess carcinogenic properties. Moreover, the stools produced by the high-fat, low-fiber Western diet tend to be relatively small—the fecal transit time is considerably longer than it would be for those on a high-fiber diet. Consequently, this longer fecal transit time allows for increased formation of potential carcinogens in the colon and also exposes the colonic mucosa to a more concentrated form of these substances for a prolonged period of time.[13]

Vegetarian dietaries, especially the vegan diet, usually include significantly greater quantities of fiber than meat-based diets. One study which compared the intestinal transit time of 24 lacto-ovo vegetarians and 24 meat eaters found a mean difference of 28 hours between the two groups: The mean intestinal transit time for the vegetarian group was 49 hours whereas this time for the meat-eating subjects was 77 hours.[14]

DIET AND HEART DISEASE

The carnivore's diet mainly consists of meat and is, consequently, very high in cholesterol and saturated fats. Carnivorous animals are not adversely affected by the large quantities of cholesterol and saturated fats they consume. Conversely, the vegetarian species has a very limited ability to metabolize these food components properly.[15] This does not really create a problem for most vegetarian animals since cholesterol and saturated fats do not exist in the foods they would normally eat. There is, however, a considerable segment of the human population whose intake of cholesterol and saturated fats is far in excess of what their bodies are able to utilize. While cholesterol is an essential component in the production of bile acids and certain hormones, the adult body has the capacity to synthesize all the cholesterol it requires.[16] Our bodies are protected from excessive increases in cholesterol to some extent by virtue of the fact that our capacity to absorb this substance is limited. Thus, a considerable portion of this unneeded dietary cholesterol is simply passed through the gastrointestinal tract into the feces.[17] However, the intestine does absorb as much as 40 percent of this dietary cholesterol, adding to the supply which is produced by biosynthesis.[18] The human body is normally able to metabolize its own cholesterol as well as some portion of that which is derived from food. However, the heavy consumption of animal products which is common in many affluent countries tends to raise the serum cholesterol* to such excessively high levels that the body is not capable of properly metabolizing

---

* The term "serum cholesterol" refers to the cholesterol in the blood, which is composed of both the cholesterol which is taken into the body from dietary sources (e.g., meat, eggs, dairy products), and that which is synthesized by the body itself.

this substance. A portion of the cholesterol settles on the inner lining of the arteries, creating fatty streaks referred to as "atheromata."* Through the course of many years, a continuous high intake of cholesterol and saturated fats results in a continuous accumulation of these deposits (plaques) on the inner walls of the arteries. This degenerative process is referred to as "atherosclerosis."

The heart obtains its oxygen and other essential elements from the blood which comes through the coronary arteries. When these arteries contain substantial deposits of plaque, the passage through which blood is sent to the heart is thus constricted, reducing the amount of blood received by this organ. The heart's ability to function

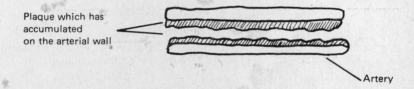

Plaque which has
accumulated
on the arterial wall

Artery

is thus impaired. This condition may result in what is commonly referred to as a "heart attack." The flow of blood to a particular part of the heart may be stopped entirely if a thrombus (blood clot) becomes lodged in one of the coronary arteries. This condition is referred to as a "coronary occlusion." Apoplexy (stroke) is caused by a thrombus which becomes lodged in an artery leading to the brain, resulting in a cutoff of blood to a particular part of that organ. As atherogenesis becomes more advanced, a person becomes more susceptible to these various types of occlusive disorders: since the passage through the arteries is constricted as a result of the accumulated plaque deposits, a thrombus is more likely to become lodged within this narrow channel than in one which is wider. Additionally, while the precise mechanism is not clearly understood, it is widely believed that the development of the thrombus itself is facilitated by the relatively large quantity of saturated fats in the diet.[19]

Prior to World War II, atherosclerosis was regarded primarily as part of the aging process. The food shortages experienced during

---

* Studies conducted as early as 1910 noted the high lipid and cholesterol content of atheromata.

that war prompted several researchers to examine data on how changes in dietary habits affected the health of various population groups. Evidence linking heart disease with cholesterol and saturated-fat intake developed as an incidental part of these investigations. One study published in 1946 on "relief diets" showed that serum cholesterol levels became lower when vegetable protein was used to replace protein from animal sources.[20] Several European researchers reported that the mortality rate from heart disease had declined in their respective countries during the war years. Animal foods, particularly meats, were in short supply during this period. These researchers further noted there was a considerable rise in heart disease mortality when animal foods were more plentiful after the war had ended.[21] One study, in particular, cited a steady rise in the mortality rate for heart disease among the Norwegian population from 1927 until 1940. A sharp reversal in this trend began in 1941, which continued for the duration of the war. When animal foods became more abundant after the war had ended, the mortality rate for various forms of heart disease rose again to its prewar level, reflecting the increased cholesterol and saturated-fat intake.[22]

Further evidence on the relationship between diet and heart disease was developed throughout the 1950s. Three U.S. Army doctors who conducted autopsies on Korean and American soldiers killed in the Korean War found that 77.3 percent of the 300 Americans they examined had developed atherosclerosis. This condition did not exist in the Korean soldiers, whose diet was relatively low in cholesterol and saturated fats as contrasted with the American diet. Apropos of this report is a study showing that the diet of American soldiers stationed in Korea contains nearly three times as much fat as the diet of Korean soldiers. The Americans obtain their protein from meat, eggs and dairy products—foods that are high in cholesterol and saturated fats—whereas the principal sources of protein in the Korean diet are rice and beans. The Koreans were found to have considerable lower serum cholesterol levels than the Americans. When a group of 67 Korean soldiers were put on the U.S. Army diet there was a significant rise in their serum cholesterol levels.[23]

It is now generally recognized that diet is a significant risk factor in the development of heart disease. Epidemiological studies show that the mortality rate for heart disease in various countries tends to correlate with the per capita dietary intake of cholesterol and saturated fats in those countries. A statement released in 1973 by the American Heart Association notes:

> In well-documented population studies using standard methods of diet and coronary disease assessment, no populations habitually subsisting on low saturated fat diets have an appreciable amount of coronary disease. This evidence suggests that a high saturated fat diet is an essential factor for a high incidence of coronary heart disease and that other risk factors are important contributory causes.

Cholesterol Intake Related to Mortality Rate[24]

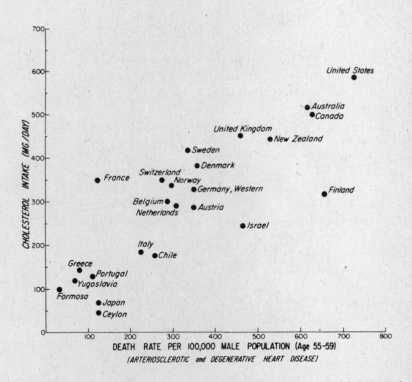

The mortality rate for heart disease compared with mean daily intake of cholesterol for 24 countries. The mortality rate is represented in deaths per 100,000 population in men aged 55–59 from the year 1955 through 1956.

It is recognized that the data derived from such investigations do not permit unequivocal conclusions. Nevertheless, the evidence is strong to show that elevated levels of lipoproteins containing cholesterol and triglyceride to lead to accelerated rates of atherogenesis. At a cholesterol level of 250 mg./100 ml. or higher—common in American adults—the risk of developing coronary heart disease is twice that of persons with levels under 220 mg./100 ml.[25]

A joint policy statement of the American Medical Association's Council on Foods and Nutrition and the Food and Nutrition Board of the National Academy of Sciences—National Research Council notes that serum cholesterol levels in most American men and women are undesirably high and that this is a significant factor contributing to the high incidence of coronary heart disease in the United States.[26] Heart disease is the leading cause of mortality in the United States, accounting for 54 percent of all deaths in this country. Conversely, the mortality rate for coronary heart disease in Japan is very low. The typical Japanese diet contains very little cholesterol. The proportion of the total caloric intake derived from fat is also quite low,

Serum Cholesterol Levels and Intake of Saturated Fat[27]

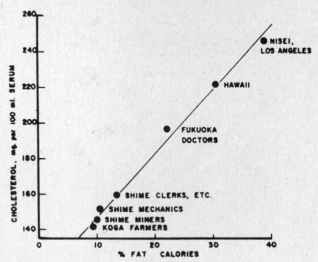

Mean serum cholesterol levels compared with the percentage of calories derived from fat in the diets of 284 Japanese men aged 40–49 years. Diet is largely determined by income and dietary habits in a given region.

and much of this is in the form of unsaturated fats. Epidemiologists have discounted race as a possible factor, noting that the incidence of heart disease is considerably greater among Japanese living in regions outside Japan where diets are high in cholesterol and saturated fats than among the native Japanese population.

A study of second-generation Japanese who live in the United States found that, having adopted the typical American diet, these Nisei had serum cholesterol levels similar to those of American Caucasians and that heart disease was the leading cause of mortality for both races.

Finding that the Caucasian community in South Africa has a considerably higher mortality rate from coronary heart disease than the Bantu population, there was some speculation that race was a possible factor. A 1955 study of dietary habits of the Bantu, Mulatto, and Caucasian peoples in the Cape Town area helped to disprove this notion. It was found that the mean serum cholesterol levels for each of these three groups corresponded to their intake of animal foods high in saturated fats. The Caucasian group had the highest consumption of animal foods and the highest serum cholesterol level. The use of animal foods was lowest in the Bantu group, which also

The Effect of Dietary Habits on Serum Cholesterol Levels[28]

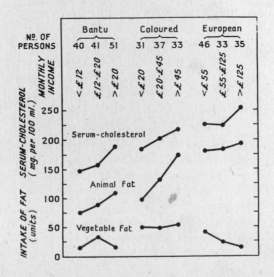

had the lowest serum cholesterol level. The Mulatto group was intermediate in respect to the use of animal foods and serum cholesterol levels. As part of this study each of these three groups was subdivided according to income. It was found that dietary habits, particularly the use of animal foods, was largely related to the income for each of the racial groups as a whole and within the subdivisions of each of these groups. Significantly enough, both the intake of saturated fats and serum cholesterol levels were similar in the Bantu and Mulatto subgroups whose income was the same. Likewise, the Mulatto and Caucasian subgroups with similar income levels had similar serum cholesterol levels, which again corresponded to their use of animal foods high in saturated fats.

Epidemiological studies indicate that there is a possible relationship between the incidence of heart disease and the percentage of the total caloric intake derived from carbohydrates. Some researchers believe this correlation is simply due to a relatively low consumption of saturated fats, since a relatively large proportion of the total caloric intake is derived from carbohydrates. These researchers thus feel that carbohydrate intake is an incidental factor in determining serum cholesterol levels and the incidence of heart disease. However, while acknowledging that the intake of saturated fats is a factor in such studies, some researchers believe that the relatively large quantities of fiber consumed on a high-carbohydrate diet actually inhibits fat absorption, which, in turn, tends to reduce the serum cholesterol level. The relationship between fiber intake and serum cholesterol levels has been demonstrated in clinical studies; these have shown that the serum cholesterol level is substantially reduced by increasing the consumption of high-fiber foods.[29] It has even been suggested that there is a better correlation between crude fiber intake and serum cholesterol levels than is found in the saturated/polyunsaturated fat ratio and serum cholesterol levels.[30]

Although the precise physiological principle by which saturated fats elevate the serum cholesterol level is not known, several hypotheses have been set forth to explain this mechanism in view of what is already known about the cholesterol cycle in the human body. It is believed that saturated fats facilitate the absorption of cholesterol from the intestine, since this process appears to be largely dependent upon the simultaneous absorption of such fatty acids.[31] Cholesterol is more soluble in saturated fats than in the highly unsaturated fats. Moreover, it is particularly significant to note that polyunsaturated fats have a tendency actually to lower serum cholesterol. Two of the mechanisms which are believed to account for the cholesterol-lowering effect of polyunsaturated fats are: (1) polyunsaturated fats seem to inhibit cholesterol biosynthesis and (2) they appear to inhibit the absorption of dietary cholesterol.

One study demonstrated the changes in serum cholesterol levels of 13 men when there was a significant reduction in their intake of saturated fats. The mean serum cholesterol level of these subjects was reduced by 21 percent when 85 percent of the saturated fat in their diet was replaced with a polyunsaturated fat. The total fat content of both diets was maintained at the same level—38 percent of the total caloric intake.[32]

The relationship between the concentration of low-density lipoproteins in the blood and serum cholesterol levels is of particular interest. Lipoproteins are produced when fatty acids combine with protein. These protein-lipid complexes serve as a transport mechanism whereby cholesterol is carried in the blood to various tissues in the body. The cholesterol constituent of the low-density lipoprotein (LDL or beta) molecules is considerably greater than that of the smaller, high-density lipoprotein (HDL or alpha) molecules. It is widely believed that diets containing large amounts of saturated fats and cholesterol tend to increase the concentration of low-density lipoproteins. It is particularly significant to note the apparent relationship between high concentrations of low-density lipoproteins and high serum cholesterol levels.[33] One study compared the lipoprotein composition in meat eaters and vegetarians ranging in age from 18 to 60 years. The meat-eating subjects included 92 men and 78 women. The vegetarian group consisted of 59 men and 64 women. There were no significant differences in the concentration of low-density lipoproteins in the vegetarian and flesh-eating women who were under 50 years of age. These findings were consistent with previous studies which have shown that low-density lipoprotein concentrations tend to remain low in women prior to menopause. However, there were highly significant differences in the concentration of low-density lipoproteins between the vegetarian and flesh-eating women over 50 years of age and between the groups of vegetarian and flesh-eating men for all age categories. The flesh-eating subjects had higher concentrations of low-density lipoproteins than the vegetarian subjects.[34] Another study conducted with 150 monks from the Benedictine and Trappist orders demonstrated that the flesh-eating Benedictines had significantly higher concentrations of low-density lipoproteins and higher serum cholesterol levels than the Trappists, who were lacto-ovo vegetarians.[35]

Aside from diet, there are several other risk factors associated with heart disease. For instance, persons over the age of 35 are more susceptible to heart disease than persons who are younger; men are more likely to develop heart disease than women; heredity also appears to be a factor which predisposes certain people to this disease. We are not able to control heredity, our sex, or the aging process. We are, however, able to control our diet. Many researchers as well as organizations such as the American Heart Association have concluded that lowering the serum cholesterol level in the body would significantly reduce one's risk of developing heart disease. A report of the Inner-Society Commission for Heart Disease Resources recommended that Americans should reduce their daily intake of cholesterol by more than 50 percent and that: "Intake of less than 10 percent of total calories from saturated fats is of critical importance for attainment of optimal serum cholesterol levels for most people."[36] This could be achieved by reducing the total proportion of fats in the diet and by replacing a large portion of saturated fats with polyunsaturated fats.

Various studies have shown that the percentage of the total fat intake derived from saturated fats tends to be significantly greater in meat-based diets than in lacto-ovo vegetarian diets. Conversely, the percentage of the total fat intake derived from polyunsaturated fats tends to be significantly less in meat-based diets than in lacto-ovo vegetarian diets.[37] These differences are even more pronounced in comparisons of meat eaters and vegans. One study demonstrated that the mean percentage of the total fat intake derived from saturated fats in the meat-eating subjects was more than two times greater than that of the vegan subjects. Moreover, the proportion of polyunsaturated fats to the total fat intake was more than twice as great for the vegans as for the meat eaters.[38] Actually, the extent of this differential is quite predictable, since the fats of most plant foods are highly unsaturated whereas most animal foods contain saturated fats.

Cholesterol, being a universal constituent of animal tissue, is consequently found in all animal foods. However, while cholesterol was recently found to be present in algae, it does not exist in any other form of plant life. Therefore, the vegan diet does not include any dietary cholesterol whatsoever. Dairy products and eggs constitute the principal source of protein for lacto-ovo vegetarians. Notwithstanding the cholesterol content of these foods, the total intake of dietary cholesterol tends to be significantly lower in the lacto-ovo vegetarian diet than in the typical meat-based diet in the affluent countries, which usually includes large quantities of dairy products and eggs as well as flesh foods.

The total intake of cholesterol and fat as well as the polyunsaturated/saturated fat ratio in a given diet is reflected in the serum cholesterol level. Several studies have demonstrated that lacto-ovo vegetarian adults tend to have significantly lower serum cholesterol levels than flesh-eating adults.[39] Comparisons of vegans and lacto-ovo vegetarians have shown that vegans tend to have significantly lower serum cholesterol levels than their lacto-ovo counterparts.[40]

DIET AND BONE DENSITY

Various studies have shown that after an increase in bone mass from infancy through pubescence there is a gradual and steady decrease in bone mass after this period, which continues throughout life.[41] This degenerative process, referred to as osteoporosis, may begin in men at the age of 45 and in women as early as age 35.[42] One hypothesis on the reason for this bone dissolution is that a portion of the phosphate in bone is utilized as a buffer base when there is an excess of acid ash in the body. Phosphate is generally thought to be an important part of the body's mechanism for maintaining pH homeostasis, i.e., it serves to regulate the acid-alkaline balance in the body.[43] It has been suggested that a possible correlation exists between meat consumption and the occurrence of osteoporosis, since flesh foods are a primary source of acid ash. Corroboration of this hypothesis is found in a controlled study on the incidence of osteoporosis among vegetarians and meat eaters. A group of 25 lacto-ovo vegetarians and another group of 25 flesh eaters were used for this study. Each group consisted of 8 males and 17 females, all ranging in age from 53 to 79 years. The results of this study showed that the bone density of the vegetarian subjects was significantly greater than that of their flesh-eating counterparts in all age catego-

ries. It was even found that the average bone density of the 70–79-
year-old vegetarians was greater than that of the 50–59-year-old flesh
eaters. It was also discovered that, while there was a decrease in
bone density for both groups, this decrease was less pronounced in
the vegetarian subjects. Additionally, this report noted that no further
decrease in bone density seemed to occur in the vegetarian subjects
after the age of 60, whereas the flesh eaters experienced a continuous
decline in bone mass.[44]

4

The Meat Industry, the Consumer, and the Law

THE MEAT INDUSTRY AND YOUR HEALTH

Being part of the dead body of some animal, meat is highly susceptible to bacterial contamination. Consumers Union conducted tests on hamburger, frankfurters, and sausages from different parts of the United States, which revealed that substantial quantities of these meat products contained unacceptably high levels of bacteria.[1] Dr. Richard Novick of the Public Health Research Institute, in his testimony at congressional hearing on Food Safety and Quality, noted: ". . . many studies have been done to show that the meat we buy is grossly contaminated with both coliform bacteria and salmonella."[2]

MEAT INSPECTION

The various hygienic problems associated with flesh eating (such as bacterial contamination and chemical residues) are controlled to some extent by meat inspection. There are, however, serious deficiencies in the meat-inspection procedures which are presently followed in the United States. Thorough inspection of meat is simply not practical. Animals are slaughtered and inspected in assembly-line fashion. An inspector in a poultry plant has less than three seconds to examine each bird.[3]

43

A joint FAO/WHO study on meat hygiene noted: "Normal meat inspection procedures (masseter and cardiac muscle cuts), even when performed with meticulous care, cannot give complete assurance of safe meat when carcasses are only lightly infected with cysticerci."[4] The lack of systematic microscopic examinations for trichinae has been raised as a point of contention by various consumer groups and public-health organizations. If trichinoscopical examinations were made as a routine procedure, slaughterhouse operations would be greatly hampered. Moreover, samples from hogs that are lightly or moderately infected with trichinosis may not even be detected with a trichinoscope.[5] Dr. Myron G. Schultz of the Center for Disease Control in Atlanta, Georgia, estimates that 100,000 trichinae-infected hogs are processed in the United States each year.[6] Noting that about 360 servings are obtained from a single hog, Dr. Robert H. Moser estimates that each year about 40 million servings of trichina-infected pork are consumed in the United States.[7] Actually, this is a conservative estimate in view of the fact that a considerable quantity of pork is combined with the meat of other animals in processing sausage.

There are 1,300 serotypes within the genus *Salmonella*. While all serotypes are considered potential pathogens for humans, twelve of these account for 78 percent of all documented cases of human infections. Most people who contract salmonella poisoning recover within a few days. They experience nausea, diarrhea, abdominal cramps, fever, and sometimes vomiting followed by chills. Because the symptoms of this disease are similar to intestinal influenza symptoms and because of the temporary nature of the illness, many people do not actually seek medical attention and do not realize that their illness was caused by eating salmonella-infected meat. It is estimated that each year about two million Americans contract salmonella poisoning. In a report titled *An Evaluation of the Salmonella Problem*, the National Research Council of the National Academy of Sciences stated: "Salmonellosis is one of the most important communicable disease problems in the United States today."[8]

Notwithstanding the fact that salmonellosis is the most common disease contracted by human beings from livestock and their products, detection of salmonella bacteria is not actually required as part of USDA meat-inspection procedures. Slaughterhouses, particularly poultry-processing plants, provide an ideal environment for the spread of salmonella bacteria. A survey of one cattle slaughterhouse showed that 87 out of 359 carcasses examined (24 percent) were contaminated with salmonella.[9] One study published in *Poultry Science* reported that while only a small number of birds entering a processing plant were infected with salmonella, as much as 90 percent of the dressed product was found to be contaminated with salmonella.[10] Another study found that 95 percent of the poultry from one federally inspected plant was contaminated with salmonella.[11] The National Academy of Sciences cites measures that could be taken to ameliorate the salmonella problem but concludes that the cost of instituting such reforms would be prohibitive:

> Traditional animal husbandry practices allow ample opportunity for the spread of salmonellosis within flocks and herds, but certain modern innovations are likely to exacerbate the situation. For example, increased use of contaminated animal by-products to feed poultry and swine (e.g., meat and bone meal, fish meal, and poultry meal) exposes more animals to infection; and greater crowding of animals into feeding lots, broiler houses, and holding pens increases the likelihood of spread from one animal to another. No less significant is the long-standing practice of crowding animals together in vehicles during transportation and holding them in dirty pens while awaiting slaughter. Numerous studies have demonstrated the rapid spread of salmonellae under these circumstances.
>
> To eradicate salmonellosis from domestic animals will require radical and very expensive changes in management practices all the way from breeding to slaughter; it is therefore unreasonable to expect complete elimination of all salmonella infections in the foreseeable future.[12]

Since the federal meat inspection program offers little protection from salmonella contamination, meat consumers should take appropriate measures to protect themselves from salmonella poisoning.

Salmonella poisoning poses a threat to meat eaters who do not exercise a certain degree of caution in cooking meat adequately. Interestingly enough, fresh meats, including poultry, cannot be subjected to temperatures that would be sufficient to kill salmonella bacteria and yet retain the quality and appearance of unprocessed meat.[13] Foods not normally cooked by the consumer at high temperatures (e.g., precooked foods) as well as foods that are not cooked at all (e.g., salad vegetables) may become contaminated with salmonellae in a number of ways. Such foods may be contaminated by kitchen utensils, cutting boards, the counter top, or one's hands that have come into contact with salmonellae-infected meat. Precooked, processed meats are frequently contaminated by butchers who handle raw meat.[14]

The American Public Health Association, composed of federal, state, and local public-health officials, feels that the public is misled by U.S. meat inspection seals, which certify a product's wholesomeness, since current inspection procedures do not require detection of salmonella and other potentially harmful bacteria. This false sense of security was stressed in a suit filed by the American Public Health Association and others which would compel the USDA to require meat labels to include a warning that would read in part: "Caution. Improper handling and inadequate cooking of this product may be hazardous to your health." The Agriculture Department claimed it would be unfair to stigmatize the meat industry by warning consumers of the potential hazards associated with flesh eating.

Aside from the various deficiencies in U.S. meat inspection procedures, many of the federal meat inspection regulations that do exist are not strictly enforced. Dishonest meat inspectors are bribed to overlook violations while conscientious meat inspectors are harassed by packing-plant supervisors who are more concerned with profit margins than with the health of those who use their products. Some federal inspectors have been subjected to verbal abuse. Others have actually been physically assaulted.[15] Aside from the lowering of meat inspection standards which results from such instances of bribery or harassment, many federal meat inspectors readily acknowledge that if the presently constituted U.S. meat inspection regulations were strictly enforced, no meat processor in America would be able to continue doing business.[16]

In judging the policies of the USDA it is important to bear in mind that this agency represents the interests of both food producers and food consumers—an obvious conflict of interest. Consequently, this agency is forced to make compromises in its commitment to the public's well-being in order to preserve the financial integrity of the meat industry. The USDA is notorious for its lax enforcement of meat inspection regulations. The General Accounting Office, which oversees federal regulatory activities for Congress, has issued reports citing the USDA's failure to take quick action against slaughterhouses where serious violations existed. One such report noted that out of

40 slaughterhouses which had been cited for violations over a period of several years 30 had not remedied the situation. The GAO officials reported finding carcasses of cattle and hogs that were contaminated with cockroaches, flies, rodent feces, and rust. Among the violators were several major meat-packing companies, including Swift, Wilson, John Morrell, Armour, Carnation, Cudahy & Stark, and Wetzel.[17]

Aside from the USDA's lax enforcement of regulations governing meat-industry operations as set forth in the so-called "Wholesome Meat Act," this agency has actively supported rule changes that serve to further the interests of the meat industry at the expense of meat consumers. An interesting case in point is the USDA's proposal to allow as much as 3 percent ground bone in processed meat despite 4,000 letters from consumers who opposed this idea. It is particularly curious to note that the endorsement of the Agriculture Department's proposal to allow ground bone in processed meat by USDA Assistant Secretary Carol Foreman is a complete reversal of the position Ms. Foreman had taken on this matter in her former capacity as executive director of the Consumer Federation of America.

CHEMICALS IN MEAT

Chemicals are used throughout the various stages of meat production. Although the use of chemicals such as sodium nitrite, DES, arsenic, and antibiotics poses a serious health hazard to those who eat meat, the meat industry maintains that economic benefits outweigh the health risks. For instance, nitrofurans have been characterized as "highly suspect carcinogens," based on extensive studies conducted by the Food and Drug Administration.[18] However, efforts to ban the use of nitrofurans have been stymied by drug companies that manufacture this chemical as well as by meat interests. David Phillipson, president of the Animal Health Institute and vice president of the Upjohn Company, a major drug firm, is strongly opposed to banning nitrofurans as well as various other chemicals used by the meat industry. Testifying on this matter at a hearing before a subcommittee on Agricultural Research and General Legislation, Phillipson cited an FDA study which estimates that a loss of $2.6 billion would be incurred by hog and poultry producers if furazolidones (a class of nitrofurans) were banned.[19]

SODIUM NITRATE AND SODIUM NITRITE

Sodium nitrate and sodium nitrite are used in various types of meat, including bacon, smoked ham, sausage, frankfurters, dried beef, bologna, salami, and fish. These use of sodium nitrate and sodium nitrite in meat serves two basic purposes. These chemicals retard the growth of harmful bacteria, most notably that of *Clostridium botulinum*, which causes botulism food poisoning. Sodium nitrite and sodium nitrate also give meat a fresh red color as a result of their reaction with pigments in the muscle and blood of the meat. The meat would otherwise turn an unappetizing gray or gray brown.

Dr. Charles C. Edwards, who defended the use of nitrite in meat during his tenure as commissioner of the Food and Drug Administration, conceded that sodium nitrite can be poisonous to small children, that it can deform the fetuses of pregnant women and can also cause serious harm to anemic persons. These concerns are based on the fact that nitrite is absorbed from the intestinal tract into the bloodstream, where it converts hemoglobin in the blood cells to methemoglobin. Unlike hemoglobin, methemoglobin does not carry oxygen. Consequently, when high levels of nitrite are taken into the body, the blood's ability to carry oxygen is seriously impaired. This situation is most critical in infants because the hemoglobin content of their blood is considerably lower than that of adults.

The cancer risk associated with the use of nitrite and nitrate has caused serious concern among scientists in the public-health field. Nitrite and nitrate are capable of combining with secondary and tertiary amines. This synergistic reaction produces carcinogenic substances called nitrosamines. Significantly enough, a wide variety of substances commonly ingested by human beings, including tea, wine, cereals, certain medicines, and tobacco contain secondary amines.[20]

Efforts to ban the use of nitrite and nitrate in meats have been continually thwarted by meat-industry lobbyists, who insist that the use of these additives is needed to retard bacterial growth in meat. Food additives which can cause cancer would ordinarily be banned under provisions set forth in the Delaney Amendment.* However,

---

* The Delaney Amendment to the Food, Drug and Cosmetic Act (1958) prohibits the use of food additives that have been shown to cause cancer in laboratory tests.

these chemicals were originally approved as *coloring agents* by the USDA in 1925 under the Federal Meat Inspection Act and are not subject to provisions of the Delaney Amendment to the Food, Drug, and Cosmetic Act which govern the use of *additives*.

ARSENIC

Arsenic is widely used as a growth stimulant by hog farmers and poultry producers. Despite its carcinogenic properties, arsenic residue levels of .55 ppm are permitted by the FDA. Federal law requires livestock owners to discontinue using arsenic in the animals' feed 5 days prior to slaughter so that arsenic residue levels will not exceed these standards. However, many livestock producers simply do not comply with this directive. In an ABC television documentary titled "Food: Green Grow the Profits," reporters found there was arsenic in 4 out of 5 "final food" samples that had been taken from different locations.[21] The USDA, in January, 1972, estimated that 15.5 percent of the nation's poultry contained residues of arsenic which exceeded the legal limit.[22]

DIETHYLSTILBESTROL (DES)

Diethylstilbestrol, commonly referred to as DES, is a synthetic hormone given to livestock as a growth stimulant. The USDA Economic Research Service reports that steers given DES consume 11 percent less feed while gaining 15 percent in weight.[23] DES has been used in the United States since 1954 despite studies conducted as early as 1940 which have shown this chemical to be a carcinogen. The continued use of DES was jeopardized by the Delaney Amendment. However, yielding to pressure from the meat industry, Congress approved a revision of the Delaney Amendment which was specifically designed to allow for the continued use of DES. This revised amendment, passed in 1962, permitted DES to be used provided that no residue of this chemical could be detected in any edible portion of the animal's carcass. When the USDA began using a more sophisticated technique for analyzing tissue samples in 1971, DES residue was detected. During this same period of time, further evidence on the relationship between DES and human cancer was developed. A study of several young women who had developed cancer of the vagina revealed that the mothers of these cancer victims had taken DES as an anti-abortive drug during pregnancy. Moreover, other clinical studies conducted in the United States and Great Britain demonstrated a relationship between the use of DES and cardiovascular disease.[24]

The FDA announced on August 2, 1972, that it intended to ban the use of DES as a growth stimulant for livestock. However, the ban on DES in livestock feed was not to become effective until January 1, 1973. This would enable cattlemen to use up their existing stock of this deadly drug. The ban was only effective for a year. Several drug companies that manufacture DES challenged the FDA ruling in the U.S. Court of Appeals for the District of Columbia. On January 24, 1974, the court ruled in favor of the DES manufacturers on the technicality that the FDA had failed to hold administrative hearings on the use of DES before issuing its ban on this drug.[25]

The use of DES as a growth stimulant is viewed as a serious health hazard by 32 countries, which have prohibited the use of this chemical.[26] However, the U.S. government still permits DES to be used by livestock owners to increase their profits. The FDA has estimated that a ban on the use of DES as a growth stimulant would result in an annual loss of $503 million to the beef industry.[27]

ANTIBIOTICS

Antibiotics are used to prevent and treat various diseases which affect livestock. Since 1949, antibiotics have also been used by the livestock industry as a growth stimulant. There is some controversy over the exact mechanism behind the growth-promoting properties of antibiotics. Some scientists believe that this effect is due largely to the control of certain unidentified microorganisms that in some way interfere with animal growth.[28] Significantly enough, it has been pointed out that the growth-promoting effect of antibiotics is realized only when animals are raised in crowded, dirty, heavily contaminated pens and feedlots.[29] In essence, then, the subtherapeutic use of antibiotics is viewed by the meat industry as an effective means to compensate for poor animal-husbandry practices.

The most serious problem to arise from the widespread practice of using antibiotics as a growth stimulant is that an increase in the prevalence of antibiotic-resistant bacteria is created. These antibiotic-resistant bacteria are transferred from livestock to human beings who eat their flesh. Since these bacteria have survived the antibiotics which the animal has consumed, they may well be capable of surviving antibiotics that would ordinarily be used to treat various human diseases. Moreover, the complicated workings of these antibiotic-resistant bacteria may give rise to new disease strains which are resistant to antibiotics. The following example is a case in point: In 1969, 41 babies with diarrhea and vomiting caused by a bacteria of the Escherichia coli group were admitted to several pediatric clinics in Manchester, England. Doctors unsuccessfully tried to treat them with various antibiotics. The babies died. Two microbiologists from a London research institute for intestinal diseases were sent to make a complete report on the tragedy. Their findings concluded that the death of the infants was caused by a new germ type that had developed a resistance to antibiotics through their use in animal feeds.[30]

The development of antibiotic-resistant bacteria has increased steadily since the advent of the antibiotic era. Several different types of pathogenic antibiotic-resistant bacteria have emerged within recent years.[31] It has been pointed out that the development of such bacteria types is due, in large part, to the extensive therapeutic use of antibiotics by human beings. Although it is not actually known to what extent the subtherapeutic use of antibiotics by livestock producers is responsible for the increase in antibiotic-resistant bacteria, it is most significant to note that 50 percent of all the antibiotics manufactured in the United States are used as growth stimulants for meat animals.[32] It has, of course, also been pointed out that the treatment of human disease is a more compelling reason to use antibiotics than the desire to increase the profit margin of one's business. The FDA estimates that the cost of meat-industry operations would increase $1.9 billion if penicillin and tetracyclines were not allowed to be used in swine and cattle feeds for subtherapeutic purposes.[33] This increase would naturally be passed on to the consumer.

Certainly there are many consumers who do not think the health risks associated with the use of antibiotics as a growth stimulant for livestock offsets the advantage of lower meat prices. Mary T. Goodwin, chairperson of a consumer organization associated with the Food and Nutrition Board of the National Academy of Sciences, notes that many consumers are not aware of the health hazards associated with the use of antibiotics in animal feed. Moreover, those who are aware of these hazards have no choice in the matter. Ms. Goodwin observed: "One alternative to this problem is to choose not to eat meat."[34] Indeed, this would appear to be the best solution.

HOW TAXPAYERS SUBSIDIZE
THE MEAT INDUSTRY

Government subsidization of the meat industry is considerable. The federal government gives substantial sums of money for research projects on various aspects of meat-industry operations. In 1977, the USDA spent $30 million on poultry research. When the beef industry was experiencing serious financial difficulties in 1974, the USDA agreed to purchase an additional $100 million worth of meat for the school lunch program. Columnist Murray Kempton noted it was somewhat ironic that President Nixon, who had previously attempted to cut the school lunch program's budget, was now endorsing a plan to provide this program with 45 million pounds of prime beef. However, as Mr. Kempton duly notes, Nixon's action in this matter was designed to help the nation's cattle ranchers and was certainly not prompted by a desire to provide luxury foods for schoolchildren.[35] During the same year when the U.S. government was spending $100 million to aid the American beef industry, European governments bought 5,000 tons of surplus beef at a cost of $480 million. A spokesperson for the Common Market Executive Committee stated that in the summer of 1974, 9 European governments owned 130,000 tons of meat, which was costing them more than $300,000 a day in storage charges alone.[36]

A report published by the Council on Environmental Quality in 1975 noted that 31 percent of the land used for grazing livestock is public property.[37] This represents about 373 million acres. Cattle and sheep producers tell us that this land would be "wasted" if it were not for the valuable service they provide. The livestock producers do not refer to the destruction of wildlife in these regions and the deterioration of the land itself, which is caused by their grazing animals.[38] Cattle and sheep producers do not even pay a fair market value for the privilege of using these public lands. The present fee is set at $1.51 for each animal per month for use of national resource lands and $1.60 for use of national forest lands. Efforts to set a more equitable fee for the use of these lands have been spectacularly unsuccessful. The "Grazing Fee Moratorium of 1977" (H.R. 9757), passed in 1978, placed a one-year moratorium on proposals to increase public-lands grazing fees. A statement from the director of the Congressional Budget Office on the economic impact of this moratorium noted that this failure to implement recommended grazing fee increases would result in a $5 million loss to the government for the 1978 grazing season.[39]

Despite extensive use of antibiotics and other drugs, animal disease continues to be a serious problem within the meat industry. Indeed, losses due to animal disease are a major factor in the cost of producing animals for food. Part of this expense is simply passed on to the meat-eating consumer. However, a substantial portion of these losses are defrayed by state and federal indemnity programs. When chickens raised in Mississippi were found to be contaminated by dieldrin, a carcinogenic substance, the USDA ordered the destruction of more than 50,000 of these animals. The U.S. government compensated the chicken producers for lost wages in addition to paying full market value for the chickens which had to be destroyed. These indemnity payments were estimated to cost up to $10 million.[40] Actually, this outlay is relatively small compared to the monies which are spent by the government for controlling animal diseases. Indemnity payments made by the federal government for controlling brucellosis rose from $33,350,000 for the 1976 fiscal year to $53,978,000 for the 1978 fiscal year.[41] These figures actually represent only half the total amount spent for this program since the federal government matches subsidies made by individual states on a 50 percent basis.

A bill passed by the U.S. Congress in 1974 allows producers of dairy and beef cattle as well as those who produce sheep, pigs, chickens, and turkeys to obtain loans underwritten by the federal government in amounts up to $350,000. The U.S. government will guarantee up to 90 percent of an individual producer's loan. The House Agriculture Committee stated that administrative costs alone will come to $9.4 million. The Agriculture Department estimates the federal government will incur another $80 million in costs as a result of defaults on these loans.[42] Noting that other farm programs receive only as much as $20,000 in government-guaranteed loans, a *New York Times* editorial referred to this "outrageous subsidy bill" to aid the faltering meat industry as ". . . a scandalous steal out of the public treasury for purposes directly opposite to the public interest."[43] The *Times* editorial noted that when profits from beef sales are high, the beef industry resists price controls or any other kind of governmental interference, citing the inviolability of the so-called free market system under the law of supply and demand. However, this same industry eagerly seeks financial relief from the government when profits are low.

THE MEAT INDUSTRY'S PUBLIC RELATIONS CAMPAIGN: HOW TO SELL A DEAD BODY

There are many different organizations involved in the business of promoting meat products. In addition to the various meat-packing companies which advertise their own separate brands, there are many national and statewide organizations which encourage the American public to eat more meat. There are the National Livestock and Meat Board, which promotes beef, pork and lamb; the American Sheep Industry, which promotes lamb; and 28 state beef councils, which promote beef products. Meat eating is promoted by means of advertising campaigns and the publication of propaganda booklets, which are distributed in public schools, and through lobbying efforts in the nation's capital.

ADVERTISING

The National Livestock and Meat Board creates various types of displays, banners, and posters for use in retail stores, since it has been shown that such gimmicks are very effective in influencing a shopper's purchasing decisions. An important part of the Meat Board's promotion of flesh foods is their so-called consumer information program. In one such promotional effort conducted in 1969, a poll was taken on consumer attitudes toward pork before and after a campaign to improve the image of this meat product. Before the campaign, 21 percent of those polled felt that pork was "always safe to eat." After the campaign, this figure rose to 27 percent.[44]

After stating that the California Beef Council sends press releases to some 500 newspapers and over 300 radio and television stations in California, the manager of this organization commented: "We have established ourselves as a responsible and unbiased source of information on beef and the beef industry."[45] Now how many people are gullible enough to believe that an organization set up to promote beef is an "unbiased source of information on beef and the beef industry"?

Within the past few years, many meat ads have been designed to counter adverse publicity on the various health, economic, and ecological problems associated with flesh eating. One ad sponsored by the Meat Board pictures a well-marbled cut of beef—the type that would be relatively high in calories. Curiously enough, this fatty cut of meat is pictured as part of an ad that informs the reader "why beef is great if you're watching your weight." The ad emphasizes the importance of "nutrient density," i.e., the quantity of vitamins and minerals available per caloric unit. This factor, the ad claims, "brings the virtues of beef into sharp focus." Stressing the importance of "nutrient density" for those who desire to lose weight, the ad compares beef to junk foods, which are such popular items in the American diet today.

An ad sponsored by the American Sheep Industry presents a dire warning: "No more lamb. No more wool. It could happen." Many ecology as well as animal-protection groups have raised strong objections to the sheep industry's so-called "predator control" program. Appealing to the reader's sympathy, the ad states that predators are killing "completely defenseless" lambs, which are "at their mercy." In this same vein, the ad later relates: "Since biblical times 2,000 years ago, sheep have depended on us to protect and shepherd them." What sophistry! The people in the sheep industry wish to "protect" their innocent lambs so they, themselves, will have the privilege of killing these "completely defenseless" creatures. The human predator who savors the taste of mutton or lamb chops is responsible for killing more sheep and lambs than coyotes and wolves.

There has been a great deal of controversy in recent years over the use of television commercials that are specifically designed to influence young children. Many in the consumer movement feel that such advertising takes unfair advantage of a child's naïveté. The McDonald's hamburger chain is one of the major producers of children's commercials. The McDonald's television commercials feature a variety of fantastic characters, including a clown named Ronald

McDonald, who is now said to rival Santa Claus in popularity among children.[46]

LITERATURE

Organizations such as the McDonald's hamburger chain, the Swift Meat Packing Company, the National Livestock and Meat Board, and various state beef councils publish literature to promote their products. The dissemination of this propaganda is, curiously enough, often referred to as a "consumer information" program. Much of this propaganda is distributed in the public school system. The manager of the California Beef Council notes that approximately 800 junior and senior high schools in California were involved in his organization's "consumer information" program. This represents half of the public schools in that state. He notes that in the 1974–75 school year 500,000 pieces of literature were distributed in California high schools. Over 1,000 teachers were sent beef teaching manuals, lesson plans, charts, and other such material. The California Beef Council is particularly interested in influencing the home-economics teachers in their state.[47]

The Swift Meat Packing Company has produced comic books to promote the image of meat products. One such comic book, entitled "The Winning Combination," tells the story of Bob Turner, who has been doing rather poorly on the high school basketball team. Bob's cheerleader girlfriend, Betty, informs a teacher named Jane White about Bob's poor eating habits. Miss White, Betty, and Bob go to the school nutrition exhibit, where they meet Bob's older brother, Jim. One of the displays shows the picture of a calf with a caption that reads: "You can't eat grass and alfalfa, but animals can eat it for you." Explaining the meaning of this display, Miss White comments on the efficiency of using animals as "food manufacturers": "They digest and turn these LOW-grade foods into HIGH-grade foods that we can eat!" Jim, who is obviously impressed with Miss White's wisdom, remarks: "If it weren't for our meat animals, half the land in this country would go to waste as far as human food is concerned." The nutrition exhibit has a profound effect on the lives of Bob, Betty, Jim, and Miss White. Betty is enraptured over the fact that Bob has written a report on nutrition which has been posted on the science room's bulletin board. Bob, of course, becomes a better basketball player (which also gives Betty something to cheer about). Oh, by the by, Jim marries the wise and beautiful Miss White.

A comic book entitled "The Story of Meat," published by the American Meat Institute, opens with a most provocative question: "Why couldn't the North American Indians living in a land teeming with natural resources lift themselves above their primitive stone age culture?" The American Meat Institute's answer to their rhetorical question is that these Indians "failed to domesticate livestock for their principal food necessity—meat." Indeed—are we to believe that it was the cattlemen and sheep ranchers who elevated the level of culture in the old Wild West?

The McDonald's Corporation publishes a coloring book for grammar school children which includes various cartoon characters. The purpose of this book is entertainment and could hardly be characterized as educational. If McDonald's chose to include a picture of a steer being butchered in a slaughterhouse, that would be educational. Would the children know enough to color the butcher's apron red?

The National Livestock and Meat Board has published a booklet entitled "Meat and the Vegetarian Concept" in an apparent effort to counter some of the arguments raised by vegetarians against the use of flesh foods. This pamphlet, printed in 1976, contains a curious assortment of misinformation. In describing vegetarians, the author of this pamphlet remarks: "some eat seafood." Presumably such vagary has led the writer of this pamphlet to characterize the macrobiotic diet as vegetarian even though many people who follow this regimen eat fish. The statement that no significant difference exists between the length of a carnivore's intestine and that of a human being indicates that the writer knows very little about comparative anatomy. In a section entitled "Advantages of Four Food Groups," a nutrition instructor is quoted as stating: "A vegetarian, to be adequately nourished, must have a sophisticated knowledge of nutrient sources." Thus, we must assume that the several million vegetarians in America are either malnourished or that most of those who belong to this group have a "sophisticated knowledge" of nutrition. The writer states that, within a short time after becoming a vegetarian, many people report a lack of heaviness, which is associated with meat, as well as renewed vigor. While not denying that such a sensation is a common experience among vegetarians, the writer conjectures that this phenomenon is based on psychological rather than physiological factors. In a section entitled "More than Protein," the writer lists various vitamins and minerals that are available in flesh foods. However, this person neglects to mention that all of these nutrients can be easily obtained from non-flesh-food sources.

It is particularly interesting to see how this pamphlet deals with various questions which relate to serious health hazards associated with flesh eating. The significance of numerous scientific studies linking the use of DES and nitrite to cancer is disputed. Likewise, the writer ignores the preponderance of evidence on the relationship between heart disease and the consumption of foods high in cholesterol and saturated fats. Indeed, this person seeks to show us that meat is relatively low in cholesterol by comparing the cholesterol in a *lean* cut of meat with high-cholesterol foods such as butter and eggs. Of course, it is the "juicy," well-marbled cuts of beef— not the tough, lean cuts, that are pictured in those meat ads which are designed to entice meat consumers into eating more beef. The writer does not seem to feel that the dead body of an animal is more susceptible to contamination than fruits and vegetables. Moreover, this person asserts: "Strict government and industry standards and regulations for the inspection and handling of meat insure that Americans receive healthful, clean, wholesome meat." The fallacy of *strict* government and industry standards has previously been discussed.

5

Fish and Other Marine Animals

Is any kinde subject to rape like fish?
Ill unto man, they neither doe, nor wish:
Fishers they kill not, nor with noise awake,
They doe not hunt, nor strive to make a prey
Of beasts, nor their young sonnes to beare away;
Foules they pursue not, nor do undertake
To spoile the nests industrious birds do make;
Yet them all these unkinde kinds feed upon
To kill them is an occupation,
    And lawes make Fasts, and Lents for their
    destruction.

JOHN DONNE

People who abstain from the flesh of mammals and birds are often referred to as vegetarians even if they eat various types of marine animals. The erroneous classification of such people as vegetarians is presumably due to the fact that animals such as fish, crustaceans, and mollusks are not generally regarded as "flesh" foods. Hence, if one defines vegetarianism simply as the practice of abstaining from *flesh* foods, it is conceivable that persons who eat these "sea foods" might be regarded as vegetarians. However, the term "vegetarianism" as originally coined in the 1840s denotes strict abstinence from all types of animal flesh. Although this original definition of the term "vegetarian" is generally accepted today, there are, nonetheless, a considerable number of people who make a strong distinction between

59

eating various forms of aquatic life and the eating of mammals and birds. It would, therefore, be worthwhile to examine some aspects of using "sea food."

ETHICAL ISSUES

The "venerate" class of the Albigensians abstained from all animal foods except fish. A 14th-century Dominican friar, commenting on the dietary habits of this medieval "heretical" sect, writes: ". . . they never eat flesh, nor even touch it, nor cheese or eggs or aught that is born of the flesh by way of generation or coition."[1] Fish were excluded from this injunction because the Albigensians believed fish were mysteriously created from the water itself.

There are a curious assortment of reasons that have been used to justify the practice of killing various forms of marine animals for food. The semantic distinction between fish and "flesh foods" has previously been cited. It should also be noted that many people do not feel fish are worthy of our sympathy since these creatures are considered to be devoid of both physical and emotional feelings. The term "cold fish" is a colloquialism used to describe a person who is devoid of emotion. While it is true that fish are cold-blooded animals, many people subconsciously fail to distinguish between the biological definition of the word "cold-blooded" and the meaning of this word as used to describe the deeds of obdurate villains. Indeed, this subliminal juxtaposition of cold-blooded fish with callous individuals might well serve to assuage the pangs of a guilty conscience.

Benjamin Franklin rationalized fish eating by announcing to his victims: "If you eat one another I don't see why we mayn't eat you."[2] William Paley, the prominent 18th-century English theologian, noted that many rationalizations which are frequently used to justify killing animals for food are "extremely lame," particularly those used to justify the killing of fish. Paley cites two such rationalizations in his work *Principles of Moral and Political Philosophy:* (1) Animals would "overrun the earth" if they were not killed for food. (2) Animals "are requited for what they suffer at our hands, by our care and protection." Noting the absurdity of these rationalizations as applied to killing fish for food, Paley asks: "What danger is there, for instance, of fish interfering with us, in the occupation of our element? or what do we contribute to their support or preservation?"[3] While ridiculing those who use silly rationalizations to justify killing fish, Paley describes himself as a "great follower of fishing" and adds: ". . . in its cheerful solitude have passed some of the happiest hours of a sufficiently happy life; but to this moment, I could never trace out the source of the pleasure which it afforded me."[4] James Thomson, like Paley, had ambivalent feelings about fishing. In his poem *The Seasons,* Thomson represents fishing as an "art"[5] and a "cheerful" sport[6] despite his fleeting sympathy for the "weak helpless uncomplaining wretch."[7] Thomson prefers "the well-dissembled fly" to the "tortured worm" whose "convulsive twist in agonizing folds" seems to be a disturbing sight for the tender-hearted poet.[8]

Brigid Brophy, herself a vegetarian, does not regard fishing as either an art or a cheerful sport:

> Were it announced tomorrow that anyone who fancied it might, without risk or reprisals or recriminations, stand at a fourth-storey window, dangle out of it a length of string with a meal (labelled "Free") on the end, wait till a chance passer-by took a bite and then, having entangled his cheek or gullet on a hook hidden in the food, haul him up to the fourth floor and there batter him to death with a knobkerrie, I do not think there would be many takers.
>
> Most sane adults would, I imagine, sicken at the mere thought. Yet sane adults do the equivalent to fish every day: not in panic, sexual jealousy, ideological frenzy or even greed—many of our freshwater fish are virtually inedible, and not one of them constitutes a threat to the life, love or ideology of a human on the bank—but for amusement. Civilisation is not outraged at their behaviour. On the contrary: that a person's hobby is fishing is often read as a guarantee of his sterling and innocent character.[9]

Brophy argues that our supereminence among other species does not give us the right to destroy other beings at will. Indeed, it places a special obligation upon us to "recognise and respect the rights of animals."[10]

Peter Singer, the author of *Animal Liberation,* rejects the anthropocentric notion that animals should be used to satisfy the pleasures and needs of humans regardless of the pain and suffering which are caused by this exploitation. Singer uses the term "speciesism" in referring to this subjugation, which is supposedly justified by the supereminence of *Homo sapiens* among other species. Ironically, Singer does not feel it is unethical to kill species such as oysters, clams, mussels, and scallops, since these animals presumably do not feel pain. Singer does not believe this position is inconsistent with his condemnation of speciesism, noting that the criterion he has established on the ethics of killing is not based on the superiority of a species per se, but is rather based on the species' capacity to experience pain. Singer is decidedly opposed to killing fish and crustaceans on ethical grounds. "Fish," Singer notes, "show most of the pain behavior that mammals do."[11] Although he is not quite so certain about the crustacean's capacity to feel pain, he concludes that the various crustacean species "deserve the benefit of the doubt."[12] However, Singer finds it "difficult to imagine" that the Pelecypoda class of mollusks actually experience pain. He remarks: "Those who want to be absolutely certain that they are not causing suffering will not eat mollusks either; but somewhere between a shrimp and an oyster seems as good a place to draw the line as any, and better than most."[13]

Mollusk-eating "vegetarians" are, of course, regarded as heretics by the vegetarian community at large. However, according to Singer's ethical standards, it is far worse to use dairy products and eggs than to eat Pelecypoda mollusks since milch cows, their calves, and laying hens are subjected to much pain and suffering,* whereas Pelecypoda mollusks do not appear to experience pain when they are killed for food. Notwithstanding the merits of this argument, mollusk eaters can hardly be classified as vegetarians. The term "vegetarianism" has never been defined as a philosophical system based on degrees of pain and suffering. Vegetarianism simply means the practice of abstaining from the flesh of *all* animals regardless of their capacity to feel pain.

ENVIRONMENTAL ISSUES

It was formerly thought that there existed an inexhaustible supply of fish that could be taken from the world's seas. However, it is

---

* See Chapter 1, "The Three Basic Vegetarian Diets," pp. 7–11.

now quite apparent that such is not the case. The somewhat recent use of huge fishing vessels with sophisticated equipment has been largely responsible for the serious depletion of the world's fish population which has occurred over the past several years. The catch of most commerical fish has dropped by an average of 40 percent within the past decade.[14] Many species of fish in various parts of the world are now classified as "commercially extinct." Moreover, many marine biologists believe that the worldwide fish catch cannot be expanded beyond its present level.[15] Aside from "overfishing," large numbers of fish are killed by pollution. The U.S. Department of Interior estimated that, in 1968, 15 million fish were killed by various forms of pollution in U.S. rivers, lakes, and streams.[16] Ocean dumping has become an increasingly serious problem. The Council on Environmental Quality estimated that, in 1974, 13,176,000 tons of industrial waste, sewage sludge, and construction and demolition debris were dumped in the Atlantic Ocean—up from 8,079,000 which had been dumped there in 1968.[17]

Interestingly enough, a great deal of waste is generated by the fishing industry itself. Salmon processing produces about 25 percent waste; about 35 to 40 percent waste is created by the processing of halibut; it is estimated that 65 percent of the tuna is wasted in the canning process; about 77 to 85 percent of the shrimp is wasted in processing; about 85 percent waste is created by the processing of blue crabs.[18] The total annual volume of solid wastes generated by the U.S. seafood industry is estimated to be about 1.2 billion pounds.[19] The liquid wastes that are created by fish processing are usually discharged into adjoining waters. Sometimes these wastes are discharged into municipal sewage systems.[20] The processing of oily fish such as sardines and herring creates large quantities of fat and grease wastes, which are discharged into waterways. The fat and grease content of sardine-canning waste waters are estimated to be from 1,000 to 30,000 milligrams per liter compared to 50 to 200 milligrams per liter in domestic sewage.[21]

Many environmentalists have expressed concern over the practice of killing animals that compete with human beings for food. In 1978, Japanese fishermen slaughtered over 1,000 dolphins. Although the dolphins themselves have essentially no commercial value, the Japanese fishermen defend this massacre citing the fact that the dolphin population consumes substantial quantities of fish, which interferes with the fishermen's livelihood.

HEALTH ISSUES

Since heart disease is the leading cause of mortality in the United States, many Americans are concerned about controlling the amount of cholesterol and saturated fats in their diet. Unlike most other animal foods, fish is high in polyunsaturated fats and has a relatively low cholesterol content.* Consequently, many persons who wish to reduce their intake of cholesterol and saturated fats view fish as a good "meat substitute." However, while fish may be a good meat substitute in this respect, it is hardly a good food. The pollution of various waterways, accelerated since the advent of the Industrial Revolution, creates many problems for those who eat fish. A common practice for determining the extent of pollution in a body of water is to test the pollutants found in the fish that inhabit those waters. Seth Lipsky, in an article from the *Wall Street Journal,* reports that the Dow Chemical Company has been organizing fish fries since the mid 1930s "to find out how much of certain chemicals and wastes can enter lakes and streams and still allow the fish to remain acceptable to the palate of even the most sensitive fish lover."[22] He adds: "The problem of keeping fish tasting right isn't simple." Water pollution creates far more serious problems than bad-tasting fish. Environmentalists and public health officials have been particularly concerned with the health hazards posed by chemical pollutants which exist in various bodies of water.

PCBs (polychlorinated biphenyls) are synthetic chemicals which have been widely used since the 1930s. Like DDT, PCBs possess carcinogenic properties and are widely dispersed throughout the environment. A study at the Wood's Hole Oceanographic Institute estimates that PCBs remain in the environment about 500 years—more than 100 times as long as DDT. Despite efforts to control the use of PCBs in recent years, PCB contamination levels have actually increased in various waterways, including the Great Lakes. High levels of PCBs have been found in fish that inhabit Lake Michigan, Lake Superior, Lake Huron, various lakes in New York State, and the Hudson River. One sample of rock bass taken from the Hudson

---

* It should be noted that, unlike fish, crustaceans and mollusks are high in cholesterol.

River had a PCB concentration 70 times higher than the tolerance levels deemed reasonably safe by the FDA.[23]

The New York State Department of Environmental Conservation was harshly criticized by Canadian and American scientists for its plan to build a $10 million fish hatchery near Lake Ontario. Opponents of this plan pointed out that Lake Ontario is heavily contaminated with carcinogenic chemicals such as PCBs, Mirex, Kepone, DDT, and DDE. The fish to be placed in the lake would naturally become contaminated themselves. Among the critics of this plan were members of the New York State Environmental Conservation Department's own staff. One department scientist, Dr. Ward Stone, an associate wildlife pathologist, expressed his strong opposition to this project in a memorandum dated July 23, 1976: "I find it repugnant to think that the state will put fish into Lake Ontario only to have them caught for fun, and then thrown away. Perhaps this goes with our disposable society which considers them disposable living things. I don't see how this program relates to conservation, or aids the environment, and the salmon moving toxins in the feeder streams may make for toxin problems in wildlife species that would otherwise not have them."[24] Aside from failing to recognize the inherent dangers of its plan to release hatchery-bred salmon and trout into the polluted waters of Lake Ontario, the New York State Department of Environmental Conservation has been criticized for its overall laxity in dealing with the problem of toxic substances. The department's contaminant-monitoring program, in particular, is ineffectual.

Endrin is more toxic than any other chlorinated hydrocarbon. In discussing the hazards of various chlorinated hydrocarbons, Rachel Carson remarks that endrin "makes the progenitor of all this group of insecticides, DDT, seem by comparison almost harmless. It is 15 times as poisonous as DDT to mammals, 30 times as poisonous to fish, and about 300 times as poisonous to some birds."[25] Prior to 1964, the USDA and the FDA took the position that endrin was so hazardous to human health that no endrin residue whatsoever should be permitted in fish that are sold on the commercial market. When these government agencies discovered that significant quantities of fish contained endrin residues, they simply reversed their former policy as a practical solution to this dilemma. The FDA's present tolerance level for endrin residue in fish is .3 ppm.

Bodies of water that are heavily contaminated with mercury pose a particularly serious health hazard for those who consume fish. Unlike synthetic chemicals such as DDT and dieldrin, which lose their toxicity when they are ultimately degraded into the simpler elements from which they are composed, mercury is a naturally occurring element and cannot be degraded. Moreover, mercury may be transformed into methylmercury by the actions of aquatic microorganisms within the sediment. Methylmercury is even more toxic in nature than mercury. It is also significant to note that fish have considerably higher concentrations of mercury than the waters which they inhabit since fish, particularly predatory fish, are the highest level of the aquatic food chain. Thus, if the concentration of mercury in seawater is 0.00003 ppm, the concentration in aquatic plants would be approximately 0.03 ppm and the concentration in fish would then be about 0.12 ppm.[26] The use of mercury in the chlorine manufacturing process is a major source of mercury pollution, particularly in the United Kingdom and the United States. The use of mercury for chlorine production in the United States has increased by 2,100 percent since 1946.[27]

Mercury contamination of fish was first recognized as a serious health hazard in the 1950s. During this period, more than 100 people in Minamata, Japan, were stricken with mercury poisoning, which resulted in severe nerve disorders, brain damage, paralysis, and birth defects. Within the two decades since mercury-contaminated fish was found to be the cause of this catastrophe, a total of 397 people in Minamata have been stricken with mercury poisoning, of whom 68 have died.[28] Mercury poisoning continues to be a serious problem in Japan. Within recent years, a great number of Japanese have died or become disabled as a result of eating fish that were heavily contaminated with mercury. The high per capita consumption of fish in Japan, as well as the pollution of this highly industrialized country's waterways, are major factors contributing to this problem.

Various countries have taken measures to control the problem of mercury poisoning, including the establishment of mercury tolerance levels in fish as well as placing an outright ban on fishing in certain bodies of water. The FDA forced a recall of more than one million cans of tuna in 1971 because dangerously high levels of mercury were found in these fish. In 1973, the Ralston Purina Company, producers of Chicken of the Sea brand tuna, recalled an undisclosed number of cans of this product after a woman was fatally poisoned as a result eating a tuna salad.[29] The U.S. government banned the sale of swordfish in 1971 as a result of FDA tests which showed that 95 percent of 853 swordfish samples examined contained dangerously high levels of mercury.[30] In 1967, the Swedish government banned fishing in 40 lakes where there were fish with high concentrations of mercury. Within recent years, 33 states in the United States have, likewise, banned commercial fishing in some of their freshwater bodies where fish were found to contain high levels of mercury.

Shellfish tend to concentrate pollutants to a significantly greater extent than fish. Eating shellfish that inhabit polluted waters can result in typhoid fever, infectious hepatitis, and cholera. The cholera epidemic that struck Italy in the summer of 1973 was caused by mussels that were taken from polluted waters around Italy and in North Africa. Twenty-one of the cholera victims died. Over a million Italians were inoculated. Large mussel beds in the Bay of Naples were destroyed and a complete ban was placed on the sale or importation of shellfish throughout Italy.

The presence of toxic dinoflagellates in various bodies of water creates another serious threat to shellfish eaters. Dinoflagellates are found sparsely scattered within coastal waters throughout the world. These algae are innocuous under normal circumstances. However, under certain conditions which are not clearly understood, these organisms proliferate, causing serious problems. This phenomenon, commonly referred to as "red tide," occurs periodically throughout various regions, including the North Sea, the northern Atlantic coast of America, the north Pacific coast of America from central California to the Aleutian Islands, and the coastal areas of Japan, South Africa, and New Zealand. During the few days in which vast areas of these waters abound in poisonous dinoflagellates, shellfish ingest considerable quantities of these organisms. The process by which various types of shellfish feed (filtering plankton out of the water) results in a high concentration of toxic dinoflagellates being incorporated into their bodies.

In the fall of 1972, the *Gonyaulax tamarensis* species of dinoflagellates was responsible for a major outbreak of red tide, which extended over a large section of the north Atlantic coast. Thirty-three persons suffered temporary paralysis as a result of eating shellfish that inhabited these red-tide-infested waters. The poisonings prompted the states of Maine and Massachusetts to ban shellfish for several weeks.

The *Exuviaella mariae-lebouriae* species of dinoflagellates have been responsible for several hundred cases of poisonings and more than a hundred deaths of Japanese who had eaten oysters that were taken from Lake Hamana.

Many people who enjoy seafood are not aware of the hazards associated with eating various types of marine animals, while others may be aware of these hazards but are willing to take the risks. Indeed, some seafood connoisseurs are willing to take substantial risks for the sake of gastronomic pleasures. Take, for instance, the many thousand Japanese who relish the taste of a poisonous species of puffer fish which belongs to the genus *Tetraodontidae*. These fish must undergo special preparations by licensed chefs, who are trained to eliminate the fish's deadly toxins. The standards for licensing these chefs are quite high. Only 30 percent of the candidates pass the government examination after taking a two-month training course. About a hundred Japanese die each year from puffer fish poisoning (tetrodotoxin). Most of these deaths have been blamed on persons who were not licensed to prepare this deadly delicacy.

Official regulations governing the operations of the seafood industry do not eliminate the various hazards associated with eating the many different species of aquatic animals. These regulations only serve to minimize the risks. Indeed, it would be quite impossible to inspect every fish, crustacean, and mollusk that is sold on the commercial market. Inspection procedures for fish usually entails a spot check of a few batches of fish from a particular catch. Inspection at the processing and retail levels is woefully inadequate. A study conducted by Consumers Union in 1970 revealed that in 1969 less than 2 percent of the U.S. fish-processing plants and "fishery shore establishments" were visited by federal inspectors.[31]

There has been an increasing number of smoked fish found to be contaminated with salmonella.[32] In 1966, more than 300 people were stricken with salmonella poisoning after eating salmonella-contaminated smoked whitefish which had been imported from Canada.[33] The practice of washing eviserated fish with polluted water has been a factor contributing to salmonella contamination of fish. Also, fish are sometimes packed in ice made from polluted water.

Fish often remains on supermarket shelves for long periods of time. The United States Department of Interior conducted a three-year study on the quality of frozen fish products and found that some supermarket chains carried fish that were as much as four years old.[34] In analyzing frozen fish products, Consumers Union found that 80 percent of all the brands they tested were actually rancid.[35] After finding several health-code violations that existed in a Star-Kist tuna plant, FDA inspectors simply admonished Star-Kist to rectify these unsanitary practices. These admonitions went unheeded for some time, until in the spring of 1973, more than 230 people became sick after eating decomposed tuna that was processed at this plant.

Nine persons died in 1963 from eating smoked fish contaminated with botulism. Sodium nitrite and sodium nitrate are added to various types of fish in order to inhibit the growth of *Clostridium botulinum* bacteria. In fact, the FDA even requires a minimum of 100 ppm sodium nitrite to be used in the processing of smoked chub. However, the use of nitrite poses a serious hazard because of its potential to combine with secondary amines to form carcinogenic compounds known as nitrosamines.* Since secondary amines are found naturally occurring in fish, the practice of adding nitrite to fish exposes the consumer to a cancer risk. Serious liver disorders that occurred in cattle and sheep in Norway were found to have been caused by fish meal preserved with sodium nitrite.[36] The use of sodium nitrite and sodium nitrate in smoked fish in Finland and Japan, countries with a high per capita fish consumption, is cited by some epidemiologists as a possible factor contributing to the high incidence of stomach cancer in these countries. Canada and Sweden are two countries which have banned the use of nitrite in fish because of the serious health hazards associated with this practice.

Some countries have taken measures to protect shellfish eaters. However, regulations governing the operations of the shellfish industry are hardly adequate, particularly in view of the fact that many of these regulations are difficult to enforce. An Italian court investigating the cause of the cholera epidemic that struck Italy in 1973 charged 49 medical officers and mussel growers with dereliction of duty. However, these actions were little consolation to the 94 cholera victims, 21 of whom died, or to the many thousands of others who stood in long lines waiting to be inoculated. In certain areas of the

---

* A more detailed discussion of this issue is found in Chapter 4, "The Meat Industry, the Consumer, and the Law," pp. 48–49.

United States, clams are required by law to undergo forty-eight hours of ultraviolet treatment in special processing plants. Clams sold on the commercial market are required to have stickers which prove they have been treated. However, used stickers may be purloined by enterprising clam diggers. The diggers make more money by selling these clams directly to a wholesaler than by selling them to a licensed "master digger" who is charged with the responsibility of transporting them to a treatment plant before selling to a wholesaler.[37]

Fishmongers who refer to their product as "fresh fish" are either deceitful or naïve. Arthur F. Novak of the Department of Food Science, Louisiana State University at Baton Rouge, notes: "Virtually all fish is sold as 'fresh,' although less than 25% of the product marketed could meet present minimum standards for applying such a term."[38] It is a queer notion indeed to believe that fish can, in any way, be considered fresh. Most fish sold on the commercial market are taken from polluted waters. Many commercial fishing vessels stay out on the sea for several days at a time before they bring in their catch. Fish decompose faster than any other animal. Ice itself is not always adequate to preserve dead fish. Therefore, antibiotics such as chlortetracycline and oxytetracycline are often added to the ice which is used to preserve the fish on board ship. Antibiotics are, likewise, added to the ice in retail fish markets. Despite the use of ice and antibiotics, the stench of dead fish permeates the fish market. It is an odor that only a seafood connoisseur could appreciate.

6

Diet and Economy

Were the belief one day to become general that
people could dispense with animal food, there
would ensue not only a great economic revolution, but a moral improvement as well.

MAURICE MAETERLINCK
Translation by Alfred Sutra

If true, the Pythagorean principles as to abstaining from flesh foster innocence; if ill-founded
they at least teach us frugality.

SENECA
Translation by Richard M. Gummere

The practice of raising animals for food has many serious ramifications which adversely affect the lives of people in various parts of
the world. This practice affects the general quality of our environment, our health, and the very existence of large numbers of people
in countries like India who die of starvation or malnutrition for
want of adequate quantities of food. Yet these are things that few
Americans consider when they dine on beefsteaks or ham.

PROTEIN, CALORIE, AND ENERGY
CONVERSION RATIOS

The Biblical aphorism "All flesh is grass" aptly explains the relationship between animals and plants. Certain animals eat plant foods
and are, in turn, themselves used for food. This places them higher
on the food chain, and therefore meat is referred to as a "secondary"

71

source of food. Carnivorous animals in their natural habitat kill herbivores to eat. This predator-prey relationship is widely recognized as part of the balance of nature. However, the human use of secondary foods is a distinctly different matter. The tremendous amount of time, effort, and financial resources involved in producing flesh for human consumption has made it a relatively expensive product. Moreover, unlike carnivores, human beings do not actually require meat as a necessary part of their diet.

The processing of secondary foods, e.g., raising livestock as opposed to basic agricultural production, requires additional operations and involves greater financial risks. Livestock prices are affected to a considerable extent by a bad growing season. The rancher must also be concerned with such things as floods and a large variety of animal diseases. The use of antibiotics for prevention and treatment of livestock diseases is a significant cost factor. More than half of the world's production of antibiotics is used by the meat industry just for medicated feeds alone.[1] Parasites are a common problem to the livestock industry in all countries. American ranchers often dip their livestock into a chemical solution on a regular basis to kill parasites which bore holes in the animals' hides, thus lowering their market value. The tsetse fly, peculiar to the African continent, poses a serious threat to the livestock industry of that region. Vampire bats are a serious menace to the cattle industry in the Central and South American countries, where they cause an estimated $350 million in damage each year. These bats, which are carriers of rabies, became more numerous as the cattle population was expanded in these regions.[2]

Ironically enough, many meat packers, especially those in the United States, make most of their profits from the so-called by-products (particularly hides)—not from selling edible portions of the butchered animals.[3] This is, indeed, a most significant consideration in analyzing the value of producing animals as a source of food. A "dressed carcass" prepared at the slaughterhouse represents only 62 percent of the steer's live weight.[4] The carcass is usually shipped to retail food markets in quarter sections. Further processing by the retail store eliminates even more waste. Consequently, the total volume of meat that is sold to the consumer constitutes only 42 percent of the animal's original weight.[5] The proportion of a steer that is actually used for food is even lower than this figure since the quality steaks (as opposed to ground hamburger) contains inedible material such as bone and fat. The inefficiency that is inherent in the practice of using animals for food can be analyzed, basically, in three ways: (1) protein conversion ratios, (2) calorie conversion ratios, and (3) energy conversion ratios.

PROTEIN CONVERSION RATIOS

Flesh meat is undeniably a rich source of protein. In fact, the protein content of meat constitutes its principal nutritional value. However, producing animal protein from vegetable protein is well recognized by economists as a wasteful process. The purpose of feed-lots is to fatten steers, or in cattlemen's jargon to "finish" them. The average steer gains only one pound of weight for every ten pounds of grain it consumes. The protein conversion ratio for pigs is somewhat more efficient. The pig consumes four pounds of grain for each pound it gains in weight. The differential in the protein conversion efficiency of legumes as opposed to flesh foods is even more pronounced than that found in a comparison between grains and flesh foods. A study published by the Food and Agriculture Organization of the United Nations noted that a moderately active man could be sustained for about 10 times as long on the quantity of whole wheat that could be produced on 1 acre of land than with the quantity of meat that would be obtained from utilizing this acreage for the purpose of raising beef cattle. The efficiency of using soybeans would be more than 28 times greater than for using beef, given this same set of conditions.

The phenomenon of reduced efficiency from eating higher on the food chain is also found in aquatic environments:

> Most of the fish that we eat are carnivorous. There are great losses at each stage of conversion so that, in round numbers, 1,000 pounds of protein in the original plants yields 150 pounds of protein in the herbivores that eat them but only 22 pounds in the carnivores that eat the herbivores. These carnivores are often too small to be useful as human food; they are eaten by a larger one. Consequently, only two or three pounds of protein are finally harvested.[6]

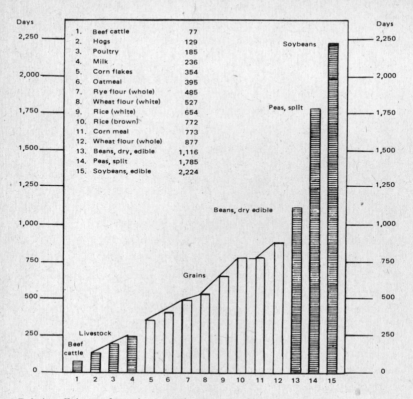

	Days			Days

1.	Beef cattle	77
2.	Hogs	129
3.	Poultry	185
4.	Milk	236
5.	Corn flakes	354
6.	Oatmeal	395
7.	Rye flour (whole)	485
8.	Wheat flour (white)	527
9.	Rice (white)	654
10.	Rice (brown)	772
11.	Corn meal	773
12.	Wheat flour (whole)	877
13.	Beans, dry, edible	1,116
14.	Peas, split	1,785
15.	Soybeans, edible	2,224

Relative efficiency of protein conversion per acre of land from various protein sources in terms of number of days of protein requirement by a moderately active man[7]

Actually, this protein conversion ratio of 1,000 pounds of plant food used to produce 2 or 3 pounds of fish protein for human consumption does not even take into consideration the fact that as much as one-third of the international fish catch is used as livestock feed.[8] Feeding animal protein to livestock that are used for meat production adds yet another link in the food chain, further reducing the efficiency of protein conversion. The largest purchaser of fish protein on the world market is the United States, which uses two-thirds of this product for manufacturing animal feed. Ironically, less fish is consumed directly by the entire population of western Europe than by the U.S. livestock industry. In fact, American livestock use even more marine protein in the form of meal than is consumed directly by the people of Japan, where fish has traditionally been a prominent part of the diet.[9]

CALORIE CONVERSION RATIOS

The wastefulness of eating higher on the food chain, as represented by calorie conversion ratios, is even more pronounced than the protein inefficiency created by such diets. Crops such as grains or legumes have a relatively higher protein yield per acre than other types of foods. However, root crops produce considerably higher calorie yields per acre than the grains or legumes. United States Department of Agriculture statistics, for instance, note that 2,400 pounds of wheat can be produced on 1 acre of land. The potato yield per acre is 20,000 pounds. However, if the amount of grains that can be grown on one acre of land is diverted to use as feed for steers, the amount of beef produced would be only 168 pounds. It is noted in another statistic that, in terms of calorie units, a rice-and-beans-based diet would feed 20 times more people than a meat-based diet.[10]

It is important to consider calorie conversion ratios, along with protein conversion ratios, when analyzing the efficiency of plant versus animal foods. Insufficient calorie intake adversely affects protein utilization and metabolism. Dietary protein is used to provide energy when calorie intake is deficient and, consequently, unavailable for this use. Therefore, insufficient calorie intake impairs the utilization of proteins that might be included in meager diets.[11] When the interrelationship between calorie and protein requirements is realized, the inefficiency created by using meat as a source of food becomes even more apparent. An FAO/WHO committee report comments on this fact, noting:

> When intakes of both energy and protein are grossly inadequate, the provision of protein concentrates or protein-rich food of animal origin may be a costly and inefficient way of improving the diets, since energy can generally be provided more cheaply than protein of good quality. This is an important point in planning programmes for meeting the needs of vulnerable groups in developing countries. Clearly, energy and protein needs should be considered together in planning for the nutritional improvement of populations whose diets are deficient in either.[12]

Considering the relatively low per acre yields for protein foods in general, it is significant to note that many people in the more affluent countries, especially Americans, consume a great deal more protein than they actually require to be properly nourished. Currently, the annual per capita consumption of meat in the United States is 254 pounds, among the highest in the world.[13] Nearly a ton of grain is annually required for the average American diet. However, only 7 percent of this amount represents grain that is eaten directly by Americans in the form of bread, cereals, baked goods, and related foodstuffs. The other 93 percent is used to feed livestock.[14] As much as 80 percent of the corn that is grown in the United States is used for animal feed.[15] Dr. Vernon Youngs, director of the U.S. Department of Agriculture's National Oat Quality Center at the University of Wisconsin, reports that only 5 to 10 percent of the oats produced in the United States is used directly by the American public; the other 90 or so percent is used in animal feeds.[16] Professor Georg Borgstrom has estimated that the livestock population in the United States alone consumes enough plant food to feed 1.3 billion people.[17] A similar situation exists in Great Britain, where it is estimated that 80 percent of the farm acreage is used for feeding livestock while only 20 percent is used in producing food that is used directly by the human population.[18] Considering the fact that there are as many animals raised for meat as there are people in the world,[19] it is not surprising that FAO statistics show that 50 percent of the international grain harvest is fed to livestock.[20] Most of the world soybean crop is produced for animal feed. Only 3 percent of this protein-rich legume is used directly for human consumption.[21] Even excluding the food requirements of other farm animals, the world's cattle population consumes a quantity of food equivalent to the calorie needs of 8.7 billion people.[22]

The wasteful practice of feeding grain to livestock is by no means a recent custom. Ancient Egyptian records show that cattle were fed with loaves of bread.[23] There are also various passages in the Bible which allude to grain-fed livestock. King Solomon kept grain-fed cattle as well as cattle that obtained their food exclusively by grazing. It is noted that the former were fatter than the ones that foraged in pastures.[24] Notwithstanding Solomon's extravagant dining habits, food has generally been in short supply for most people throughout the course of history. The practice of raising livestock has long been recognized as an inefficient means of food production. During periods of famine caused by adverse weather conditions or war the livestock population was usually reduced so that more food would be available to feed the hungry people.

During the long periods of famine in medieval Europe, livestock were systematically slaughtered. When food became scarce in Denmark because of the German blockade in World War I, much of that country's livestock were slaughtered. Dr. Hindehede, a nutritional research advisor to the Danish government, recommended this course of action. At the end of a two-year period, Dr. Hindehede noted that, in addition to conserving the food supply, there was also a dramatic improvement in the health of the four million Danish people, who had been forced to live on a predominantly vegetarian diet during this time. The livestock of west and central Europe were reduced by as much as 20 percent during World War I. This represents a total of 6 million beef cattle, 16 million pigs, and 22 million sheep that were slaughtered en masse for the sake of food-production efficiency.[25] At this time citizens of the United States were formally requested by their government to observe beefless Tuesdays and porkless Thursdays.

The situation in Germany was somewhat different. There was a very good German harvest at the outset of the war. The Germans were also confident of winning the war within a relatively short period of time because of the initial success of their military campaign. Furthermore, the Germans relied on the rich farmland in occupied territories as a potential food supply to supplement their own production. It was ostensibly for these reasons that the German government did not wish to force its people to adopt an austerity diet. Both cattle and hogs were fed with grains to provide quality meats for the German people. By the time Germany was reconciled to a war that would be longer than anticipated, that nation's grain supply was already exhausted. The Germans had also miscalculated their ability to force farmers in occupied territories to produce adequate quantities of food to feed both the armed forces and the civilian population.

The principle of reducing meat consumption to improve the efficiency of food production was an important aspect of the war effort during World War II. There was a large-scale effort to reduce the livestock population in Europe at that time. In Denmark, the number of pigs declined from 3 million to 1 million, while the poultry population in that country declined from 29 million to 11 million. The number of poultry in The Netherlands dropped from 33 million to less than 4 million, and a full two-thirds of the pigs in that country were destroyed. The Soviet Union's cattle population was reduced by about 33 percent while there was an 88 percent decline in the number of their pigs.[26] The citizens of various European countries were advised to grow and eat more peas and beans to compensate for the shortages of animal protein. Similarly, Americans were encouraged to grow "victory gardens" and to reduce their consumption of meat.

Special provisions were made for vegetarians in various European countries when food was rationed in times of war. During both World Wars I and II, Dutch vegetarians were given larger rations of dairy products in lieu of meat. Official membership in the Vegetarian Society of the Netherlands was used to determine who was actually a vegetarian. Mrs. Eikeboon-Broekman, current secretary of De Nederlandse Vegetariërsbond, recalled that when the ration plan was first announced at the outset of World War I, there was a great influx of new members in the vegetarian society. However, there was a drop in membership after the ration program was terminated. Again, when the same ration program was put into effect during World War II, there was a dramatic increase in the number of people joining the vegetarian society of the Netherlands. Mrs. Eikeboon-Broekman observed that the drop in membership when rationing was finally terminated in 1949 indicates that many Dutch people had opted to forgo meat in order to take advantage of the larger ration of dairy products that was alloted to vegetarians at that time. Great Britain continued its food rationing program for several years after the war had ended. The British rationing plan, like the Dutch program, allowed those persons who were registered as vegetarians to receive special rations of cheese. Brian Gunn-King, a native of Northern Ireland who is presently the secretary of the International Vegetarian Union, noted that many meat eaters actually registered as vegetarians since they were willing to forgo meat in order to obtain the special cheese rations that were alloted to vegetarians during this period. The British ration program was finally terminated in 1954. The British government was hardly concerned with the fact that many people receiving the special cheese rations were not bona fide vegetarians.

The purpose of the program was, after all, to achieve greater calorie conversion efficiency in their food production. Despite the fact that, in this respect, dairy products such as milk or cheese are less efficient than vegetable protein, they are, nonetheless, certainly more efficient than meat.

While these various food rationing programs were successful, they unfortunately had the effect of reinforcing the concept that living without meat is a hardship despite the obvious fact that flesh food is certainly not a necessity. Indeed, except in times of famine, people who abstained from flesh foods were considered peculiar. George Bernard Shaw was once ridiculed at a dinner party by G. K. Chesterton, a connoisseur of food. The portly Chesterton commented: "Looking at you, Shaw, people would think there was a famine in England." Shaw retorted: "And looking at you, Chesterton, people would think that you were the cause of it."

Notwithstanding his humorous intent, there is a great deal of truth in Shaw's remark. The inefficiency involved in meat production severely limits our ability to make more food available to use directly instead of feeding it to livestock. Lester Brown, an economist with the Overseas Development Council, has calculated that if Americans reduced their annual consumption of meat by only 10 percent it would save approximately 12 million tons of grain. This amount would be enough to offset the entire grain deficit of India and constitutes the equivalent of food that could be used directly to feed as many as 60 million people.[27] The question of reducing meat consumption to relieve world starvation became the focus of much controversy at the 1974 World Food Conference that was held in Rome.

ENERGY CONVERSION RATIOS

The advent of the Industrial Revolution resulted in a population shift from rural areas to the cities. This trend continued, creating a situation in which a large segment of the population—urban dwellers—became dependent on an ever-dwindling number of farmers for their most basic need—food. Before moving to the cities, these people had been able to produce at least part of the food they used. However, the Industrial Revolution, which was responsible for the diminution of the agricultural labor force, was also responsible for innovations in farming which compensated for this loss. The use of farm machinery greatly increased the efficiency of agricultural production in terms of the work hours expended. Even greater efficiency was achieved in the 20th century, when fossil fuel was utilized to power a wide variety of farm machinery that had now been developed, including tractors, harvesters, and irrigation pumps. Petroleum, in addition to its use as a source of energy, also had come to be used as a basic element in the manufacturing of fertilizer. This was viewed as yet another method of improving agricultural efficiency.

Events in the early part of the 1970s, particularly the massive increases in petroleum prices, prompted economists to reappraise traditional standards for evaluating the efficiency of agricultural production. Energy-intensive farming practices are undeniably efficient in terms of work hours. However, in a time when the availability of petroleum and food are no longer taken for granted, many economists cite the low efficiency of our contemporary agricultural practices in terms of energy conversion ratios as a cause for concern. The energy conversion ratio is an equation which measures the quantity of energy derived from food in terms of calorie units against the amount of energy expended in its production. It has been estimated that in the earlier part of this century the energy content of food was somewhat greater than the amount of energy required to produce it. However, efficiency as measured by energy conversion ratios steadily declined, and by 1970 nearly 9 calories were used to produce 1 calorie of food.[28]

It is readily apparent that flesh, a secondary source of food, is considerably less energy efficient than primary food sources. Ranchers often point out that their inefficient use of grain is, to some extent, offset by the fact that cattle are able to utilize grass as a source of food. Furthermore, it is asserted that much of the land that is used for grazing purposes is actually unsuitable for crop production. However, the amount of food obtained by cattle from grazing does not compensate for the basic inefficiency of meat production. Many countries that have developed a large livestock industry, such as the United States and the Soviet Union, do not maintain their herds exclusively by grazing. The animals that are used for food are fed grains in addition to the food they obtain by foraging. As much as 93 percent of the cereal grain produced in the United States is used to support the livestock industry in this country despite the considerable period of time these animals spend grazing on rangeland.[29] Proposals have been made to reduce the amount of grains that are now given to livestock and to rely more on grazing, in view of the fact that the feedlot system requires 60 to 70 percent more energy per pound of protein produced than if the steer lived on forage.[30] This suggestion, however, would be difficult to implement for the following reasons:

1. The amount of grain fed to animals is a principal factor in determining the quality of the meat product. Cattle that are fed sufficient quantities of grain produce the tender, juicy cuts of meat that are highly favored by most people who eat meat. Grass-fed cattle produce a lower-quality beef product, which is lean and tough to chew. The aroma quality is also adversely affected.[31] Z. L. Carpenter, a "meats specialist" from Texas A & M University, outlined other disadvantages of grass-fed cattle at a symposium sponsored by the American Society of Animal Science in 1975 on "The Role of Livestock in a Hungry World." He cited such things as higher processing cost, unappetizing yellow fat and dark muscle color, more rapid spoilage, and overall consumer skepticism about the product's desirability.[32] Some cattle ranchers actually use plastic pellets which remain permanently in the steer's stomach. This serves to curb the animal's appetite for roughage, thereby creating a higher-quality meat.[33]

2. Even if there were widespread consumer acceptance of tough, less flavorful beef, cattle ranchers would still be less than enthusiastic about eliminating grain from their feeding program. Feed grains represent a considerable expense to the cattlemen. Eliminating the use of feed grains to any significant extent would, therefore, seem to create a substantial saving. However, it takes a longer period of time for cattle to reach a desirable market weight when they are maintained on a grass diet than when grains are used in their feeding program. The average grain-fed American steer, for instance, is ready for slaughter within a 14- to 16-month period. However, it requires significantly more time to raise cattle in South America, where steers are grass-fed. Despite Argentina's excellent rangeland, it takes 26 months for the cattle raised in that country to reach market weight.[34] The flora of the regions used for grazing livestock in Brazil is seriously deficient in minerals, such as lime and other important nutrients.[35] Vegetation is so sparse in Brazil that a single steer may need to graze over an area of 37 acres in order to obtain its sustenance.[36] Consequently, Brazilian cattle require as much as 5 years of prepara-

tion before they are slaughtered for food.[37] It is evident that any substantial reduction in the use of feed grains would adversely affect the American ranchers' turnover.

3. Proposals to change from grain feeding to grass feeding on any kind of large scale fails to take into consideration the fact that our land resources which could be used for such a purpose is limited. Despite the claim that nearly half of the world's productive land is not being used, it would not be feasible, in terms of cost, to bring a considerable portion of this land into use. Also, as the world's population steadily rises, more land will be required for cultivation of crops, housing, and recreational areas. One analysis of grazing land costs in the United States reports that the prohibitive price of potential grazing land in the Northeast is due to the high demand for recreational areas.[38]

4. It would hardly be reasonable to expect new grassland areas to be used as the exclusive source of nourishment for enormous numbers of livestock over an extended period of time without adversely affecting the quality of the environment. The question of allocating a significantly greater portion of land for pasturage has not really been adequately studied. The issue of grazing as a cause of erosion is analyzed in greater detail in Chapter 7, "Ecology and Vegetarianism."

5. Grazing is not possible during much of the winter season except in certain climatic regions, like California, that have no significant seasonal temperature variation. Farmers compensate for this loss by producing hay. The process of making hay involves cutting and drying grass, alfalfa, or clover. Much of this is stored to be used by cattle during the winter. Like grazing, the practice of making hay would appear to provide a source of food that is both practical and efficient. However, the use of hay as fodder can hardly be considered efficient when analyzed in terms of energy conversion. Traditional methods used in making hay are estimated to waste 45 percent of the carbohydrate and 32 percent of the protein content in grass.[39] This waste can actually be reduced to a minimum of 5 percent for carbohydrates and 7 percent for protein if the grass is dried in an oven as soon as it has been cut.[40] The drying method, however, is more costly in terms of both labor and fuel—a fact that would reduce rather than improve efficiency as measured by energy conversion

ratios. Another factor to be considered in winter feeding is that cattle burn up more calories during cold weather than in the summer. As a result, they require more feed and additional protein supplements.[41]

6. Finally, cattle are the least efficient of all livestock in terms of protein, calorie, and energy conversion ratios. Even if the cattle industry succeeded in changing to grass feeding on a large scale despite the problems already mentioned, this would still not affect the grain requirements of nonruminant animals, such as pigs and poultry.

When all aspects of food production are analyzed it becomes increasingly apparent that waste is unavoidable in the meat industry. No attempts that are made to ameliorate this inefficiency can ever really alter, to any significant extent, the low returns for protein, calorie, or energy conversion.

SUPPLY, DEMAND, AND OTHER COST FACTORS

The inefficient nature of meat production is certainly a factor in the relatively high retail price of this item. The inefficient use of fuel and human labor, as represented in energy conversion, naturally translates into higher production costs. The cost of meat is also affected by the principle of supply and demand. There are various other factors which affect not only the price of food but its availability in general. It is important to remember that these factors affect all foods, but meat as a secondary food source is affected to a significantly greater extent. It would therefore be useful to examine some of these issues in greater detail, illustrating their relevance to contemporary problems.

PETROLEUM

The recent quadrupling of petroleum prices in the course of a few years has had a profound effect on food production. The relationship between petroleum and food is highly significant, as noted in the previous section on energy conversion. It is particularly disconcerting to note that a major food-producing country like the United

States has reversed its position as an exporter of energy in the past two decades. The United States must now import 15 percent of its energy needs and as much as 35 percent of the petroleum it uses.[42]

INCREASED COST OF LABOR

The number of work hours and the need for skilled labor contribute to the high cost of meat. Processing meat involves increased costs in such areas as transportation or simply raising crops, since the ultimate consumer is twice removed. Furthermore, producing meat, as opposed to using foods directly, involves a more extensive operation, including feedlot operators, slaughterers, veterinarians, meat inspectors, and meat cutters. The Amalgamated Meat Cutters Union, in particular, has created additional expenses for the meat industry as a result of various regulations designed to benefit its members. For instance, retail stores are generally required to have their meat cut, wrapped, and priced inside the store itself, instead of using a central facility for this task, which would be a more efficient operation. Contracts also usually require the store to maintain a butcher on duty whenever meat is being sold even though it has already been cut, wrapped, and priced.[43] One study of supermarket operations in Ohio revealed that meat cutters actually spend less than half of their time doing skilled work.[44] The butcher is usually the highest-paid person in a supermarket, next to the store manager.

Unfortunately, the high cost of meat production is often unwittingly subsidized by the vegetarian consumer. It is standard policy in most supermarkets to compensate for low profits or even sustained losses on meat sales by raising the prices on other items.[45] This can be accomplished with little or no consumer opposition since these other commodities are relatively less expensive than meat.

POPULATION

The world's capacity to produce more food appears to have nearly reached its peak. The world population, however, continues to grow at an alarming rate. This has created a disastrous situation in which the amount of food capable of being produced cannot possibly fulfill the increased demand for this essential commodity. According to long-term trend calculations made by the U.S. Department of Agriculture, world grain consumption is growing at an annual rate of 1.4 million tons faster than world grain production.[46] This situation has been further complicated by recent crop failures in various parts of the world, which have reduced production while the demand for food continues to increase unabated.

INCREASED DEMAND FOR MEAT

It is most ironic that in a time when the world is experiencing a food crisis the per capita consumption of meat is rapidly increasing in many countries throughout the world. The annual per capita consumption of meat in West Germany, for example, rose from 144 pounds in 1960 to 192 pounds in 1972. There was a 94 percent increase, from 70 pounds to 136 pounds, in per capita meat consumption by Italians over this same period. There has also been a significant increase in the per capita meat consumption in such countries as Spain, Japan, France, Canada, Yugoslavia, and the Soviet Union.[47] Americans have doubled their per capita consumption of beef and poultry products in the past two decades.[48]

The Soviet purchase of nearly one-fifth of the total U.S. wheat supply in 1972 strongly affected the world market for this commodity. Soaring prices had a particularly bad effect on the American meat industry. The sharp increase in the cost of feed grains resulted in higher meat prices for the retail consumer. The price of meat became an issue of major concern for the American public. When asked by a reporter what Americans could do to curb the rising cost of meat, President Nixon replied: "Don't buy meat!"[49] Indignation over further increases in the price of meat precipitated the famous 1973 nationwide meat boycott. The boycott, which lasted a full week, actually caused many meat-packing plants to suspend their operations temporarily. Aside from the issue of higher meat prices, there were more serious ramifications to the so-called Russian wheat deal. As a result of its depleted grain supply, the United States was forced to reduce the shipment of this commodity to needy countries. The issue of starving people being deprived of food prompts one to make an inquiry into the nature of the Soviet Union's actual need for American wheat. The principal reason for the Soviet grain purchase was to maintain its faltering livestock industry. It is known, in fact, that 60 percent of the grains and soybeans purchased by the Soviets

was allocated specifically for feeding their livestock.[50] The present
Soviet policy of expanding meat production during a period of severe
crop shortages is unprecedented. Previously, the Soviet government
had reacted to food shortages by reducing the number of livestock,
thus making more food available to the people. During a major
crop failure in 1963, for instance, the hog population was reduced
to 41 million from its previous level of 70 million.[51]

The Soviet government has now made a token gesture to ameliorate
the present food crisis. As of May, 1976, the restaurants and cafeterias
in Moscow do not serve meat for one day (Thursday) of each week,
while there are two meatless days each week in the city of Kiev.[52]
While the Soviet Union endeavors to avoid what it considers austerity
measures (a severe reduction in meat consumption), Americans are
forced to pay more for their foodstuffs made with grain and the
people in developing countries learn to equate the law of supply
and demand with malnutrition and death.

WEATHER CONDITIONS

Weather is a significant determining factor in food production,
as evidenced by recent crop failures in various parts of the world.
Adverse weather conditions impair food production in some of our
best agricultural regions. Studies conducted by the U.S. Department
of Agriculture show that within an 8-year period (1967–75), 125
of the 254 counties in Texas have been designated as disaster areas
in four or more years; in Iowa, 29 of the 99 counties; in Nebraska,
35 out of 93 counties; and in Illinois, 34 of 102 counties. Oklahoma
has 5 counties that have been declared disaster areas in seven years
within this 8-year period.[53] Over the short span of the past 5 years,
several regions of the world have experienced major crop failures
as a result of adverse weather conditions. Africa, India, the Soviet
Union, the United States, and several European countries have all
been affected. In 1976, Great Britain experienced its worse drought
since 1727. Dr. Walter Orr Roberts, one of the leading authorities
on climate, believes there is ample evidence to conclude that major
crop failures will occur in the near future.[54] His theory, which is
supported by many other scientists, is based largely on phenological
studies, which indicate there is a pattern to weather changes, particularly as such changes relate to the occurrence of drought.

While there is little that can be done to alter the course of adverse weather conditions, there is something that can be done to ameliorate the problem of food shortages created by such natural occurrences. We can, for instance, significantly increase the world grain reserves by reducing meat consumption. World grain reserves have steadily declined over the past several decades and are presently at dangerously low levels. The fact that American grain reserves have already been seriously depleted is cited as a principal reason for the parsimony that characterizes current U.S. food assistance programs.

FERTILIZER

Fertilizer is used to improve the efficiency of crop yields. The increased demand for this commodity has been caused, in part, by the inefficient nature of meat production. The use of feed grains for animal consumption severely diminishes the amount of food that could be made available to people directly. Thus, the necessity to produce higher crop yields to feed both animals and people has required a significantly greater use of fertilizers. Chemical fertilizer is even being used to improve the efficiency of grazing land. It was concluded from one 3-year study in Scottsbluff, Nebraska, that fertilized rangeland produced about 10 pounds more beef per acre than rangeland that was not fertilized.[55] The world use of fertilizers in 1938 was less than 10 million metric tons. The amount that was used in 1974 rose to more than 80 million metric tons.[56] Estimates for 1976 indicate a 25 to 30 percent increase in the use of fertilizer over the previous year.[57] One economist estimates that the use of chemical fertilizers may triple in the next thirty years.[58] The sharp increase in the demand for fertilizer has caused fertilizer prices to rise considerably on the world market in recent years. The cost is often prohibitive to countries with the greatest need—the developing nations.

Actually, the notion that the use of chemical fertilizers is a highly efficient method of improving crop yields is not altogether correct. The percentage of increase in crop yield is significantly lower than the additional quantity of fertilizer needed to obtain this better productivity. For example, in 1949 the average farm in the state of Illinois used about 20,000 tons of fertilizer nitrogen to produce a corn yield of about 50 bushels per acre. Statistics for this same area show that in 1968 about 600,000 tons of fertilizer nitrogen were used to produce an average of about 93 bushels per acre.[59] The total agricultural production for the entire nation between 1949 and 1968 increased by about 45 percent. During that same period the annual use of fertilizer nitrogen had increased by about 648 percent.[60]

LOSS OF AGRICULTURAL LAND

Despite the need for greater productivity as a result of population growth and the increased demand for meat, the amount of agricultural land in the United States continues to decline. This problem is particularly significant in view of the U.S. position as one of the world's principal food-producing countries. New York State alone is estimated to have lost 11.4 million acres of cropland by 1972 over a 10-year period. The total number of farms in the state declined 32 percent within this period of time.[61] One study published in 1975 that was prepared by the Citizens' Advisory Committee on Environmental Quality reported that "more than 54 million acres of cropland were converted to irreversible uses during a recent 20-year period."[62] This was due, in large part, to urban expansion, including development projects such as housing, highways, airports, power plants, solid waste disposal sites, shopping centers, and reservoir construction. The committee's report further noted that each year 2.4 million acres of agricultural land in the United States is converted to non-agricultural uses.[63] This loss is offset to some extent by land-reclamation projects, which annually create an additional 1.25 million acres of land which formerly could not be used for agricultural purposes.[64] Aside from the fact that this amount falls short of the total number of acres lost, long-term use of this new cropland presents serious environmental problems. Some of these disadvantages are outlined in the Sixth Annual Report of the Council on Environmental Quality:

> Some 400,000 acres of cropland added each year is irrigated land dependent on dammed or diverted water or deep wells. In time, energy development in the Northern Great Plains and other water-scarce western areas may place competing demands on the water that this cropland requires. Other new cropland is created from coastal wetland "potholes"

that serve important functions for fish and wildlife populations. Draining of wetlands for new cropland continues to destroy these important biological resources, especially in Florida and the upper Midwest. Finally, bringing new cropland into production requires extensive use of commercial fertilizers, as do continued increases in productivity of land already under cultivation. In addition to water quality problems created by fertilizer runoff into streams, there are other important implications of continued dependency on commercial fertilizer, including resource problems because fertilizer is made of natural gas or petroleum.[65]

Optimists refer to recent increases in U.S. food production despite the Midwestern droughts of the early 1970s. However, it is important to consider several factors if we are to properly evaluate both the quality and quantity of our future food supply. American farmers have been producing more food in response to increased demand for food products on the international market. This tremendous upsurge in demand for food was precipitated by crop failures that occurred in various parts of the world in addition to the increased demand generated by population growth. Consequently, several million acres of land that had formerly been left idle are now being cultivated. It is significant to note that the government program to pay farmers for restricting production was phased out in 1973.[66] More land is still available that could be used to increase productivity further. However, much of this land is of questionable value. A recent study reported that 50 percent of the agricultural land presently available is "marginal or worse."[67] It is then evident that we are confronted with a situation where the demand for food continues to rise while our capacity to increase productivity continues to become more and more limited.

Concern for increasing productivity in terms of crop yield, i.e., return per acre, and overall production, overshadows the important issue of the product's nutritional quality. Indeed, quality is often sacrificed in order to obtain higher yields, as evidenced by the lower protein content found in certain hybrid strains. While there has been a significant improvement in wheat yield, the protein content of this wheat has declined by as much as 25 percent over the past several decades.[68] This is due to the fact that the plant's cells increase in bulk, mainly starch, thereby reducing its protein component.

A reduction in meat consumption would relieve the strain on our agricultural resources, improving the quality as well as the quantity of crops that are cultivated for our use as food.

EATING TO SURVIVE: FOOD AND THE POOR

Some consider food as a basic right while others view it as a commodity that should be put on the open market and sold to the highest bidder. The debate over this controversy has become more intense in recent years. Large-scale crop failures and the continuing rapid population growth have been major factors contributing to higher food prices as well as to the availability of food in general. Increase in the cost of food has a far more serious effect on the poor than on any other segment of the population. Malnutrition is the principal factor contributing to infant and child mortality in developing countries, where 25 to 30 percent of the population die before the age of four.[69] The poor in the affluent countries are also affected by food distribution policies based on supply and demand. A government report issued in 1974 by the staff of the U.S. Senate Select Committee on Nutrition and Human Needs stated: "Spot reports from communities around the nation indicate death from malnutrition on the increase due to food/price spiral. Reports from St. Louis show elderly are dying because of lack of food. In Chicago, a survey showed that large numbers of people of all ages were going hungry each day with many more malnourished, or undernourished because of poverty diets."[70]

It has been previously noted that any significant reduction in meat consumption would make more grain available on the world market. Exactly how this additional quantity of food would actually be distributed is another matter, which, alas, is an issue to be determined by politicians and the international grain speculators. However, by making more food available, the bargaining position of the rich and powerful grain dealers would be seriously undermined and American government officials would no longer be able to cite our dwindling grain reserves as a reason for reducing food shipments to starving people in other parts of the world. Such realizations have prompted religious leaders of various Christian denominations to issue appeals calling on their members to abstain from meat on certain days of each week. One such appeal was made by Paul Moore, Jr., the Episcopal Bishop of the Diocese of New York. A pastoral letter that contained his request to observe "meatless Wednesdays" was presented to the diocese's 200 churches in November, 1974.[71] A similar appeal for abstinence from meat on Wednesdays had previously been issued by Cardinal Cooke, the Roman Catholic Archbishop of New York. Bread for the World is a political lobby organization that promotes legislation favoring increased food assistance to needy countries. The founder and current president of this organization is Reverend Eugene Carson Blake, former head of the World Council of Churches. Aside from his lobby activities, the Reverend Mr. Blake recognizes the need to deal with the food problem at its most basic level and has, therefore, encouraged all the members of his organization to abstain from eating meat on Mondays, Wednesdays, and Fridays.[72]

There is much evidence to indicate that developing countries could, to some extent, lessen their dependence on food assistance by eliminating wasteful practices. Livestock raising, for instance, is obviously an inefficient means of producing food. However, many developing countries continue to tolerate or even encourage meat production. It is not uncommon to find cattle or goats in various parts of Africa. The actual meat yield per animal for cattle raised on that continent is astonishingly low—6 times less than would normally be obtained from American beef cattle.[73] These low yields and the widespread damage caused to agricultural land as a result of grazing hardly justify the practice of raising livestock in Africa. Even more areas in Africa would be used for producing cattle if successful methods could be found for controlling the tsetse fly.

The Brazilian government has been attempting to expand its cattle industry despite the country's poor terrain, which is ill suited for use as grazing land. Ironically, much of Brazil's beef is exported to the United States in an effort to achieve a more favorable balance of trade.[74] Mexico and Venezuela are now involved in developing their poultry industry, which has made it necessary for them to import large quantities of fish meal.[75] Bad food policy is partially responsible for the malnutrition that exists in those countries. A UNICEF report on nutritional standards stated that more than half of all childhood deaths that occurred in Latin America are related to malnutrition.

While it is clearly evident that raising livestock is an inefficient means of producing food, the question of the relative value of vegetable protein, compared to that of meat protein, is an issue which is often raised. It is asserted that meat protein is of a higher quality than any single source of vegetable protein. This is an altogether specious argument, since there are a wide variety of ethnic foods that use more than one source of vegetable protein, thus constituting a complete protein combination. Arroz y frijoles (rice and beans) or tacos (tortillas made with corn and stuffed with pureed beans) are commonly used in the Latin American countries. Soybeans are often eaten in combination with rice in the Asian countries. Tahini (sesame paste), a traditional Middle Eastern food, is often used with pita, a slightly leavened bread that is made with wheat. Hummus (ground chickpeas) also provides a good-quality protein when combined with pita bread. Ground chickpeas are often mixed with tahini. Hummus bi tahini, as this mixture is called, is also commonly used with pita bread. Megadarra (lentils with rice) is another popular Middle Eastern dish. Vegetable protein combinations that are popular in Italy include pasta con lenticchie (pasta with lentils) and pasta e fagioli (pasta and beans).

Kwashiorkor, a protein deficiency disease, is most commonly found in the developing countries and occurs more frequently in children than adults. Various studies of kwashiorkor show that people afflicted with this malady use very little or no animal protein, especially meat. Some people have, therefore, naïvely concluded that kwashiorkor is caused by a lack of animal protein in the diet. A more thorough examination of this problem reveals that the diet of kwashiorkor victims consists predominantly of root crops affording little, if any, nutritional value in terms of protein. Furthermore, kwashiorkor is usually remedied by providing the victims with skim-milk powder in combination with grains and/or legumes. It is also common to remedy this disease by using plant proteins exclusively, usually grain and legume mixtures.[76]

It is important to control nutrition-related diseases like kwashiorkor with large-scale preventive programs instituted as part of national policy. Many countries have now established programs to improve the nutritional value of food by fortification. The practice of supplementing standard food items with vitamins, minerals, and/or amino acids is of particular importance to the poor, since the high cost of conventional foods may preclude them from maintaining desirable nutritional standards. In the United States, products such as breakfast cereals, bread, and macaroni are commonly fortified with vitamins and minerals. Practically all milk produced in the United States is required to be fortified with vitamin D. Margarine is similarly required by government regulations to contain vitamin A supplementation. The British government instituted regulations in 1964 that require all bread to contain established minimum quantities of iron, thiamine (vitamin B_1), and nicotinic acid.[77] Other countries, including India and Japan, have developed sophisticated programs to create inexpensive sources of complete protein. The Japanese fortify such foods as bread, rice cakes, and bean noodles with amino acids that would normally be deficient in such products. Bread that has been fortified with synthetic amino acids or peanut flour provides an inexpensive source of complete protein for Indian citizens with limited financial means.

There are two basic methods used to produce complete protein foods through fortification. Flour produced from legumes (e.g., soybeans, chickpeas) can be mixed with grain flours. Another method would be simply to add synthetically produced amino acids to processed grain products such as bread or cereal. These amino acids can be produced by a process of either chemical synthesis or by fermentation. Grains that do not contain sufficient quantities of amino acids can be effectively fortified for this deficiency. The protein value of wheat is increased by 66 percent with the addition of lysine; cornmeal by 70 percent with lysine and tryptophan; and rice by 78 percent with lysine and threonine supplementation.[78] Protein supplementation is considerably less expensive than conventional protein sources. The cost of fortifying wheat with soy flour, for instance, is one-tenth the cost of obtaining the same quality of protein from milk.

American legislators from the coastal states have tried to promote fish protein concentrate as a product that would be suitable for use in protein fortification. This effort, initiated in the 1960s to benefit their constituents from the fishing industry, did not succeed for a variety of reasons. Processing costs were higher than anticipated. There were also serious objections to the fact that whole fish, including eyes, scales, viscera, and even some intestinal contents would be used in processing this high-protein fish powder. Fish-protein concentrate has never achieved any degree of popular acceptance in the United States. Furthermore, a United Nations committee that was established to evaluate the feasibility of using this product to fortify foods in developing countries concluded that it should not be used since other methods of protein fortification were considerably less expensive.[79]

It would be most helpful if nations established a nutritional education program for their citizens. Such a program would enable people to select foods on the basis of their nutritional merit. The late president of Chile, Salvador Allende, was particularly dedicated to improving the nutritional standards for the people of his country. The national public health education program that had been initiated before Allende took office was given greater priority under his regime. Special efforts were made to supply poor women and children with milk supplements. Also, as of January 12, 1972, meat was not allowed to be sold four days (Monday through Thursday) of each week because of food shortages. One outcome of the Chilean nutritional policies was that there was a significant reduction in disease and death related to infant malnutrition.[80] This progress would undoubtedly have been more pronounced if the dedicated efforts of the Allende regime had not been sabotaged by the American Central Intelligence Agency.

The need for a large-scale nutrition educational program in the United States is evidenced by the great popularity of hot dogs, soda pop, pizza, hamburgers, and French fries. At the present time, one-third of the American adult population is classified as overweight. A substantial segment of the American public has been aptly characterized as overfed and undernourished. It is particularly interesting to note that poor people often spend as much money on food as those people who are better off, or even more, and at the same time are eating less nutritious meals than their wealthier counterparts. Economist Dr. Walter Heller notes that low income groups spend as much as 40 percent to 50 percent of their total income on food.[81]

Because of the naïve belief that flesh food is indispensible as a source of protein, many people who can ill afford meat nonetheless feel compelled to include substantial amounts of it in their diet. The purchase may be costly but this is simply regarded as an investment in good health. One of the most disturbing commentaries on the high regard afforded meat is that some people who are too poor to buy regular meat have resorted to using pet food. Dr. Michael Jacobson, co-director of the Center for Science in the Public Interest

(Washington, D.C.), estimates that one-third of all dog food that is sold at inner-city stores is actually bought for human consumption.[82] It is ironic that, in their desperation to feed themselves, people are spending more money by using pet food than if they were to obtain their protein from vegetable sources. Pet food, in addition to costing more than most vegetable protein foods, is also taxed and cannot be purchased with food stamps.

The cost differential between conventional meat sources and vegetable protein is quite pronounced, particularly when analyzed in terms of protein values. Calculations made by Consumers Union in 1971 showed that the price per pound of actual protein value for ground beef was as much as $4.18 per pound; ground chuck as much as $5.17 per pound; ground round as much as $6.78 per pound; and ground sirloin as much as $7 per pound.[83] The so-called "fast-food" eating establishments have become increasingly popular in recent years. Service, of course, accounts for part of the price that is paid for hamburger, which is one of the principal items sold at such places. Nonetheless, the actual price per pound of protein for these hamburgers is substantially higher than the cost per pound of protein for sirloin steak prepared at home. Interestingly enough, the relatively low protein value of frankfurters ("hot dogs") makes them even more expensive than sirloin steak in terms of per pound protein cost. Calculations made in 1972 by Consumers Union showed the average cost per pound of protein for all-beef frankfurters was $7.94.[84]

Reflecting on the numerous factors that contribute to the inefficiency of meat production, it is not really difficult to account for the high cost of this product. When people discover that quality protein can be obtained from a wide variety of vegetable sources they should have no need to complain of the high price the merchant exacts for his pound of flesh.

FOOD, ECONOMY, AND WAR

Human beings are among the few animals that kill members of their own species. Indeed, they are the only species that has conducted such killing on an organized basis and has continued in this endeavor to perfect carnage as an art. It would, of course, be absurd to attribute the cause of war to any single factor. However, it is undeniable that competition for food has inevitably led to conflict, and that this struggle for survival has been a significant factor in the historical development of organized warfare. It is in this respect that meat eating is either the underlying cause of armed conflict or at least one of several factors contributing to the exacerbation of a pre-existing problem. The reason why meat, in particular, has created such problems is that the practice of raising livestock requires a much greater use of resources. The basic problem is simply that people are forced to compete with animals for food—a most precarious situation when food is in short supply. As the continued increase in both the human and livestock populations made the competition for limited resources more intense, conflicts arising out of territorial disputes became more common.

The Bible contains numerous examples of conflict situations that are directly attributable to the practice of raising livestock, including contested water rights, bitter competition for grazing areas, and friction between agriculturists and nomadic herdsmen. The more settled agricultural communities deeply resented the intrusion of nomadic tribes with their large herds of cattle, sheep, and goats. These animals were considered a menace. Aside from the threat to the crops themselves, large herds of livestock caused much damage to the general quality of the land as a result of overgrazing. It was ostensibly for this reason that the Philistines, whose primary agricultural pursuits were corn and orchards, sought to discourage nomadic herdsmen from using their territory by filling in many of the wells in the surrounding area.[85]

One of the earliest accounts of strife among the herdsmen themselves is found in the story of Lot and Abram:

> And Lot also, which went with Abram, had flocks, and herds, and tents. And the land was not able to bear them, that they might dwell together: for their substance was great, so that they could not dwell together. And there was a strife between the herdmen of Abram's cattle and the herdmen of Lot's cattle.[86]

Abram moved westward to a region known as Canaan while Lot journeyed to the east, finally settling in Sodom. Such peaceful agreements, however, were not always possible. There are several references in the Bible to clashes between the Israelites and Midianites. The Midianites were wealthy Bedouin traders who owned large numbers of livestock, as did the Israelites, who brought their herds with them when they left Egypt.* Livestock require vast areas of land for grazing. They also need water, which has never been abundant in that region of the world. The strain thus placed on the land's resources is mentioned in Judges 6:4: "And they encamped against them, and destroyed the increase of the earth." The depletion of resources created by the people and livestock moving into this territory is described in Judges 6:5 by a singularly appropriate simile: "For they came up with their cattle and their tents, and they came as grasshoppers." Another passage informs us that after a particularly vicious battle with the Midianites the Israelites augmented their herds with the livestock of their slain captives. This included 675,000 sheep and more than 72,000 beeves.[87]

A strikingly frank reference to the causal relationship between flesh eating and war, in terms of land use, is found in Deuteronomy 12:20:

> When the Lord thy God shall enlarge thy border, as he hath promised thee, and thou shalt say, I will eat flesh, because thy soul longeth to eat flesh; thou mayest eat flesh, whatsoever thy soul lusteth after.

There is a similar straightforward reference to the relationship between flesh eating and war in Plato's *Republic*. While engaged in a dialogue with Glaucon, Socrates comments that a vegetarian diet is conducive to peace as well as good health:

> They will feed on barleymeal and flour of wheat, baking and kneading them, making noble cakes and loaves; these they will serve up on a mat of reeds or on clean leaves, themselves reclining the while upon beds strewn with yew or myrtle. And they and their children will feast, drinking of the wine which they have made, wearing garlands on their heads, and hymning the praises of the Gods, in happy converse with one another. And they will take care that their families do not exceed their means; having an eye to poverty or war.

---

* The Pharaoh had originally refused to let Moses take the Israelites out of Egypt unless the livestock they had raised was left behind for the Egyptians. Moses refused to accede to this demand: "Our cattle also shall go with us; there shall not an hoof be left behind" (Exodus 10:26).

But, said Glaucon, interposing, you have not given them a relish to their meal.

True, I replied, I had forgotten; of course they must have a relish—salt, and olives, and cheese, and they will boil roots and herbs such as country people prepare; for a dessert we shall give them figs, and peas, and beans; and they will roast myrtle-berries and acorns at the fire, drinking in moderation. And with such a diet they may be expected to live in peace and health to a good old age, and bequeath a similar life to their children after them.[88]

Glaucon remains skeptical that people would be satisfied with such fare. He asserts that people will desire the "ordinary conveniences of life," including pig's flesh. Socrates replies that it is in the people's best interest for them to avoid things "not required by any natural want." In the ensuing dialogue Socrates comments on the consequence of exceeding one's needs:

. . . and there will be animals of many other kinds, if people eat them.

Certainly.

And living in this way we shall have much greater need of physicians than before?

Much greater.

And the country which was enough to support the original inhabitants will be too small now, and not enough?

Quite true.

Then a slice of our neighbours' land will be wanted by us for pasture and tillage, and they will want a slice of ours, if, like ourselves, they exceed the limit of necessity, and give themselves up to the unlimited accumulation of wealth?

That, Socrates, will be inevitable.

And so we shall go to war, Glaucon. Shall we not?

Most certainly, he replied.[89]

While Glaucon concedes that flesh eating may contribute to armed conflicts, he does not actually endorse the proposition that vegetarianism should, therefore, be adopted. Indeed, Plato's contemporaries may have agreed with the premise set forth by Socrates but, nonetheless, felt that the privilege of eating meat was well worth the cost—war.

The history of the European spice trade would seem to confirm that there is indeed a relationship between war and large-scale consumer demand for foods not required by what Plato refers to as "natural want." Aside from their general use as flavoring agents, spices were of vital importance to meat preparation. Before the process of mechanical refrigeration was developed in the 20th century, meat was usually preserved by the process of salting. Using various combinations of spices to offset the saltiness of meat, thus making it palatable, became a popular practice in medieval Europe. The demand for spices was a significant factor in European colonial endeavors. Competition intensified, contributing to the exacerbation of serious disputes that already existed among various European nations. Efforts in the 17th and 18th centuries by the Dutch, Portuguese, English, and French to expand their spice trade resulted in warfare as well as the subjugation of native peoples by these imperialist powers. The Dutch wrested control of the Spice Islands* from the Portuguese in the middle of the 17th century. The British and the French, former allies in expelling the Dutch from all but a few small parts of India, struggled to enhance their power over the regions they controlled in that country. Despite attempts to maintain a cordial relationship, armed conflict between these two powers became inevitable. The British became the dominant power in India but were finally forced to relinquish their control in 1947, largely as a result of the successful passive-resistance campaign directed by a vegetarian ascetic—Mahatma Gandhi.

Shepherds have traditionally been depicted in both art and literature as a peaceable lot. However, there were inevitable disputes between farmers and shepherds over territorial rights. This situation was aggravated by the fact that sheep posed an even greater threat to the land than cattle because they clipped grass closer to the ground, sometimes tearing it out by the roots. The Spanish sheepowners' guild known as the Mesta dominated Spain's political affairs for several centuries (A.D. 1200–A.D.1500) and was the source of much internal strife within that country. The Mesta's sheep not only destroyed pastureland by overgrazing but were also allowed to rampage through cultivated fields. The peasant farmers could hardly expect the monarchy to rectify this injustice since sheep raising dominated

* Ceylon, Malacca, Sumatra, Java, Celebes, and the Moluccas.

medieval Spanish commerce and was the government's principal source of revenue during this period.

There was considerable animosity among shepherds, cattlemen, and crop farmers in 19th-century America. The Homestead Act of 1862 encouraged more people to settle in the West. The very nature of livestock raising in the United States at that time required vast areas of land for grazing and moving the animals along designated trails to their final destinations. Hence the proliferation of farming communities became a serious threat to the livestock industry. This situation became worse when the farmers put up barbed-wire fences, a practice that became popular in the 1880s. Aside from the conflict between livestock herders and farmers, there were bitter feuds between cattlemen and sheepmen, including such conflicts as the "Tonto Basin War" in Arizona, the "Holbrook War" in Montana, the "Blue Mountain War" in Colorado and the "Big Horn Basin Feud" in Montana.

We are presently confronted with a rather precarious situation in which a few select regions of the world are the principal suppliers of various commodities that are essential to the entire process of food production. The Middle East region, for example, dominates the world petroleum market. Petroleum is needed to power farm machinery in addition to its use as a fertilizer base. Despite the relatively large amount of petroleum produced in the United States, this country is, nonetheless, highly dependent on Middle East oil. The U.S. Secretary of State Henry Kissinger commented in 1975 that military intervention "could not be ruled out" in the event of another Arab oil embargo. His comment indicates the extent of American dependency on Arab oil and the desperate lengths the U.S. government will go to obtain it. Morocco is the leading producer of phosphate, an important element in fertilizer production. Within the period of a few years in the early 1970s, Morocco more than quadrupled its price for phosphate. The large world demand for phosphate prompted Morocco to invade the Spanish Sahara when the Spanish relinquished control of the region in 1975. A determined guerrilla force of Saharan nationals are presently battling the Moroccan aggressors, whose sole interest in this region is its phosphate reserves.

We know from past experience that the United States is fond of using its position as a major food exporter to manipulate the policies of foreign governments. The most striking example of this practice is evidenced by the successful U.S. "destabilization" effort in Chile. A project initiated by the American Central Intelligence Agency to create dissatisfaction among Chilean truckers resulted in widespread food shortages. The Allende regime was then rebuffed in its attempts to make a cash purchase of vitally needed U.S. wheat. However, in less than a month after a successful Chilean coup that was abetted by the U.S. government, the new fascist regime was given a large shipment of American wheat on generous credit terms despite Chile's unstable economy.

A report prepared in August, 1974, by the American Central Intelligence Agency cites several ominous trends in weather conditions and population growth. The authors of this report indicate there is substantial evidence to support the belief that food shortages will become more acute as a result of a major cooling trend. This trend will adversely affect food production in most regions of the world. The report further predicts that only the United States and Argentina will remain unaffected by these unfavorable weather trends. As a result, such a situation "could give the United States a measure of power it had never had before—possibly an economic and political dominance greater than that of the immediate post–World War II years."[90] The study warns, however, that countries adversely affected by these weather changes may resort to desperate measures, including "nuclear blackmail" and "massive migration backed by force." The report concludes that we have the potential to compensate for future large-scale famines that may be far worse than the present food crisis. It is duly noted that if the anticipated marked and persistent cooling trend occurs there would not be enough food to feed the world's population "unless the affluent nations make a quick and drastic cut in their consumption of grain-fed animals."[91] The CIA's analysis of the relationship between meat eating, food shortages, and armed conflict echoes Plato's prophetic commentary on this issue.

7

Ecology and Vegetarianism

Has God, thou fool! work'd solely for thy good,
Thy joy, thy pastime, thy attire, thy food?
Who for thy table feeds the wanton fawn,
For him as kindly spread the flow'ry lawn:
Is it for thee the lark ascends and sings?

ALEXANDER POPE

Every aspect of meat production, from raising livestock to slaughterhouse operations, presents serious ecological problems. It is, therefore, important to examine these environmental issues thoroughly and give serious consideration to the long-range consequences of using animals as a source of food.

FEEDLOTS

The feedlot has become an increasingly important part of the meat industry in recent years. It is estimated that, at the present time, about 82 percent of the beef cattle produced in the United States are sent to feedlots prior to slaughter. Just three decades ago, only 30 percent of American cattle were processed in this manner.[1] The feedlot operation involves an intensive feeding program in which cattle are encouraged to eat large quantities of grains. This is done to prepare the animal for market more quickly. Additionally, increasing the animal's consumption of grain (as opposed to forage) enhances the quality of its meat. In fact, the grading standards for meat are largely determined by the quantity of feed grain the animal has received.

The concentration of waste in feedlot areas presents a particularly serious problem: water pollution. The large quantities of manure that accumulate in feedlot areas cannot be readily transformed into humus, since the natural rate of this transformation is limited. Instead, the nitrogenous waste is converted to soluble forms, e.g., ammonia and nitrate. This material may then leach into ground water beneath the soil or it may be washed into surface waters by the rain or melting snow. The pollution of waterways often results, with excessive growth of aquatic plant life. The nitrates in runoff material contribute to this aberrant growth process, known as "eutrophication." The eventual decay of these aquatic plants (algae, in particular, have a very short life span) creates bad odors and places a severe strain on the water's oxygen supply. This, of course, has an adverse effect on fish and other forms of marine life. A heavy spring rainfall in 1967 caused tons of wastes from Kansas feedlots to be washed into receiving streams, killing an estimated 300,000 to 500,000 fish.[2]

A report prepared for the Office of Research and Monitoring of the U.S. Environmental Protection Agency was highly critical of the manner in which feedlot owners deal with the pollution problem caused by feedlot wastes, noting: "Emphasis has been on cheapness rather than adequacy of method."[3] One farming trade publication had advocated the use of abandoned strip mines for feedlots. It was argued that the streams in these areas were already polluted by runoff from the mines. Even the United States Department of Agriculture had, at one time, actually encouraged beef producers to locate their feedlots on hillsides near streams expressly for the purpose of efficiently channeling concentrated feedlot waste into the water.[4] Several states have recently enacted laws regulating animal waste, but as one Environmental Protection Agency official notes, ". . . there has been little public scrutiny of the feedlot pollution problem."[5] The EPA is actually reluctant to enforce pollution regulations since pollution control is very costly and the small feedlot owners, in particular, would not be able to absorb this additional expense. These regulation problems are responsible for the current situation, in which feedlot runoff is estimated by the Agricultural Research Service of the USDA to be as much as 50 times higher than public health standards permit.[6] One study conducted by associates of Ralph Nader found that the food industry was one of the leading contributors to pollution in the United States and that this was largely due to animal waste.[7] American livestock produce two billion tons of waste each year—more than twenty times that of human derivation.[8]

There are no ideal solutions to the control of pollution caused by feedlot waste. Fluidizing these wastes would place a heavy burden on local water-treatment facilities. A process of concentrating or drying feedlot wastes would greatly increase equipment and power costs. Incineration would create a serious air-pollution problem.[9] It has been suggested that manure from cattle feedlots could be collected and transported to various crop-growing farms for use as fertilizer. However, the cost involved in time, labor, and equipment needed to move a ton of manure, in addition to the cost of the manure itself, is considerably higher than the cost of a ton of commercial fertilizer.[10]

FERTILIZER

We have become increasingly dependent upon chemical fertilizers to improve crop yields as part of our endeavor to meet the growing demand for food. Environmentalists have expressed concern over various problems that have been created by the extensive use of fertilizers. One such problem is the fact that fertilizer production is energy intensive. The world use of energy is increasing at a rate of nearly 6 percent annually—three times the rate of population growth.[11] The increased demand for energy in the United States has effectively lessened public opposition to a wide variety of programs that have been severely criticized by environmentalists, including the Alaskan pipeline project, strip mining, and the expansion of nuclear power.

The extensive use of fertilizer has created major water-pollution problems because various constituents of fertilizer, particularly nitrogen, are not entirely retained in the soil and are easily washed into surface waters by rain or melting snow. As previously noted, eutrophication is caused by nitrogen runoff. Children as well as livestock have become ill and, in some instances, have even died from drinking water with high levels of nitrates.[12]

WATER

Despite the fact that three-quarters of the earth's surface is covered by water, the insufficiency of this vital resource is considered to be the principal constraint on efforts to expand world food production. The reason for this seemingly ironic situation is that 97 percent of the earth's water is seawater. Because of its high saline content it is not suitable for use as drinking water or for irrigation purposes. Only 3 percent of the earth's water is classified as fresh water, and the vast proportion (98 percent) of this is contained in the polar ice caps, primarily in the region of Antarctica and Greenland. It is generally agreed that any attempts to utilize this water would have disastrous consequences, e.g., massive flooding and unpredictable changes in weather patterns.[13]

It would naturally be assumed that the continuous increase in population would create a greater demand for water. It is significant to note that the percentage of increase in water usage is actually much greater than the percentage of increase in population growth. The U.S. trend in water consumption serves as a useful illustration of this fact. The population of this country increased 165 percent from 1900 to 1970. During this same 70-year period, water usage increased by 285 percent.[14] Economists and food-production experts who attended the 1974 World Food Conference in Rome generally agreed that the next global crisis would be a water shortage.

Significantly greater quantities of water are required for processing meat than for growing crops that are used directly by the human population. More water is needed to produce feed grains as well as that which is consumed by the livestock. Actually, the amount of water required to produce various food crops is determined by the type of crop that is grown. One pound of wheat, for example, requires 60 gallons of water while the same quantity of rice requires from 200 to 250 gallons of water. The amount of water that is used to produce one pound of meat ranges from 2,500 to as much as 6,000 gallons.[15] The slaughterhouse operation in itself requires an incredible amount of water. One hundred million gallons of water are used every day in just one slaughtering plant that processes chickens. This is equivalent to the amount of water needed to service a community of 25,000 people.[16]

Aside from the issue that meat production requires significant quantities of fresh water, the disposal of slaughterhouse waste contributes to the pollution of our waterways. A report published in 1973 by the National Industrial Pollution Control Council states: "The disposal of rumen content generated in cattle slaughterhouses is a problem only slightly less urgent than that of ground manure disposal."[17] Data from a 1972 study of waste disposal in the meat industry noted that 2,957 combined slaughtering and processing plants in the United States routinely discharge about 70 percent of their waste water into city sewers. The other 30 percent is treated before being discharged into receiving streams. This study further notes that meat-industry waste waters are from 5 to 10 times as polluted as domestic sewage and contain significantly higher concentrations of nitrogen, phosphorus, and grease.[18] One study of wastes from the meat-packing industry in Omaha, Nebraska, cited the fact that meat-packing companies located in that city discharged over 100,000 pounds of grease, carcass dressing, casing cleaning, intestinal waste, paunch manure and fecal matter from viscera into the sewer system each day.[19] Omaha's sewer system empties into the Missouri River.

GRAZING

The practice of grazing animals has resulted in destruction of large areas of land throughout the world. There is ample evidence to indicate that the quality of the environment is impaired in regions used for the purpose of grazing livestock. Foraging animals not only trample the ground but also reduce the amount of herbage in the area. The combination of trampling and depletion of plant cover loosens the soil, making these grazing areas particularly vulnerable to erosion. Furthermore, cattle paths are continuously enlarged by windstorms and rainfall since there is no protective plant cover to hold the soil in place. Simple cattle paths in such diverse regions as Africa and the United States have created gorges 30 feet deep.[20]

"Overgrazing" is a euphemistic term used to describe the destructive effects of livestock grazing. Throughout the course of history overgrazing has been a principal cause of erosion in various parts of the world. Much of this was caused by the early nomads who wandered from one region to another in search of better grazing

This erosion in an area of Utah was caused by overgrazing. (Photo courtesy of the Bureau of Land Management)

land. Various nomadic peoples with their herds of livestock created vast areas of barren land in China.[21] Similarly, nomadic tribes were largely responsible for the deterioration of large tracts in the Middle East region, including the Sinai Desert.[22] The expansion of early agricultural civilizations actually did little to prevent the continued deterioration of the land within their borders. Early agricultural communities in Italy, Greece, and India continued to raise animals for food despite the fact that, unlike nomads, there was certainly no need for them to do so. The sheep and goats that were commonly kept in these countries destroyed much of the vegetative cover in the areas where they grazed. This contributed to erosion, as is evidenced by the large stretches of barren land presently found throughout these countries. A considerable portion of Spain was devastated by the powerful sheep industry, the Mesta, which dominated the agricultural life of that country for several centuries. Their sheep destroyed cultivated land as well as territory used for grazing. The Mesta, in fact, was so influential that it succeeded in persuading the Spanish monarchy to outlaw the tilling of any new areas of land that were not already under cultivation. The disallowance of any further cultivation of arable land by peasants was in effect until the middle of the 16th century.

Various conservation programs have been initiated in the 20th century in an attempt to control the extent of erosion caused by grazing. One such program started in the United States was known as the Taylor Grazing Act. This legislative act, passed in 1934, was designed to curb the large-scale deterioration of public lands that were used by ranchers for grazing their livestock. Much of the Great Plains region had been severely damaged as a result of overgrazing— one of the major causes of the catastrophic dust bowl of 1934, which devastated large sections of Colorado, Kansas, Oklahoma, New Mexico, and Texas. Despite the havoc caused by this event, U.S. ranchers were loath to comply with provisions of the Taylor Grazing Act. It had remained, for the most part, an ineffectual piece of legislation. The administrative functions of the Taylor Grazing Service (1934) and the General Land Office (1812) were combined in 1946 to form the present Bureau of Land Management. The U.S. Council on Environmental Quality, in its sixth annual report, published December, 1975, noted that the BLM like its predecessor, the Taylor Grazing Service, has not been able to effectively control the deterioration of land which is under its jurisdiction:

> In more than 3 decades of assigning grazing privileges, it has been handicapped by the lack of an organic act which would clearly establish its powers and define the purposes for managing its lands. Operating under this handicap, BLM has found it difficult to carry out the conservation aims of the Taylor Grazing Act.[23]

A study prepared in 1975 by the U.S. Department of Interior, Bureau of Land Management, reported that 50 percent of the grazing land under its jurisdiction was considered to be in only fair condition. Another 28 percent was rated poor, and 5 percent was deemed bad.

The erosion of this area in St. Joe National Forest, Idaho, was caused by overgrazing. (Photo courtesy of the USDA Forest Service)

Only 15 percent of this land was rated good and a scant 2 percent was characterized as excellent.[24] Elaborating on their classification of range conditions, the BLM noted that the substantial portion of land characterized as fair was decidedly "unsatisfactory." There has been a substantial reduction in forage plants that have been replaced by lower-quality perennial grasses, weeds, and shrubs, or by bare ground. Rangeland that is rated poor has lost most of its vegetative cover and topsoil, exposing it to erosion. Grazing areas considered to be in bad condition have lost most of their topsoil, contain sparse amounts of low-value plants, and are subject to the perils of erosion.[25]

Extensive grazing in various countries has resulted in severe erosion or a general deterioration in the quality of the land used for this purpose. Such abuse of these lands creates a particularly serious problem for those nations which desire to expand their food production as a matter of necessity. Extensive grazing has been a principal factor contributing to the severe soil erosion that has occurred in Africa, the South American countries of the Andes, as well as the Middle East region. Land which was formerly under cultivation in these regions is now being abandoned because it is no longer productive.[26] Various studies have shown that the annual precipitation is only 10 to 12 inches in a particular region of Australia. The practice of raising sheep in such areas naturally aggravates the situation. Several years ago the Australian government attempted to ameliorate the problem of overgrazing by making provisions for ranchers to double their acreage. However, instead of grazing their livestock over a greater land area, as the government intended, the ranchers expanded their livestock population in an effort to increase their profits.[27]

The environmental problems that are an inherent part of meat production cannot be easily resolved by scientific technology. Indeed, technology sometimes creates more problems than it solves. The use of rinderpest vaccine in Africa provides an interesting illustration of this point. Rinderpest, often referred to as "cattle plague," is a viral disease that is highly contagious. It first appeared on the European continent in the 17th century. The disease, however, was not known in Africa until 1889, and has been effectively controlled there by the use of a vaccine. As a result of the successful vaccination program, there has been a significant increase in the number of cattle raised in Africa. The deterioration of grazing land was accelerated by this increase in the cattle population. The large-scale destruction of land was aggravated by a six-year drought that recently affected the Sahelian region, which includes Chad, Mali, Mauritania, Niger, Senegal, and Upper Volta.

WILDLIFE

There are many people who are not really concerned with the general issue of animal welfare but are, nonetheless, outraged by the killing of animals which are classified as endangered species. A great many species are already extinct—some as a direct result of their use as food by humans. One such example is the dodo bird. Actually there were three different types of dodos, each species inhabiting one of three islands (Mauritius, Réunion, and Rodriguez) in the Indian Ocean. The existence of dodo birds was first recorded in the early 1500s by Portuguese sailors. The dodo, which weighed about 50 pounds, was quite incapable of defending itself and could not flee from its enemies, since it lacked the ability to fly. Large numbers of these birds were killed by human beings for food. Additionally, pigs that were brought to the islands destroyed a significant portion of the dodos' eggs, creating a severe decline in the dodo population. The Mauritius species became extinct by about 1681; the dodo that inhabited Réunion became extinct sometime between 1746 and 1750; while the species that was indigenous to the island of Rodriguez existed until sometime between 1790 and 1800.

Before it became extinct, the Steller's sea cow inhabited the coastal waters and shallow bays of the Commander Islands in the Bering Sea. Russian sealers, who were first to record the existence of these creatures in 1741, estimated the entire population of this species to be about 5,000. The meat of the Steller's sea cow was considered a delicacy by Russian sealers, who exterminated the entire species in less than 3 decades (by 1768) after the initial discovery.

The Labrador duck has been extinct since 1875. This species formerly inhabited the coastal regions of northeastern Canada. Migrating south for the winter, these ducks traveled down the Atlantic coast as far as Chesapeake Bay. The extermination of the passenger pigeon has been largely attributed to the American westward expansion in the latter half of the 19th century. As passenger pigeons became a popular food item, the numbers of this species rapidly diminished. Millions were slaughtered each year and shipped by railway cars to be sold in city markets. There is no record of passenger pigeons existing in a wild state after the year 1904. The last known member of this species died in 1914 at the Cincinnati Zoo. Another bird to become extinct as a result of its use as food was the heath hen. Indigenous to the west-central Great Plains region of the United States, this species had become extinct by about 1932.

The exploitation of the various wildlife species has resulted in a marked reduction in their numbers. Concern over the declining duck population prompted the Soviet government to impose a ban on duck hunting in 1970. Aside from the large number of waterfowl killed by American hunters directly, more than 2½ million other birds die each year as a result of lead poisoning.[28] This is caused by the large number of lead pellets which, having missed the hunters' targets, fall into the wetland areas and are ingested by waterfowl foraging for food. A single number-six shotgun shell contains 280 pellets. It is estimated that 1,400 pellets are expended for every bird that is killed.[29]

The significant decline in the population of various marine animals has been attributed primarily to "overfishing." The Pacific sardine lives along the coasts of North America from Alaska to southern California. Sardines, once a major part of the California fishing industry, are now considered to be "commercially extinct." When they were more abundant these sardines had been used for cattle feed and fertilizer in addition to their use as human food. Another species classified as "commercially extinct" is the New England haddock. Ecologists have also been concerned about the significant reduction in finfish, the Atlantic bluefin tuna, Lake Erie cisco, and blackfins that inhabit Lakes Huron and Michigan. Shellfishery, one of the oldest industries in Cape Cod, Massachusetts, is presently in a state of serious decline. As of 1974 it has been necessary for nearly every Cape Cod town to hire its own shellfish warden to enforce the quota restrictions that have been placed on the gathering of shellfish, including clams, oysters, and scallops.[30]

Ecologists are well aware of the possibility that various animals may be added to the list of species that have become extinct as a result of being exploited for the purpose of providing food for human beings. Additionally, there has been widespread concern over the large numbers of animals killed as an incidental factor in the normal course of various food gathering operations. For instance, more than 200,000 porpoises are killed annually by fishermen seeking tuna in the Pacific.[31] Since yellowfin tuna frequently travel with porpoises, both species are consequently trapped in the tuna fishers' nets. Despite the fact that porpoises are of no value to the tuna fishers, any significant effort to avoid killing them would necessarily create a substantial increase in the cost of this operation. Similarly, the destruction of sea turtles is incidental to Caribbean shrimp operations. A recent U.S. government report cites the "rapidly disappearing" sea turtle population as a cause for concern.[32]

Some animals are killed because, as carnivores, they compete with the human predator for the right to kill other animals for food, including wild game and domesticated species that are raised by livestock ranchers. Alaskan hunters are most eager to reduce the wolf population in their state because this animal is a predator of moose. This creates a situation in which wolves are directly competing with human beings for food. Carnivores, such as cougars, coyotes, and wolves are considered a menace to the cattle and sheep industries, and livestock ranchers have been engaged in a large-scale campaign to exterminate these "varmints." The ranchers refer to their practice of killing these animals as a "control measure." Two species of wolves are now classified as endangered, and very few wolves are presently found in the United States except for the state of Alaska and the northeastern part of Minnesota. The relatively small numbers of eagles in the United States is largely due to the destruction of this species by livestock ranchers, particularly those in the sheep business.

The herbivorous fauna that inhabit rangeland areas pose another kind of threat to the livestock industry. These animals compete with cattle and sheep for the flora of these regions, which serves as their source of food. It is for this reason that large numbers of kangaroos are being exterminated in Australia while in the United States livestock ranchers seek to destroy such animals as wild horses, wild burros, deer, elk, antelope, and prairie dogs. One Nevada rancher commented that if the wild horses that roam public rangeland could be eliminated "we could make this cattle country again."[33] Unhappily, American ranchers have been engaged in a campaign to do just that. This situation became known to the general public as a result of the widespread publicity that was given to a gruesome incident that occurred in 1973. Pursuing a herd of some 50 to 60 wild horses, members of the Idaho Cattlemen's Association caused 12 of these animals to fall off a cliff, plunging two hundred feet to their death.

Federal legislation designed to protect wild horses and wild burros was enacted into law in 1971. However, Public Law 92–195, commonly referred to as the Wild Free-Roaming Horse and Burro Act, is not without loopholes which ranchers can use to their advantage. The livestock industry is, nonetheless, obviously annoyed by this federal mandate. The New Mexico Livestock Board, in open defiance of this law, claimed ownership of the wild horses under provisions of the stray laws of their state. A three-judge federal panel in Albuquerque, New Mexico, acting at the behest of livestock ranchers, declared the Wild Horse and Burro Act unconstitutional on February 28, 1975. Other states dominated by the livestock industry, including

Idaho, Nevada, and Wyoming, filed briefs in support of the action taken by the New Mexico Livestock Board. More than a year later, on June 17, 1976, the U.S. Supreme Court, in a unanimous decision, overturned the New Mexico ruling. Speaking for the Supreme Court in its decision, Justice Thurgood Marshall stated that the authority of Congress as it relates to public lands "necessarily includes the power to regulate and protect the wildlife living there." Various animal-welfare organizations monitoring the wild-horse situation claim that, aside from the loopholes that exist within Public Law 92–195 itself, many livestock ranchers ignore this law altogether. It is known, for instance, that in the states of Idaho, California, Utah, and Wyoming, bands of livestock ranchers are illegally killing wild horses.[34]

Prairie dogs, like the wild horses, are regarded as pests by the livestock industry. The use of poison has been a popular method of controlling the prairie-dog population. The "Mexican prairie dog" and the "Utah prairie dog" are now on the official endangered-species list issued by the U.S. Department of the Interior.

It is noted that livestock grazing is largely responsible for the widespread reduction of herbage along deer migration routes.[35] This provides hunters with one of their favorite rationalizations for killing deer: these animals will starve to death unless some of them are killed by the hunters. It has also been shown that stream habitat is adversely affected by the livestock industry.[36] The Audubon Society has been particularly critical of grazing practices that result in the organic pollution of wetlands and a reduction in nesting coverage. This organization cites one example in which a population of one thousand prairie chickens that inhabited a particular region completely disappeared within an eight-year period after livestock grazing in that area had increased.[37] A report entitled "Effects of Livestock Grazing on Wildlife, Watershed, Recreation and Other Resource Values in Nevada," issued in 1974 by the U.S. Department of the Interior, Bureau of Land Management, noted: ". . . uncontrolled, unregulated or unplanned livestock use is occurring in approximately 85% of the state, and damage to wildlife habitat can be expressed only as extreme destruction."[38] Another Bureau of Land Management study that was prepared in 1975 cites the fact that 33 species officially designated as endangered, inhabit rangeland which is under the jurisdiction of this bureau. The report acknowledges that "public land management at the existing level may not insure the survival of these endangered species."[39] Can one really expect cattle ranchers to be genuinely concerned with the survival of rangeland fauna, especially if these animals pose a threat to the efficiency of livestock operations?

CONCLUSION

A growing number of people have become acutely aware of the wasteful use of our natural resources, the destruction of our wildlife, the problem of pollution, and the general deterioration in the quality of our environment. Inevitably, the meat industry will be forced to correct some of its practices. Should we really be consoled by the thought that corrective programs are better late than never? Even then, measures such as pollution control will, at best, only serve to ameliorate the problem and cannot be regarded as a real solution. Furthermore, the cost of maintaining such programs will adversely affect the efficiency of meat-industry operations; the consumer can expect to pay more for flesh foods, since the industry itself will certainly not be willing to absorb these additional costs. Persons who are seriously concerned with the general issues of ecology can avoid this economic and moral dilemma by refusing to support an industry which contributes to a deterioration in the quality of our environment.

8

Killing for Food

To a man whose mind is free there is something
even more intolerable in the sufferings of animals than in the sufferings of men. For with
the latter it is at least admitted that suffering
is evil and that the man who causes it is a crimi-
nal. But thousands of animals are uselessly
butchered every day without a shadow of remorse. If any man were to refer to it, he would
be thought ridiculous.—And that is the unpar-
donable crime. That alone is the justification
of all that men may suffer. It cries vengeance
upon all the human race. If God exists and toler-
ates it, it cries vengeance upon God. If there
exists a good God, then even the most humble
of living things must be saved. If God is good
only to the strong, if there is no justice for the
weak and lowly, for the poor creatures who are
offered up as a sacrifice to humanity, then there
is no such thing as goodness, no such thing as
justice. . . .

ROMAIN ROLLAND
Translation by Gilbert Cannan

Approximately 134 million mammals and 3 billion birds are slaughtered annually in the United States for human consumption. These
animals are not killed for our survival but rather because we have
acquired a taste for their flesh. In our "civilized" societies the slaughter of animals for food is not only an accepted practice, it is an
established custom.

POULTRY

In large-scale production chickens are subjected to miserable conditions during the short time they are allowed to live.* They are crowded together in large poultry houses. Many die of stress. In order to prevent cannibalism which results from overcrowding, the chickens are often "debeaked." Slightly more than one half of the upper portion of the beak is cut off and the lower part of the beak is blunted which makes it difficult for the bird to grasp the feathers or skin of other chickens.

Male chickens are sometimes castrated. Two advantages are cited for this practice: (1) these capons gain weight more quickly, and (2) the flesh is made more tender. An average of about 5 percent of the cockerels who are castrated die as a result of this operation.[1] Only the cockerels of certain breeds are commonly used for capon production, e.g., White Plymouth, New Hampshires, or crosses of these breeds. It is not economically practical to raise cockerels of small breeds such as Leghorns. Therefore, they are usually destroyed at the hatchery.

It is recommended that chickens should be starved for about 12 hours before they are to be killed.[2] This allows time for their intestines to become relatively empty, making the task of eviscerating much easier.

Chickens are killed in an assembly-line process. As they hang upside down by their feet, a mechanical conveyer moves them past a sharp blade which cuts through their jugular vein. The blood is allowed to drain for a period of time. They are then sprayed with scalding water which serves to loosen their feathers before they are moved on to a mechanical de-feathering device. In the smaller-scale chicken processing plants the chickens are slaughtered manually—the slaughterer cuts the throat of the chickens as they pass by him, suspended by their feet on a conveyer line. After cutting each chicken's throat, the slaughterer quickly inserts a knife into the bird's mouth and pushes it upward to pierce the brain. This "debraining" process loosens the feathers, making it easier to pluck the bird.

---

* Most broilers are shipped to market for slaughter when they are six to eight weeks old. The "roaster" is a broiler that is fed for a period of twelve weeks or longer and is consequently more expensive.

The chickens in the foreground have just been slaughtered and the blood drained from their bodies. The ones in the background have been scalded and are set to pass through a mechanical de-feathering device. (Photo courtesy of the Humane Society of the United States)

In some plants, the birds are rendered unconscious by means of an electric stunning device before they are actually killed. Many slaughtering plants cut the chickens' throats while they are fully conscious. The British Humane Slaughter Association noted that of all birds that have their throats cut while conscious, 2 out of 5 go to the scalding tank alive.[3]

Foie gras is produced by putting a funnel in the goose's mouth. Food is cranked down its throat by a screw device within the funnel. Some places now use electric motors to force the food through the animal's gullet. These creatures are subjected to this force feeding three times a day, since they cannot otherwise be induced to overeat.

BEEF CATTLE

Long before they ever reach the slaughterhouse, beef cattle are subjected to various indignities and outright cruelty. Cattle ranchers in the United States have traditionally branded their calves with a red-hot iron as a means of establishing ownership. Although cattle rustling is not nearly so common as it had been in the previous century, branding continues to be a common practice, particularly among owners of purebred stock. Purebred cattle registry associations actually require that each animal recorded in the herd books be permanently marked and identified. Male calves are castrated to make them less aggressive. Moreover, the meat of these sexually altered steers is considered to be a better quality than that of a bull.[4] Calves are dehorned to prevent injuries they might cause each other, especially to avoid marks on their precious hides, which will later be sold to the leather trade.

Cattle are fed all sorts of nonfood items as a cost-saving measure. An article in *Successful Farming Magazine* reported that farmers could save $4.10 per head on 500 pounds of feedlot grain by replacing soybean meal with urea. A large chemical company in Chicago has devised a "protein conversion hydrolizer." One of their ads reads: "For a world running short of low-cost, high-protein animal feed, Chemetron has an answer. Chicken feathers. And hog hair, or animal hide scraps, horns and hooves." The ad claims the ANCO Hydrolizer "produces 18,000 pounds per hour of wet, granular meal from chicken feathers that's up to 88% protein, and 89% digestible."

This calf is being branded and castrated by three cowboys on a Utah ranch. (Photo courtesy of the USDA)

Some farmers found that they could cut their feed cost as much as 50 percent by mixing feed grains with chicken litter. In addition to being fed their own excrement, cattle are also given the blood of other animals killed at the slaughterhouse, cement dust, and ground newsprint mixed with sawdust and molasses. It is a common practice to feed garbage to hogs. The only stipulation that the government makes is that the garbage must first be cooked to avoid the danger of trichinosis. In 1969 the U.S. government gave a grant to Rutgers University for a two-year garbage feeding study.

Many animals die before they ever reach the slaughterhouse. The Council for Livestock Protection notes that out of every 100 million pigs farrowed, 30 million die before they reach marketable age. In 1971, 200,000 hogs and 39,000 calves died in transit.[5] Stress is a common problem for all livestock animals since they are regarded as expendable commodities, not living creatures. Consequently, they are not afforded any comforts that would cause the rancher to incur extra expenses. Sows are confined in stalls so small that they are not even able to move around. Livestock animals are forced to stand in tightly packed trucks for their long journey to the slaughterhouse. One pamphlet printed for the benefit of ranchers recommends the use of nonskid floors in trucks to eliminate the need for bedding. The trucks which transport these animals to their death are infamous for their poor ventilation. The animals are subjected to extreme heat in the summer and the bitter cold temperatures of winter. Hogs and lambs are known to huddle together in cold weather. In doing so, they sometimes die of suffocation on the way to market.[6] Hot weather, particularly when the relative humidity is 80 percent or higher, is also a major cause of sickness and death in livestock en route to the slaughterhouse.[7] John C. MacFarlane, executive director of the Council for Livestock Protection, noted that the amount of meat lost each year through careless handling and brutality would be enough to feed a million Americans for a year. Ranchers regard it as a normal course of business that some animals will die in the livestock trucks. It is a calculated loss. These animals are destined to die anyway—some just die a little sooner.

Upon entering the slaughterhouse, the cattle are reluctant to proceed. Electric prods which shock the animals and crude clubs are used to move them along. There are various methods used to slaughter them. The use of a sledgehammer to smash the animal's skull is perhaps the crudest method used in the slaughtering process. The cattle are driven, one at a time, through a narrow passageway. As each beast reaches its final destination, a gate closes behind it, confining the animal to a small area. The helpless creature is then struck on the head with a sledgehammer, which smashes its skull and renders it unconscious. However, it sometimes takes several blows on the head to knock the huge beast unconscious. If the animal twists its head suddenly, the hammer will come down on the victim's eyes, creating a bloody mess.[8] Cutting the throat of a fully conscious animal is another cruel method of slaughter. U.S. law stipulates that for sanitary reasons an animal must be off the "killing floor" at the time it is slaughtered. It is therefore shackled with heavy chains around one leg and hoisted into the air. To be suspended in the air by one leg is very painful for a four-legged animal, especially a heavy animal like a steer. It remains hanging from 3 to 5 minutes and sometimes as much as half an hour, twisting and bellowing in

The slaughter of steers in a Texas abattoir. These steers were made unconscious before they were bled to death. (Photo courtesy of the Humane Society of the United States)

pain.[9] It is difficult to cut the animal's throat while it is moving about. The slaughterer must hold the beast in a more stationary position. One method used is to place a clamp in its nostril.[10] The animal, if it persists in moving violently about, often has its nostril torn apart. Another method that the slaughterer uses is simply to gouge the animal's eyes out.[11] The head of a steer, being quite large, affords no sure grip except for the eye sockets. The steer is then killed by slitting its bulky throat, cutting through the jugular vein, gullet, and windpipe. Blood gushes from the huge throat and continues to drain out of the now lifeless body.

One method of slaughter considered somewhat painless is the use of the captive bolt pistol. After the animal is driven into a small enclosure, the muzzle of a large gun is placed to its forehead. There are two types of captive bolt pistols. One model drives the bolt through the muzzle with tremendous impact, causing a concussion. The animal remains senseless for several minutes. While it is still unconscious, the animal is bled to death. The other type of pistol shoots a bolt that actually penetrates the animal's skull and retracts again inside the pistol. A wire is then forcefully inserted through the hole and moved about to insure destruction of nerve centers in the brain. Electric stunning is another means used to render the animal unconscious before it is actually killed. The electric stunning device consists of two electrodes placed on each side of a two-pronged instrument. The tongs are firmly pressed to the sides of the animal's head just beneath the ears. The electric current passes through the brain, paralyzing the beast and rendering it unconscious. The animal must then be bled to death within seven minutes before it regains consciousness.

The issue of kosher slaughter, in particular, has generated a great deal of controversy. Many orthodox Jewish rabbis feel it is necessary to maintain the traditional method of kosher slaughter—cutting the throat of a fully conscious animal. They have sternly opposed all efforts to compel kosher slaughter plants to render the animals unconscious prior to the painful process of shackling, hoisting, and throat-cutting. It should be duly noted that not all orthodox rabbis subscribe to the notion that rendering an animal unconscious is antagonistic to the rules of Jewish ritual slaughter. It is a theological question that is open to interpretation. Even more important, however, is the serious constitutional questions which have been raised by this issue. The orthodox rabbis who subscribe to the notion that animals must be slaughtered while fully conscious defend their right to continue this barbaric practice by raising the issue of religious freedom. However, the U.S. government has been most inconsistent in dealing with the whole issue of religious freedom. For instance, polygamy is outlawed even though this practice had been permitted by the Mormon Church. The Amish people are harassed because of their defiance of compulsory-education laws, which they view as a violation of their religious principles. Voodoo sects are in violation of animal-cruelty laws when they kill various types of animals as part of their strange religious rites. Outlawing religious practices contravenes constitutional guarantees of religious freedom. However, the tolerance of certain religious practices would contravene the moral standards of American society. Which then has precedence?

Apropos of this issue, Friends of Animals and the Society for Animal Rights have pointed out that many people have scruples about eating the flesh of animals slaughtered by cruel methods. However, these people have no choice in the matter. A considerable portion of the meat that comes from kosher slaughtering plants is marketed as non-kosher. Meat consumers should be entitled to know how their victim was killed. These consumers might then assuage the pangs of a guilty conscience. They should not, however, consider themselves humane, compassionate people since slaughtering animals for food is not necessary in the first place. Indeed, the term "humane slaughter" is a misnomer. The word "humane" encompasses such qualities as kindness, tenderness, mercy, and compassion—hardly an apt description of people who eat the flesh of slaughtered animals to tickle their taste buds.

9

Sense Perception and Reality

A dead cow or sheep lying in a pasture is recognized as carrion. The same sort of a carcass dressed and hung up in a butcher's stall passes as food!

JOHN HARVEY KELLOGG, M.D.

Though 'twill to hunger give relief,
there's nothing picturesque in beef.

WILLIAM COMBE

Our perception of the food we eat is an important factor in our dietary preferences. Food that has an unappetizing appearance is usually rejected. Similarly, most people will refuse to eat food that has an unpleasant odor or a bad taste. These matters are, to some extent, subjective in nature. Many vegetarians regard flesh eating as a loathsome practice. If we accept the premise that flesh eating is, indeed, unnatural to our species, we must then ask: How have the sensory faculties of so many people been corrupted in such a way that they find the sight, taste, and smell of roasted corpses a pleasurable experience?

SIGHT AND OLFACTORY SENSES

The sight of cattle or sheep peaceably grazing in pastures is perceived differently by vegetarians than by meat eaters. Commenting

125

on the ugly reality of this seemingly pleasant pastoral scene, Shelley proclaims: "The very sight of animals in the fields who are destined to the axe must encourage obduracy if it fails to awaken compassion."[1] It is logical to believe that most people would not find the sight of dead animals at all pleasing. Yet these same individuals fail to reconcile the gruesome image of the slaughterhouse with their gourmet meals of filet mignon or roast lamb. How many flesh eaters, if given the choice of living next to a fruit stand or to a slaughterhouse, would actually choose the latter? Which is more pleasing to the sense of sight: the variety of fruits and vegetables of many different glowing colors or the butcher with the carcass of a steer slung over his shoulder, his white apron besmirched with the blood of his victim? Which is more pleasing to our olfactory senses: the sweet, rich aroma of oranges, apples, strawberries, and pungent spices blended from a variety of herbs or the odor of a cadaver, rotting by the minute? Thoreau, in addition to citing ethical objections to the practice of flesh eating, also alludes to such sensory considerations: ". . . there is something essentially unclean about this diet and all flesh, and I began to see where housework commences, and whence the endeavor, which costs so much, to wear a tidy and respectable appearance each day, to keep the house sweet and free from all ill odors and sights."[2]

We become conditioned to the aesthetic values of our society to a degree—but not completely, only to a degree. Many meat eaters will tell you that they love the smell of roast beef, but soon after cooking it they bring out a room deodorizer, scented like some flower or herb, in an effort to cover the odor of the smoldering corpse. It is interesting to note that "room deodorizers" or "air fresheners," as they are sometimes called, are often made to imitate the scent of flowers, herbs, or fresh fruits. No enterprising manufacturer has yet produced a room deodorizer or any incense that imitates the odor of any kind of cooked meat. Would anyone really want a living room that smells like fish or barbecued beef?

THE AUDITORY SENSE

The impassioned protestations of animals awaiting their impending doom is most disturbing to hear. This is more than just an unpleasant noise. The bleating of sheep, the bellowing of steers, the clucking of chickens and the squealing of pigs are a challenge to the conscience of the slaughterer, who, alas, does not seem to heed these sounds of agony. He has become inured to his gruesome task. There is a moving passage in Upton Sinclair's *The Jungle* describing the sounds of a slaughterhouse:

> At the same instant the ear was assailed by a most terrifying shriek; the visitors started in alarm, the women turned pale and shrank back. The shriek was followed by another, louder and yet more agonizing— for once started upon that journey, the hog never came back. Meantime, heedless of all these things, the men upon the floor were going about their work. Neither squeals of hogs nor tears of visitors made any difference to them; one by one they hooked up the hogs, and one by one with a swift stroke they slit their throats. There was a line of hogs, with squeals and a life-blood ebbing away together; until at last each started again, and vanished with a splash into a huge vat of boiling water.[3]

Ovid's Pythagoras notes that butchers are impervious to the mournful pleadings of calves and kids despite the fact that their cries are so similar to the cries of a human child:

> Deaf to the Calf that lies beneath the Knife,
> Looks up, and from her Butcher begs her Life:
> Deaf to the harmless Kid, that e'er he dies
> All Methods to procure thy Mercy tries,
> And imitates in vain thy Children's Cries.[4]

One must necessarily become callous to endure the sounds of the slaughterhouse. Isaac Bashevis Singer's "The Slaughterer" is the story of a man who was not able to make such an adjustment:

> Barely three months had passed since Yoineh Meir had become a slaughterer, but the time seemed to stretch endlessly. He felt as though he were immersed in blood and lymph. His ears were beset by the squawking of hens, the crowing of roosters, the gobbling of geese, the lowing of oxen, the mooing and bleating of calves and goats; wings fluttered, claws tapped on the floor. The bodies refused to know any justification or excuse—every body resisted in its own fashion, tried to escape, and seemed to argue with the Creator to its last breath.[5]

Even the farmer who kills hogs and chickens to provide food for his own family has, like the professional slaughterer, become inured to the dreadful cries of his victims. In China, where storytelling is a finely developed art, there is a record of one particular storyteller who inspired the awe of his listeners by his uncanny ability to imitate seven distinct sounds of a pig in the successive stages of its slaughter.[6] Could this man's macabre talent really be appreciated by people who are not accustomed to killing the animals they eat?

The slaughterer acts on behalf of the meat-eating consumers who can quietly dine on the animals that have been killed for their enjoyment. Table talk or dinner music is a pleasant diversion which helps them to forget the nature of their meals. These people would much rather listen to Percy Grainger's "Country Gardens" while dining than the agonizing sounds of animals that are killed to satisfy their appetites. Voltaire, who was himself a meat eater, asks: "Where is the barbarian who would roast a lamb, if it conjured him by an affecting speech not to become at once an assassin, an anthropophagus?"[7] Meat eaters do not wish to be disturbed by such hypothetical fantasies. They are thankful that, in reality, their victims never protest the injustice done to them but lie in dead silence upon a dinner plate. Besides, as Marcus Cato noted: "It is a difficult task, O citizens, to make speeches to the belly, which has no ears."[8]

THE SENSE OF TASTE

An individual's food preferences are a most interesting issue to analyze. It is generally acknowledged that individual differences in eating habits are largely based on sociological conditioning. Snake meat is eaten in some western communities while most people from the eastern part of the United States would find this repugnant. Similarly, most Americans would be repelled by a number of foods which are popular in other regions of the world: Puppies are eaten in West Africa; the natives of Central America and Siam eat grubs and worms; the French consider snails a delicacy. We acquire a taste for the foods we eat. Our perception of meat, in particular, is influenced to a great extent by other members of our society who continually refer to meat as a highly desirable food. Many people in affluent societies look upon meat as indispensable to a good standard of living. The inculcation of this belief has reassured people that they are wise to eat meat and, at the same time, has caused them to view vegetarianism as a peculiarity. George Bernard Shaw, who was often questioned on his curious eating habits, responded: "Why should you call me to account for eating decently? If I battened on the scorched corpses of animals, you might well ask me why I did that." Porphyry, in noting that people have resorted to cannibalism in times of famine, implies that the need to survive mitigates the odious nature of this practice. He is, however, appalled by the notion that people can actually find pleasure in eating dead bodies whether it be people or animals.[9]

THE TACTILE SENSE

One might normally shudder at the thought of touching a corpse, yet this is something that meat eaters have become accustomed to as part of their daily routine. Like Porphyry, Plutarch expresses amazement that human beings have not only developed such a habit but actually find much delight in what he considers a perversity:

> For my part I rather wonder both by what accident and in what state of soul or mind the first man who did so, touched his mouth to gore and brought his lips to the flesh of a dead creature, he who set forth tables of dead, stale bodies and ventured to call food and nourishment the parts that had a little before bellowed and cried, moved and lived.[10]

The meat eaters' attitude in this regard has remained the same throughout the course of history. The flesh eaters of the 20th century remove the object of their desire from its polyethylene shroud, perceiving an item of food rather than a mutilated corpse.

THE SIXTH SENSE

It is evident that the strong feelings expressed by some vegetarians on the matter of flesh eating is the result of their sensitive natures. "A man of my spiritual intensity," remarked Shaw, "does not eat corpses." There is an element of truth in Shaw's sarcastic witticism,

Frontispiece from Sydney Whiting, *Memoirs of a Stomach,* W. E. Painter
(London), 1853.

for despite the worldliness of his wealth and arrogance, Shaw did
not wish to be the cause of death and suffering. Gandhi, who had
been raised as a vegetarian, was tormented by his conscience after
having eaten goat's meat out of youthful curiosity. He experienced
recurrent nightmares in which a live goat bleated mournfully from
within his own body.[11] Leonardo da Vinci, who had become a vegeta-

rian primarily for ethical reasons, observed that meat eaters are "burial places"—that their bodies become graveyards for the animals they devour. Ovid, in *The Metamorphoses,* had previously made this same analogy, noting that the bowels of animals are entombed in the bowels of humans. Ovid referred to meat eaters as people who are "maintained by murder, and by death they live." This oxymoron perhaps best expresses the sentiments of vegetarians who are disturbed by the realization that people obtain their sustenance from death.

Animals must necessarily die to satiate the flesh eater's appetite. Sometimes these people will even acknowledge their appreciation of the animal's sacrifice by eulogizing the victim after the completion of the meal: "That chicken was very good! Yes, indeed, it made an exemplary meal." Meat eaters eulogize the victim while refusing to acknowledge their complicity in the murder.

It appears then that some people become vegetarians because of a heightened spiritual awareness. They wish to transcend the standards of the masses who salivate at the sight of dead animals that are cut up and served on a dinner plate.

10
Vegetarianism in Literature

The advantage of a reform in diet is obviously greater than that of any other. It strikes at the root of the evil. To remedy the abuses of legislation, before we annihilate the propensities by which they are produced, is to suppose that by taking away the effect the cause will cease to operate. But the efficacy of this system depends entirely on the proselytism of individuals, and grounds its merits, as a benefit to the community, upon the total change of the dietetic habits in its members. It proceeds securely from a number of particular cases to one that is universal, and has this advantage over the contrary mode, that one error does not invalidate all that has gone before.

PERCY BYSSHE SHELLEY

And there are the ideas of the future, of which some are already approaching realization and are obliging people to change their way of life and to struggle against the former ways: such ideas in our world as those of freeing the labourers, of giving equality to women, of ceasing to use flesh food, and so on.

LEO TOLSTOY
Translation by Aylmer Maude

The subject of vegetarianism is discussed in the writings of many notable figures from ancient times up through the present era. Some of these people were strict vegetarians themselves, some followed the vegetarian diet sporadically, some abandoned the vegetarian diet after a period of time, and many espoused vegetarianism but never actually adopted the vegetarian diet.

DEVOUT VEGETARIANS

PORPHYRY (232?–304?)

Porphyry, like his esteemed teacher, Plotinus, was a devout vegetarian. However, unlike Plotinus, who did not deal with the issue of vegetarianism in his writings, Porphyry wrote a lengthy treatise on this subject. In fact, this work, titled *De Abstinentia,* is among the few manuscripts of Porphyry to survive Constantine's censorship campaign. It is most interesting to note that the arguments on the advantages of vegetarianism as set forth in this treatise are clearly addressed to "contemplative philosophers." Porphyry does not expect to sway "plebeians and the vulgar" to his cause.

In Book I of *De Abstinentia,* Porphyry asserts that those who abstain from flesh foods will experience a greater spiritual consciousness: ". . . the eye of the soul will become free, and will be established as in a port beyond the smoke and the waves of the corporeal nature."[1] Discussing the relationship between flesh eating and immolation in Book II, Porphyry claims that animal sacrifice was often used as a pretext for flesh eating. He cites as proof the fact that various deities were commonly offered only a small portion of the slain animal[2] or were otherwise alloted inedible parts of the victim.[3] Book III is a philosophical discourse on justice as it relates to the rights of animals.

LEONARDO DA VINCI (1452–1519)

There are various references to Leonardo da Vinci's vegetarianism and his tender regard for animals in the writings of his contemporaries. One of Leonardo's more notable biographers was Giorgio Vasari, a younger contemporary of the great artist. Vasari had never actually met Leonardo da Vinci but obtained a great deal of information on his life from Francesco Melzi of Milan, who was a confidant and pupil of da Vinci. Vasari refers to da Vinci's love of horses as well as his peculiar habit of buying birds from merchants in order to release them. Da Vinci's reputation for kindness to animals is also noted in a letter from Andrea Corsali that was written to Giuliano de Medici in 1515. Corsali, who was visiting India at this time, makes a comparison between the practices of a particular religious sect he finds there and the attitudes of da Vinci: ". . . they do not feed on anything which has blood, nor will they allow anyone to hurt any living thing, like our Leonardo da Vinci."[4]

Da Vinci's notebooks contain numerous references to the injustice of killing animals for food:

Endless numbers of these animals shall have their little children taken from them, ripped open, and barbarously slaughtered.

(Of sheep, cows, goats, and the like)

The time of Herod will come again when little innocent children will be taken from their mothers, to be put to death with terrible wounds, most cruelly inflicted.

(Of young lambs, slaughtered for meat)

How foul a thing this is: to see the tongue of one animal stuffed in the guts of another.

(Of sausage made of calf tongue)

How cruel for one whose natural habitat is water to be made to die in boiling water.

(Of boiled fish)

Endless generations of fish will be lost because of the death of this pregnant one.

(Of a fish served with its roe)

Oh, how many chicks will never come to birth!

(Of eating eggs)

Living as they do in communities, whole populations are destroyed so that we can have their honey. Thus will many great nations be destroyed . . . and multitudes deprived of their food and stores; and they will be most cruelly submerged, swept under, drowned by invading armies, out of their minds. Oh, Justice of God! Why dost thou not awake and protect thy misused creatures?

(Of bees)[5]

The milk will be taken from the tiny children.

(Of beasts from whom cheese is made)[6]

This is only a partial selection of passages from da Vinci's notebooks which deal with the subjects of vegetarianism and animal cruelty. It is quite evident that da Vinci was a vegetarian primarily for ethical reasons and that he was deeply disturbed by the practice of killing innocent beings "for the benefit of your gullet, with which you have tried to make of yourself a grave for all animals."[7] It is particularly interesting to note that da Vinci condemned the practice of using eggs, cheese, and honey. One might therefore conjecture that he was a vegan.

LEO TOLSTOY (1828–1910)

Tolstoy was converted to vegetarianism in the autumn of 1885 by a man named William Frey, who had come to visit him at Yasnaya Polyana. In discussing the subject of vegetarianism with Tolstoy, Frey seems to have emphasized the ethical aspects of vegetarianism but also cited anatomical differences that exist between human beings and carnivores as proof that we are vegetarians by nature.[8] When Frey noted that the slaughter of animals for food was unnecessary, Tolstoy is reported to have remarked: "How good that is! How good!"[9] Aside from Tolstoy himself, two of his children, Mary and Tatiana, also became vegetarians as a result of Frey's influence.

Although Sophia Tolstoy did not approve of her husband's vegetarian diet, she nonetheless humored him with special vegetarian meals. She concealed the cost of high-priced items since Tolstoy disapproved of extravagance.[10] Like Sophia, the Tolstoy family governess, Anna Seuron, took a dim view of Tolstoy's vegetarianism: "The Count took up these manias only in the spirit of penitence, to subdue his flesh and elevate and enlighten his spirit."[11] Notwithstanding Anna Seuron's comments, it is quite apparent that Tolstoy had adopted the vegetarian diet out of his compassion for animals. Indeed, various sources, including Anna Seuron, have related that Tolstoy renounced hunting at about the same time he took up the vegetarian diet. Moreover, it is the ethical aspect of vegetarianism that is emphasized in Tolstoy's writings which deal with this subject.

Tolstoy's most extensive discussion of vegetarianism is found in his essay "The First Step." This piece was written in 1892 as a preface to the Russian edition of Howard Williams's *Ethics of Diet,* which had originally been published in English.

The underlying theme in the section of "The First Step" which deals with vegetarianism is that because people are inherently good (as Tolstoy believed), flesh eating is "simply immoral, as it involves the performance of an act which is contrary to moral feeling— killing."[12] Tolstoy connects the issue of intemperance and the ethical question of killing for food with the concept that flesh eating is immoral because it involves a perversion of our true nature: "So strong is man's aversion to all killing. But by example, by encouraging greediness, by the assertion that God has allowed it, and above all by habit, people entirely lose this natural feeling."[13] Commenting on the moral implications of this deviation from one's "natural feeling," Tolstoy writes:

> This is dreadful! Not the suffering and death of the animals, but that man suppresses in himself, unnecessarily, the highest spiritual capacity— that of sympathy and pity towards living creatures like himself—and by violating his own feelings becomes cruel. And how deeply seated in the human heart is the injunction not to take life![14]

Tolstoy asserts that people who are sincere about effecting "moral progress" must necessarily transcend society's standards since these standards are established by "those who are accustomed to be led by public opinion rather than by reason."[15] Tolstoy notes that vegetarianism in itself is but one of many issues that must be dealt with in the struggle to bring about moral progress. Vegetarianism is, nonetheless, an issue of particular importance because "it is a sign that the aspiration of mankind towards moral perfection is serious and sincere, for it has taken the one unalterable order of succession natural to it, beginning with the first step."[16]

Tolstoy's vegetarian proselytes included a motley assortment of groups and individuals. Vegetarianism was the rule of order within the so-called Tolstoyan Christian communes which were established in various parts of Russia.[17] Peter Verigin, the spiritual leader of the Dukhobors, was so impressed with Tolstoy's views that many of Tolstoy's ethical teachings, including vegetarianism and passivism, were adopted as part of Dukhobor doctrine.[18]

GEORGE BERNARD SHAW (1856–1950)

Accounts of George Bernard Shaw's conversion to vegetarianism are found in various magazine articles and letters written by Shaw himself. Shaw recollects that he became a vegetarian in either 1880 or 1881 and cites Shelley's poetry as a prime influence in his decision to adopt this diet.[19] Since Shelley's references to vegetarianism in his poetry emphasize the ethical issue, we might well assume that Shaw renounced flesh eating out of a sense of compassion for animals. Indeed, in an article he wrote in 1901, Shaw plainly refers to his identification with Shelley's view that flesh eating is a barbarous practice: "It was Shelley who first opened my eyes to the savagery of my diet; but it was not until 1880 or thereabouts that the establishment of vegetarian restaurants in London made a change practicable for me."[20] In another account, Shaw relates that he was first exposed to the subject of vegetarianism through Shelley's poetry and dramatically asserts: "But of course the enormity of eating the scorched corpses of animals—cannibalism with its heroic dish omitted—becomes impossible the moment it becomes conscious instead of thoughtlessly habitual."[21] Either Shelley's poetry had not actually made Shaw fully conscious of "the enormity of eating scorched corpses of animals" or his statement here is somewhat disingenuous, since there was a significant lapse in time between Shaw's exposure to the vegetarian issue and the time when it became "practicable" for him to adopt this diet.

On various occasions, Shaw rejected efforts by doctors to have him abandon the vegetarian diet. However, in each of these cases, the doctor's prescription of flesh foods was somewhat frivolous. Shaw responded in kind. On one occasion, Shaw sought medical attention for a boil that had developed on his cheek. However, he failed to accept the doctor's ludicrous diagnosis of his condition: "Barton immediately diagnosed constitutional decay from vegetarianism. But my cheek is now as fair and soft as of yore."[22] On another occasion, doctors advised Shaw that he should start eating meat to improve his constitution and thus hasten his recovery from a bone infection that had developed from a serious foot injury. Shaw did not take this directive very seriously. He proclaimed with mock solemnity: "Life is offered to me on condition of eating beefsteaks. . . . But death is better than cannibalism. My will contains directions for my funeral which will be followed not by mourning coaches, but by herds of oxen, sheep, swine, flocks of poultry, and a small traveling aquarium of live fish, all wearing white scarfs in honor of the man who perished rather than eat his fellow creatures."[23] Actually, Shaw was convinced that the exhausting schedule he had maintained for the past three years working as a London theatre critic in addition to writing plays was the real cause of his weakened condition. Indeed, Shaw's own diagnosis proved to be correct: "I did not change my diet; but I had myself carried up into a mountain where there was no theatre; and there I began to revive."[24]

In view of the fact that Shaw's discussion of ethical vegetarianism is so frequently presented with an air of self-righteousness, it is curious to note that he does not even mention the issue of ethics in his printed post card headed "Vegetarian Diet."* This postal card, in fact, notes that Shaw's principal objection to flesh eating is that this practice creates "an unnecessary waste of the labor of masses of mankind in the nurture and slaughter of cattle, poultry, and fish for human food."[25] Shaw makes this same point in his 1914 essay "Killing for Sport": "Slaughter is necessary work, like scavenging; but the man who not only does it unnecessarily for love of it but actually makes as much of it as possible by breeding live things to slaughter, seems to me to be little more respectable than one who befouls the streets for the pleasure of sweeping them." One of Shaw's characters in *Back to Methuselah* jokingly remarks that in ancient times the practice of flesh eating did not necessarily involve a waste of labor. People killed animals "as a means of killing time, and then, of course, ate them to save the long and difficult labor of agriculture." It, indeed, seems incongruous for an "out-and-out Shelleyan" and ardent antivivisectionist to presume that the question of wasted labor involved in killing animals for food is paramount to the ethical issue.

Shaw, in commending vegetarianism to various friends, often cited

---

* Owing to the large volume of mail he received from his admirers, Shaw had printed a series of more than 30 different post cards with stock replies. These printed postal cards dealt with questions that were frequently raised about Shaw's views on various topics.

the hygienic benefits to be derived from adopting this diet. In a letter dated November 22, 1910, he advises an ailing Hungarian friend to try the vegetarian diet. After stating that vegetarianism should not be regarded as a cure for all sorts of disease, Shaw proceeds to tell him how some people have greatly improved their health by adopting this diet, "especially gouty, rheumatic, neuralgic people." Continuing, he states: "It improves the temper and nerves of irritable people."[26] Later, in this same letter, Shaw states that in terms of strength and energy, a vegetarian diet "seems to be positively superior to a meat diet." In another letter, written to his friend H. G. Wells, Shaw dramatically relates how a strong current had carried him a considerable distance out to sea while he was swimming one day. Shaw contends that he very well might have drowned if he had not been a strict vegetarian. To illustrate this point he cites experiments conducted by Fisher and Chittenden of Yale University in which vegetarian subjects were shown to excel their flesh-eating counterparts in a series of tests which measured strength and endurance. After presenting this testimonial on the strength-giving qualities of vegetarianism, Shaw concludes his letter with a flippant appeal: "Renounce H. G.: abstain."[27] GBS likewise propagandizes the superior strength of vegetarians in the preface to *Androcles and the Lion.* He notes that flesh-eating athletes have suffered "the most ignominious defeats by vegetarian wrestlers and racers and bicyclists."

In contrast to these various comments on the superior nature of the vegetarian diet, Shaw's printed post card on the subject of vegetarianism simply states that one can adequately maintain oneself with such a diet: "It is beyond question that persons who have never from their birth been fed otherwise than as vegetarians are at no disadvantage, mentally, physically, nor in duration of life, with their carnivorous fellow-citizens."[28] Taking a similarly modest posture on this issue in a letter dated August 15, 1946, Shaw writes: "I claim nothing for this diet except that it has kept me alive quite as effectively as a meat diet which costs more and involves an enormous slavery of man to animals and much cruelty and suffering, though the animals owe their lives to it."[29]

This low-key endorsement of vegetarianism might possibly be explained by an embarrassing and painful dilemma that Shaw faced in the later years of his life. In the year 1938, when he was 82 years old, Shaw developed pernicious anemia. He reluctantly consented to be treated with the liver injections prescribed by his doctor. Notwithstanding the fact that this was the only recognized means to cure pernicious anemia at that time, various members of the vegetarian community expressed disappointment with Shaw. Some, including Symon Gould, the associate editor of the *American Vegetarian,* regarded Shaw as an apostate. It is hardly surprising that Shaw became further alienated from those vegetarians who made extravagant claims about the hygienic and curative properties of their diet. Conversely, Shaw never accepted the extreme notion that the vegetarian diet is in any way inadequate. His printed post card on "Vegetarian Diet" written in 1947* states: "As Mr. Shaw reached the age of 82 before he experimented with liver injections after 50 years without eating flesh, fish, and fowl, the inference that his diet was insufficient is silly. He had already lived longer than most meat eaters, and is still (1947) alive."[30]

MOHANDAS GANDHI (1869–1948)

Gandhi was raised as a vegetarian by his parents, who were vegetarians themselves, being devout members of the Vaishnavas Hindu sect. Gandhi ate meat on the sly for about one year during his childhood as an "experiment." He was told by some of his classmates that eating meat would make him strong and courageous. Gandhi abandoned this experiment because he felt guilty about lying to his parents, in addition to the remorse he experienced from the realization that he was responsible for the death of innocent animals.[31]

Gandhi recalled that reading Henry Salt's book *A Plea for Vegetarianism* was a momentous event in his life. Gandhi was no longer content simply to follow the vegetarian diet; he felt compelled to promote vegetarianism as a "mission."[32] The importance Gandhi attached to vegetarianism as a moral reform is evidenced by the numerous articles he wrote on this subject. While many of these articles deal with health questions (e.g., how much to eat, raw versus cooked foods, and the nutritional value of various foods), Gandhi usually emphasized the ethical aspects of vegetarianism. In one arti-

---

* There were actually two somewhat different versions of the post card headed "Vegetarian Diet." One was written in 1947, the other in 1948.

cle, written in 1926, he inveighs against swamis who sanction flesh eating and those who are persuaded by these false prophets to abandon their principles: "This blind worship of authority is a sign of weakness of mind." He further notes: "One needs to be slow to form convictions, but once formed they must be defended against the heaviest odds."[33] Gandhi remarks that it is beneath our dignity as human beings to imitate the ways of predatory animals: "I hold flesh-food to be unsuited to our species. We err in copying the lower animal world if we are superior to it."[34] In his address to members of the London Vegetarian Society in 1931, Gandhi stated that a person should have a definite reason for becoming a vegetarian, since the adoption of this diet constitutes a significant change in one's way of life. Noting that apostasy is particularly common among those who originally abstained from flesh food for health reasons, Gandhi asserted that one's commitment to vegetarianism should have an ethical basis. He expressed the belief that "spiritual progress" depends on the willingness of people to renounce habits which afford them pleasure at the expense of another's suffering: "I do feel that spiritual progress does demand at some stage that we should cease to kill our fellow creatures for the satisfaction of our bodily wants."[35] However, while Gandhi maintained that abstinence from flesh food is "a great aid to the evolution of the spirit," he noted that such abstinence is "by no means an end in itself."[36] The significance of this statement is underlined by the fact that one of the conspirators who plotted Gandhi's assassination was, like his illustrious victim, a vegetarian.

ISAAC BASHEVIS SINGER (1904–

Isaac Bashevis Singer had actually wanted to become a vegetarian when he was a young boy but his parents would not allow him to adopt this diet.[37] Singer's father, a rabbi, told him that his scruples over killing animals were unwarranted and, indeed, somewhat impious. The rationale that he used to support this contention—that one cannot be more compassionate than God—was later used by Singer in his story "The Slaughterer." The young Singer was not impressed by this logic but realized that to remonstrate with his father on this matter would be a futile effort. Although Singer maintained an interest in vegetarianism, he did not become a vegetarian when he left home. His financial situation obliged him to accept meals from friends, which made it awkward for him to refuse dishes that were prepared with meat. However, Singer did not adopt the vegetarian diet even after he had become a successful writer. Then one day in 1962 he came home and found that his parakeet had accidentally drowned. He was deeply moved by this tragedy and came to the realization that it was inconsistent for him to be grieved by the death of this bird when he himself was responsible for the suffering and death of many other innocent creatures. Referring to the fact that he did not actually become a vegetarian until he was 58 years old, Singer remarked: "Naturally I am sorry now that I waited so long but it is better later than never."

Singer has a great passion for Jewish culture but he does not subscribe to orthodox Jewish beliefs. His interest in occultism is reflected in the many stories he has written which deal with the supernatural. They include such mystical concepts as metempsychosis and the power of incantation. Singer rejects the anthropocentric view that human beings have the prerogative to kill other animals: "We are all God's creatures—that we pray to God for mercy and justice while we continue to eat the flesh of animals that are slaughtered on our account is not consistent." Singer, interestingly enough, disagrees with the notion that vegetarianism brings one into closer harmony with Nature—a view which is held by a great many vegetarians: "Nature is cruel but we should not contribute to this cruelty. Actually, vegetarianism is a protest against the cruelty of Nature." Apropos of the association which is often made between Nature and primitivism, Singer comments: "People often say that humans have always eaten animals as if this is a justification for continuing this practice. According to this logic we should not try to prevent people from murdering other people since this has also been done since the earliest of times."

Singer makes it clearly understood that he is a vegetarian for ethical reasons. In discussing people who follow a vegetarian diet because it benefits their health, he commented: "It is good that they don't eat meat but how sad that it is for the wrong reasons. I, myself, believe that it is healthier not to eat meat, but even if eating flesh was actually shown to be good for you I would certainly still not eat it." Singer does not think that one's abstinence from flesh foods should be regarded as a sacrifice on one's part, especially since it is not necessary to our well-being: "We are obliged not to take life—we should not take the attitude that we are doing the animals a favor by not eating them. They have a right to live just as much as we have a right to live."

Singer's attitudes on the practice of killing animals for food is reflected in many of his stories. In "The Fast," Itche Nokhun finds that flesh food makes him nauseous. Nokhum developed this repugnance for meat after witnessing the slaughter of an ox by a shokhet. A somewhat elaborate discussion of flesh eating as a moral issue is found in "The Slaughterer." Yoineh Meir, the protagonist in this story, is appointed to be the town slaughterer. This is held to be a responsible position for a man of religious piety. The "soft-hearted" Yoineh Meir has serious misgivings about his new duties. Since compassion is regarded as a virtue, Yoineh Meir notes the incongruity of slaughtering innocent creatures as an act of religious piety. The town rabbi chides Yoineh Meir for his specious scruples, noting: ". . . man may not be more compassionate than the Almighty, the Source of all compassion." This reasoning mitigates his sense of guilt for a time, but eventually creates even graver doubts: "Verily, in order to create the world, the Infinite One had to shrink His light; there could be no free choice without pain. But since the beasts were not endowed with free choice, why should they have to suffer?" He questions the hypocrisy of obdurate killers praying for mercy: "How can one pray for life for the coming year, or for a favorable writ in Heaven, when one was robbing others of the breath of life?" His guilt becomes overwhelming. When he goes to the ritual bath, every neck reminds him of the slaughterer's knife. Human beings, he observes, are so very much like the animals he kills. Indeed, they have loins, veins, guts, etc. When going to bed, he thinks of the feathers and down that were plucked from fowl to make his pillow and quilt. Upon falling asleep, he has nightmares of the creatures he has slaughtered. They cry out in human voices; they plead for mercy and some curse him. Yoineh Meir is never able to reconcile the concept of God as being compassionate and just with the notion that such a God sanctions the killing of innocent animals. Yoineh Meir resolves this theological paradox by proclaiming that humans can, indeed, be more compassionate than God since: "He is a cruel God, a Man of War, a God of vengeance."

Similar sentiments are expressed by Masha in *Enemies, A Love Story*. When Herman, Masha's lover, expresses his desire to become a vegetarian, she is sympathetic but excuses her own weak will by stating that God is not a vegetarian: "God himself eats meat—human flesh. There are no vegetarians—none." Alluding to her experiences in a Nazi concentration camp, Masha bitterly proclaims: "If you had seen what I have seen, you would know that God approves of slaughter." Herman himself had been traumatized by the Nazi occupation of Poland. He identifies with animals who suffer under the yoke of their human oppressors. He compares the Bronx Zoo to a concentration camp. Indeed, the manner in which people treat animals reminds Herman of the Nazi oppression of Jews: "At every opportunity, he pointed out that what the Nazis had done to the Jews, man was doing to animals." Herman is a sensitive, intelligent man but he is also indecisive and weak-willed. He constantly wavers in his devotion to the three women who love him. We also find that he wavers in his resolve to become a vegetarian.

Several of Singer's penitents are vegetarians. One such character is Jacob in *The Slave*. Aside from observing a vegetarian diet out of penitential abstinence, Jacob questions the whole notion that God actually looks with favor on the practice of killing animals for food. When some boys ask him, "Why are you so scared of flesh?" Jacob replies: "We are flesh ourselves." When Jacob is asked what he eats on the Sabbath, he answers that his Sabbath meals are no different from the meals he eats on weekdays. Perceiving this behavior as sacrilegious, one boy comments: "You're not allowed to torment yourself on the Sabbath." Jacob responds: "Nor must one torment others." Another boy notes that the ritual slaughterer, who is highly esteemed in Jewish culture, would no longer be able to make a living if everyone became a vegetarian like Jacob. Responding to this assertion, Jacob comments: "One can survive without slaughter."

Noting the importance that Singer attaches to ethical vegetarianism along with the fact that several of his stories include references to vegetarianism and animal cruelty, one might suspect that he is moralizing. Singer, however, denies that any of his works are didactic in nature: "I am not a writer with a message. I try to write a good story—somehow the message comes out by itself, and the message which comes out automatically by itself is stronger than the message which you plan."

INCONSTANT VEGETARIANS

GEORGE GORDON BYRON (1788–1824)

Byron frequently fasted and would often live exclusively on a diet of biscuits and water for extended periods of time. Thomas Moore reports that Byron rarely ate breakfast before three or four o'clock in the afternoon and that this meal generally consisted of one or two raw eggs, plain biscuits, and a cup of tea. There were several different reasons for Byron's sporadic adherence to this self-imposed scanty diet.

Byron is reported to have stated on one occasion: "I have no palate: one thing is as good as another to me."[38] In a letter to Lord Blessington, apologizing for not attending his dinners, Byron remarked: ". . . your banquets are too luxurious for my habits."[39] However, these remarks are somewhat misleading, since Byron was by no means totally indifferent to gourmet dining. He would occasionally indulge himself with rich foods after having maintained an abstemious diet for long periods of time. On one such occasion he remarked: ". . . for several months I have been following a most abstemious régime, living almost entirely on vegetables; and now that I see a good dinner, I cannot resist temptation, though to-morrow I shall suffer for my gourmadise, as I always do when I indulge in luxuries."[40] Byron had told Lady Blessington that eating "as others do" not only made him ill but impaired his mental faculties as well.[41] In a letter to Moore dated January 28, 1817, Byron related that he was "obliged" to eat simple meals for health reasons but that he did not always strictly adhere to this diet: "The remedy for your plethora is simple—abstinence. I was obliged to have recourse to the like some years ago. I mean in point of diet, and, with the exception of some convivial weeks and days (it might be months now and then), have kept to Pythagoras ever since."[42] Byron himself had sponsored several lavish dinners at his home in Pisa during the years 1821 and 1822. The menu for one such banquet lists an incredible assortment of foods, including several different kinds of flesh foods. The first course included pork with lentils, boiled capons, beef, and a fish stew. The second course consisted of such items as a veal dish, roasted capons with sauce, roasted woodcocks, a fricassee of poultry in gravy, and baked fish.

Although Byron held the rather curious notion that flesh eating disposes people to ferocity,[43] it would be difficult to believe that the poet's sporadic adherence to a vegetarian diet was actually based on ethical considerations. Trelawny recalls that during a voyage to Greece in 1823, he and Byron whiled away the time by pistol shooting: ". . . empty bottles and live poultry served as targets; a fowl, duck, or goose, was put into a basket, the head and neck only visible, hoisted to the main yard-arm: and we rarely had two shots at the same bird."[44] Actually, these birds would have been killed anyway, since they were meant to be used as food for the people on board ship. Byron, however, had no intention of eating the birds he killed. Aside from occasionally eating fish, Byron was committed to following a vegetarian diet at this time.

PERCY BYSSHE SHELLEY (1792–1822)

The fact that Shelley attached great importance to vegetarianism as a necessary reform is evidenced by the dogmatism that marks the first sentence of his essay "A Vindication of Natural Diet": "I hold that the depravity of the physical and moral nature of man originated in his unnatural habits of life." Alluding to Greece's mythological Golden Age and the creation myth which is part of the Judaic-Christian heritage, Shelley continues: ". . . the mythology of nearly all religions seems to prove that at some distant period man forsook the path of nature and sacrificed the purity and happiness of his being to unnatural appetites." Citing this association between flesh eating and moral degeneration, Shelley asserts that the question of diet is inextricably linked to the issue of social reform. Shelley's second essay on vegetarianism also places a great emphasis on the relationship between the treatment of animals and the moral fiber of society. He compares the killing of innocent animals for food to the hideous nature of war and the gross injustice of slavery. After citing several odious practices, such as bleeding calves to death in order to obtain whiter and more tender veal, Shelley asks: "What beast of prey compels its victim to undergo such protracted, such severe and such degrading torments?" While Shelley considers gluttony in itself to be a vice, he expounds on the ramifications of such profligacy, citing the impairment of one's health in addition to the suffering that is inflicted on innocent animals.

It appears that Shelley developed an interest in vegetarianism during his brief stay at Oxford University (October, 1810, through March, 1811). Commenting on Shelley's eating habits during this period, Thomas Jefferson Hogg reports that his friend's food was "plain and simple as that of a hermit, with a certain anticipation, even at that time, of a vegetable diet."[45] While Shelley had not strictly adhered to a vegetarian diet at this time, he nonetheless seemed convinced that it was wrong to kill innocent animals for food and had often raised this issue as a topic for discussion.[46]

Shelley and his wife Harriet both took up the vegetarian diet six months after they were married. Their enthusiasm in adopting this diet is expressed in a letter which Harriet wrote to Elizabeth Hitchener, dated March 14, 1812:

> You do not know that we have forsworn meat & adopted the Pythagorean system; about a fortnight has elapsed since the change and we do not find ourselves any the worse for it. What do you think of it? Many say it is a very bad plan but as facts go before arguments we shall see whether the general opinion is true or false—we are delighted with it & think it the best thing in the world; as yet there is but little change of vegetable, but the time of year is comming on when there will be no deficiency.[47]

Although Harriet does not give details on the reason for their adoption of the vegetarian diet, her reference to the "Pythagorean system" indicates that the ethical factor was a prime consideration.

The various accounts of Shelley's eating habits given by people who knew him certainly suggest that his diet was woefully inadequate. It is quite likely that Shelley's poor health can be attributed, at least in part, to nutritional deficiencies. Although his poor state of health may be blamed on a grossly inadequate diet and not vegetarianism per se, Shelley was very much concerned that his bad example would discourage people from adopting the vegetarian diet. This concern is noted in a letter Shelley wrote to Leigh and Marianne Hunt in June of 1817:

I know not how, I have so constant a pain in my side, and such a depression of strength and spirits, as to make my holding the pen whilst I write to you an almost intolerable exertion. This, you know, with me is transitory. Do not mention that I am unwell to your nephew; for the advocate of a new system of diet is held bound to be invulnerable by disease, in the same manner as the sectaries of a new religion are held to be more moral than other people, or as a reformed parliament must at least be assumed as the remedy of all political evils. No one will change the diet, adopt the religion, or reform parliament else.[48]

Peacock relates that on one occasion he found Shelley ill in bed. Peacock at this time suggested that Shelley's vegetarian diet was the cause of this illness. Shelley, however, adamantly rejected this notion.[49]

Hogg relates that Shelley as well as various other members of the vegetarian "church"* at Bracknell occasionally ate meat on the sly. Hogg's statement that Shelley did not strictly adhere to the vegetarian diet is corroborated by accounts on this matter which are found in the writings of Peacock and Trelawny. Shelley, his second wife Mary, and Peacock traveled up the Thames in August, 1815. Peacock recounts that during this trip he persuaded Shelley to eat some mutton in order to restore his failing health. Peacock claims that Shelley continued to follow his prescription for a week "He lived in my way for the rest of our expedition, rowed vigorously was cheerful, merry, overflowing with animal spirits, and had certainly one week of thorough enjoyment of life."[50] Commenting or the general nature of Shelley's lapses, Peacock states: "When he was fixed in a place he adhered to this diet consistently and conscientiously. . . . While he was living from inn to inn he was obliged to live, as he said, 'on what he could get'; that is to say, like other people."[51] Peacock, who was clearly hostile to his friend's vegetarianism, claims to have perceived a marked improvement in Shelley' health during those periods when the poet was impelled to eat, a Peacock puts it, "like other people." While Shelley offered such ex cuses for his backsliding, he remained a staunch advocate of th

---

* Many of Shelley's friends at Bracknell were vegetarians. Peacock and Hogg bot facetiously refer to this group as a "church."

vegetarian diet. Perhaps it was a tinge of conscience that prompted him to write the following lines in *Alastor or the Spirit of Solitude:*

> If no bright bird, insect, or gentle beast
> I consciously have injured, but still loved
> And cherished these my kindred; then forgive
> This boast, beloved brethren, and withdraw
> No portion of your wonted favour now![52]

HENRY DAVID THOREAU (1817–1862)

Thoreau abstained from flesh foods during a few brief periods of his life but was never totally committed to vegetarianism. When someone once urged him to become a strict vegetarian, Thoreau retorted: "The man who shoots the buffalo lives better than the man who boards at the Graham House."[53] Thoreau, however, also rejected the dogmatism of those who believe that flesh food is necessary for proper nutrition.

> One farmer says to me, "You cannot live on vegetable food solely, for it furnishes nothing to make bones with"; and so he religiously devotes a part of his day to supplying his system with the raw material of bones; walking all the while he talks behind his oxen, which, with vegetable-made bones, jerk him and his lumbering plow along in spite of every obstacle. Some things are really necessaries of life in some circles, the most helpless and diseased, which in others are luxuries merely, and in others still are entirely unknown.[54]

Thoreau's writings which deal with the issue of flesh eating are quite indecisive. He even appears to contradict himself at times. Thoreau's ambivalence on the question of killing animals for food can be explained, in part, by his belief in the dualistic nature of human character. Thoreau maintains that we possess a predatory instinct, which is part of our primitive nature. However, those who have cultivated their spiritual nature (like Thoreau himself) are disturbed by the notion that killing animals for food is justifiable, notwithstanding our predacious instinct: "I found in myself, and still find, an instinct toward a higher, or, as it is named, spiritual life, as do most men, and another toward a primitive rank and savage one, and I reverence them both. I love the wild not less than the good."[55] Commenting on his interest in fishing, Thoreau writes: ". . . the catching of the dinner was as much a social exercise as the eating of it."[56] Contrasted with his enthusiastic endorsement of this "social exercise," another comment on fishing is apologetic in tone: "I have actually fished from the same kind of necessity that the first fishers did. Whatever humanity I might conjure up against it was all factitious, and concerned my philosophy more than my feelings." Continuing, he adds: "I did not pity the fishes nor the worms. This was habit."[57] Thoreau confesses that he is vexed by scruples over killing these innocent creatures:

> I have found repeatedly, of late years, that I cannot fish without falling a little in self-respect. I have tried it again and again. I have skill at it, and, like many of my fellows, a certain instinct for it, which revives from time to time, but always when I have done I feel that it would have been better if I had not fished. I think that I do not mistake. It is a faint intimation, yet so are the first streaks of morning. There is unquestionably this instinct in me which belongs to the lower order of creation; yet with every year I am less a fisherman, though without more humanity or even wisdom; at present I am no fisherman at all. But I see that if I were to live in a wilderness I should again be tempted to become a fisher and hunter in earnest.[58]

Thoreau is frustrated by the fact that he cannot lead the spiritual life he aspires to attain while succumbing to this primitive instinct to prey on other animals.

Thoreau prophesies that when people cultivate their spiritual nature they will cease to kill animals for food. In fact, he contends that such an evolutionary process is part of our "destiny":

> Is it not a reproach that man is a carnivorous animal? True, he can and does live, in a great measure, by preying on other animals; but this is a miserable way,—as any one who will go to snaring rabbits, or slaughtering lambs, may learn,—and he will be regarded as a benefactor of his race who shall teach man to confine himself to a more innocent and wholesome diet. Whatever my own practice may be, I have no doubt that it is a part of the destiny of the human race, in its gradual improvement, to leave off eating animals, as surely as the savage tribes have

left off eating each other when they came in contact with the more civilized.[59]

While Thoreau was clearly sympathetic to the ethical merits of vegetarianism he evidently did not desire to be part of the vanguard of a dietary reform movement. He was content to speculate that the "destiny of the human race" would run its course with or without him.

APOSTATES

LUCIUS ANNAEUS SENECA (4 B.C.–A.D. 65)

Included in Seneca's *Moral Essays* is an epistle to his friend Lucilius which deals in part with Seneca's adoption of the vegetarian diet and the reason for his subsequent apostasy. Seneca first brings up the issue of gluttony, expressing the belief that foods which provide no real nourishment should be avoided. He states that products such as oysters and mushrooms are foods of gluttons, "since they are not really food, but are relishes to bully the sated stomach into further eating, as is the fancy of gourmands and those who stuff themselves beyond the power of digestion."[60] Aside from the question of temperance, Seneca was exposed to the issues of hygiene, cruelty to animals, and metempsychosis through the teachings of Sotion:

> Sotion used to tell me why Pythagoras abstained from animal food, and why, in later times, Sextius did also. In each case, the reason was different, but it was in each case a noble reason. Sextius believed that man had enough sustenance without resorting to blood, and that a habit of cruelty is formed whenever butchery is practised for pleasure. Moreover, he thought we should curtail the sources of our luxury; he argued that a varied diet was contrary to the laws of health, and was unsuited to our constitutions. Pythagoras, on the other hand, held that all beings were interrelated, and that there was a system of exchange between souls which transmigrated from one bodily shape into another.[61]

Seneca relates that the transition to vegetarianism was not easy but that "at the end of a year the habit was as pleasant as it was easy. I was beginning to feel that my mind was more active."[62]

We do not know how long Seneca was a vegetarian, since he does not state at what age he actually adopted this diet. We do know, however, that he abandoned his vegetarian diet about A.D. 19 at the behest of his father. It was at this time that Tiberius Caesar promulgated ordinances against a certain cult that included vegetarianism among its precepts. Seneca notes that one's abstinence from certain kinds of animal food was viewed as "proof of interest" in this unnamed cult.

PLUTARCH (45?–125)

It is not certain that Plutarch ever was a vegetarian. However, there is evidence to suggest that he may have followed the vegetarian diet at some period in the early part of his life. His zealous vindication of vegetarianism in his two early tracts entitled "De Esu Carnium" ("On the Eating of Flesh") is, indeed, telling. Plutarch begins his first vegetarian tract with a lengthy comment on the repulsive nature of flesh eating and repeatedly refers to the notion that we are "polluting" our bodies by persisting in this ghoulish practice. Supporting his contention that flesh eating runs contrary to our nature, Plutarch cites various anatomical differences that exist between humans and the carnivorous species.*

While there is some uncertainty as to whether or not Plutarch had been a vegetarian at some point in the earlier part of his life, it is apparent that he was not a vegetarian in his later years. In his essay "Advice on Keeping Well," Plutarch recommends eating birds and fish since the flesh of these animals is "light," whereas fatty types of meats "oppress the body." Total abstinence from flesh foods is commendable but "it is hard to decline all the time." It is significant to note that Plutarch clearly indicates in this essay that he does not regard flesh as a highly desirable food:

> It is best to accustom the body not to require meat in addition to other food. For the earth yields in abundance many things not only for nourishment but also for comfort and enjoyment, some of which it grants to our use just as they are with no trouble on our part, while others we may make savoury by all sorts of combination and preparation.

---

* See Chapter 3, "Anatomy, Diet, and Disease," p. 24.

But since custom has become a sort of unnatural second nature, our use of meat should not be for the satisfaction of appetite, as is the case with wolves or lions; but while we may put it in as a sort of prop and support of our diet, we should use other foods and relishes which for the body are more in accord with nature and less dulling to the reasoning faculty, which, as it were, is kindled from plain and light substances.[63]

Plutarch's reference to flesh eating as a custom which has become "a sort of unnatural second nature" is, indeed, a weak apology when contrasted with his condemnation of flesh eating in his two vegetarian tracts, where this practice is characterized as ghoulish, unnatural, unhealthy, gluttonous, cruel, and unjust.

ALFRED TENNYSON (1809–1892)

Tennyson, in his poem "To E. Fitzgerald," recalls that he had tried vegetarianism as an experiment "for ten long weeks." It was a spiritually uplifting experience "to float above the ways of men" but, alas, Tennyson "then fell from that half-spiritual height" and never returned again to the "table of Pythagoras." It is puzzling to note that in "To E. Fitzgerald" Tennyson relates that he had been a vegetarian for ten weeks but in his commentary on this poem he states that his vegetarian experiment had lasted only six weeks. There is no apparent explanation for this discrepancy.

ALPHONSE LAMARTINE (1790–1869)

Lamartine was actually raised as a vegetarian by his mother, whose objections to flesh eating seem to have been based primarily on ethical considerations. Lamartine writes: "I have retained her firm belief, that to kill animals for the purpose of feeding on their flesh is one of the most deplorable and shameful infirmities of the human state; that it is one of those curses cast upon man either by his fall, or by the obduracy of his own perversity."[64] Noting that he retains the belief that the practice of killing animals for food is wrong, Lamartine offers a rather weak apology for abandoning his vegetarian diet at the age of twelve: "Although the necessity of complying with the rules of the society in which we live has made me eat, since then, all that other people eat, I have retained a repugnance, based on reason, to cooked flesh, and it has always been difficult for me not to see in the butcher's trade something of the executioner's occupation."[65] While he never strictly followed a vegetarian diet after the age of twelve, Lamartine always maintained temperate eating habits. During the last years of his life, in particular, he rarely ate flesh food.[66]

GUSTAV MAHLER (1860–1911)

Gustav Mahler became a vegetarian as a direct result of Wagner's advocacy of this diet in the 1880 issue of the *Bayreuther Blätter*. The 20-year-old Mahler was obviously quite impressed with Wagner's article. In a letter to his friend Emil Freund, dated November 1, 1880, he wrote: "A month ago I became a complete vegetarian. The moral effect of this way of life—a voluntary subjection of the body and its ever-increasing demands—is immense. You can understand how completely convinced I am by it when I tell you that through it I expect the regeneration of the human race."[67] Although Mahler eventually abandoned the vegetarian diet, he evidently retained a strong sympathy for the ethical aspect of vegetarianism. Commenting on Mahler's feelings of compassion for all living beings that suffer, Alma Mahler states that her husband would frequently exclaim: "How can one be happy while a single living being on earth still suffers?" However, Alma notes: "Mahler did not always live up to his convictions, but that he always wished to is certain."[68]

HUGO WOLF (1860–1903)

Hugo Wolf, like Mahler, adopted the vegetarian diet as a result of his great admiration for Wagner. Wolf, who was 22 years old when he became a vegetarian, followed this diet for about 18 months.

ADVOCATES WHO DID NOT
PRACTICE WHAT THEY PREACHED

It is particularly curious to note that some of the most forceful arguments favoring the adoption of the vegetarian diet are found in the writings of individuals who were not vegetarians themselves.

There are several passages in Pope's *An Essay on Man* that ridicule the anthropocentric notion that animals were created solely for the benefit of the human species. In this same work, there is a poignant image of an innocent lamb that "licks the hand just rais'd to shed his blood."[69] William Cowper, in a moving passage in *The Task*, refers to the frightful "persecution" of animals to satiate the "base gluttony" of flesh-eating humans.[70] Bernard Mandeville reflects: "I have often thought, if it was not for this Tyranny which Custom usurps over us, that Men of any tolerable Good-nature could never be reconcil'd to the killing of so many Animals for their daily Food, as long as the bountiful Earth so plentifully provides them with Varieties of vegetable Dainties."[71] Voltaire, after citing the merits of vegetarianism, sarcastically remarks that those of "austere virtue" have won few proselytes because "they could not prevail against butchers and gluttons."[72] Wagner dogmatically postulates that "the degeneration of the human race has been brought about by its departure from its natural food, the only basis of a possible regeneration."[73] Similarly, Goldsmith writes: "Man was born to live with innocence and simplicity, but he has deviated from nature."[74] Despite these dogmatic assertions and poignant appeals to one's sense of compassion and justice, Mandeville, Pope, Cowper, Goldsmith, Voltaire, and Wagner failed to be swayed by their own rhetoric.

WRITERS WHO SATIRIZED VEGETARIANISM

It would be difficult to determine the extent to which the general public has been influenced by various notable people who espoused vegetarianism in their writings. However, the fact that vegetarianism did enjoy a certain degree of popularity, particularly in England, is evidenced by the fact that several writers satirized the vegetarian lifestyle.

Caricatures of Shelley's vegetarian friend John Frank Newton appear in several of Thomas Love Peacock's novels. In Thomas Holcroft's *Alwyn, or the Gentleman Comedian,* a character named Handford establishes a humane asylum for animals in distress. Various people blackmail Handford into giving them money by threatening to torture their animals if he does not comply with their demands. Interestingly enough, the character of Handford in this story is patterned after Holcroft's vegetarian friend Joseph Ritson.

In Charles Lamb's "The Pawnbroker's Daughter," a butcher reads from Ritson's treatise on vegetarianism while he goes about his business. While reading a poignant passage on the slaughter of innocent lambs, the butcher is reminded that he has an order for mutton that was to have been delivered an hour ago. Returning once again to the passage on the slaughter of a lamb, he remarks: "What an affecting picture!" Other works in which Lamb satirizes vegetarianism are "Hospita on the Immoderate Indulgence of the Pleasures of the Palate" and "Edax on Appetite." In the former piece, Lamb refers to the dire predictions of Malthus in regard to food supply and population growth, while in the latter he refers to various ethical arguments on vegetarianism that are set forth in Mandeville's *Fable of the Bees.*

G. K. Chesterton makes disparaging remarks about vegetarianism in several of his essays. He rails against vegetarian moralists, lumping them with "cranks" and "ascetics" who oppose the use of tobacco and alcohol. It is curious to note that Chesterton, who characterized himself as a staunch antivivisectionist, does not seriously address himself to the question of killing for food as an ethical issue. However, in one of his many attacks on vegetarianism, Chesterton does concede that the ethical argument for total abstinence from flesh food is more compelling than the argument for total abstinence from alcohol: "There is a very strong case for vegetarianism as compared with teetotalism. Drinking one glass of beer cannot by any philosophy be drunkenness; but killing one animal can, by this philosophy, be murder."[75] This seems to be the most favorable comment on vegetarianism that Chesterton makes in any of his writings.

VEGETARIANISM AS A UTOPIAN CONCEPT

There are several works in which vegetarianism is represented as a Utopian ideal. Voltaire, in his mythological story *The Princess of Babylon,* writes about a Utopian society that exists on the eastern shore of the Ganges, where people and animals live together in peaceful harmony. Cowper, in his poem *The Task,* notes that Adam and Eve lived as vegetarians in the Biblical Paradise. Since the time of their fall from grace, there has been a marked increase in moral turpitude—humans kill some animals for sport to sate their lust for blood while other innocent creatures are slaughtered to satiate our "base gluttony." Similarly, Ovid and James Thomson harken back to the Greek mythological Golden Age, when all people lived as vegetarians. Ovid cites this idyllic period as a marked contrast to his contemporary society, where people who delight in their ghoulish "Cyclopean Feasts" are "Maintained by Murder":

> Not so the Golden Age, who fed on Fruit,
> Nor durst with bloody Meals their Mouths pollute.
> Then Birds in airy space might safely move,
> And timorous Hares on Heaths securely rove:
> Nor needed Fish the guileful Hooks to fear,
> For all was peaceful; and that Peace sincere.[76]

A similar depiction of this mythological Golden Age is found in James Thomson's "Spring" from his work *The Seasons:*

> But who their virtues can declare? who pierce
> With vision pure into these secret stores
> Of health and life and joy? the food of man
> While yet he lived in innocence, and told
> A length of golden years, unfleshed in blood,
> A stranger to the savage arts of life,
> Death, rapine, carnage, surfeit, and disease—
> The lord and not the tyrant of the world.[77]

The underlying theme in "Spring," as Thomson relates in his preface to the second edition of this poem, is the "Degeneracy of Mankind," which had begun immediately following that period known as the Golden Age. Thomson, however, negates the significance of his moral discourse on the virtues of the Golden Age in noting that his account of this period is drawn from "gaudy Fables." Thomson eliminated the term "gaudy Fables" in the 1746 edition, substituting the somewhat less derogatory phrase "fabling poets." The effect, nevertheless, is similar: one does not feel overly compelled to live as an idealist, imitating the ways of a Utopian society that exists only in fables.

While Ovid, Thomson, and Cowper wrote about Utopian societies of a bygone era, Shelley's *Queen Mab* depicts a Utopian society of a future era. In this youthful work, Shelley envisions an era in which immortal humans do not kill for food but live rather in a state of peaceful coexistence with their fellow creatures:

> And man, once fleeting o'er the transient scene
> Swift as an unremembered vision, stands
> Immortal upon earth: no longer now
> He slays the lamb that looks him in the face,
> And horribly devours his mangled flesh,
> Which, still avenging Nature's broken law,
> Kindled all putrid humours in his frame,
> All evil passions, and all vain belief,
> Hatred, despair, and loathing in his mind,
> The germs of misery, death, disease, and crime.
> No longer now the wingèd habitants,
> That in the woods their sweet lives sing away,
> Flee from the form of man; but gather round,
> And prune their sunny feathers on the hands
> Which little children stretch in friendly sport
> Towards these dreadless partners of their play.
> All things are void of terror: Man has lost
> His terrible prerogative, and stands
> An equal amidst equals: happiness
> And science dawn though late upon the earth;
> Peace cheers the mind, health renovates the frame . . .[78]

Shelley further notes that even those species of animals that had formerly been carnivores do not kill for food in this Utopian setting.

The Utopians in the H. G. Wells story *A Modern Utopia* possess a natural aversion to killing any kind of living being for food:

> In all the round world of Utopia there is no meat. There used to be. But now we cannot stand the thought of slaughter-houses. And, in a population that is all educated, and at about the same level of physical refinement, it is practically impossible to find anyone who will hew a dead ox or pig. We never settled the hygienic aspect of meat-eating at all. This other aspect decided us. I can still remember as a boy the rejoicings over the closing of the last slaughter-house.[79]

It is highly questionable whether Wells, a meat eater, would have found such a Utopian society much to his liking. Indeed, it is hard to conceive of an ideal state without meat if one enjoys the taste of meat. Yet how is it possible to reconcile our desire for flesh foods with the repulsive thought we are eating the dead bodies of innocent animals that were slaughtered to satisfy this desire? H. G. Wells offers an interesting solution to this perplexing dilemma in his story "Days of Things to Come":

> It was a very different meal from a Victorian breakfast. The rude masses of bread needing to be carved and smeared over with animal fat before they could be palatable, the still recognisable fragments of recently killed animals, hideously charred and hacked, the eggs torn ruthlessly from beneath some protesting hen,—such things as these, though they constituted the ordinary fare of Victorian times, would have awakened only disgust in the refined minds of the people of these latter days. Instead were pastes and cakes of agreeable and variegated design, without any suggestion in colour or form of the unfortunate animals from which their substance and juices were derived.[80]

Thus, while the practice of killing animals for food has not been eliminated, the Utopians avoid any feelings of guilt as a result of the illusion they have created.

Like Wells, Thomas More recognized the need to shield Utopians from the grim reality of the slaughterhouse:

> The Utopians feel that slaughtering our fellow creatures gradually destroys the sense of compassion, which is the finest sentiment of which our human nature is capable.[81]

Yet this is a curious sort of compassion—More's Utopians are flesh eaters who seek to uphold their lofty ideals by relegating the task of slaughter to slaves:

> Next to the marketplace of which I just spoke are the food markets, where people bring all sorts of vegetables, fruit, and bread. Fish, meat, and poultry are also brought there from designated places outside the city, where running water can carry away all the blood and refuse. Slaves do the slaughtering and cleaning in these places: citizens are not allowed to do such work.[82]

Thus, while More's Utopians feel that slaughtering animals for food destroys their sense of compassion—that "finest sentiment"—they do not seem to fully comprehend their culpability in the killing of these "fellow creatures."

Those who enjoy the taste of flesh would, perhaps, find such a Utopia much to their liking. While some like Shelley conceive of Utopia as a world where justice prevails, others subscribe to the notion that ignorance is bliss. Throughout the course of history, those who espoused vegetarianism as an ethical principle were regarded as idealists by their contemporaries. However, many of these people did not live up to their own ideals.

11

Vegetarianism and Religion

I do feel that spiritual progress does demand at some stage that we should cease to kill our fellow creatures for the satisfaction of our bodily wants.

It ill becomes us to invoke in our daily prayers the blessings of God, the compassionate, if we in turn will not practice elementary compassion towards our fellow creatures.

MOHANDAS GANDHI

Man walk'd with beast, joint tenant of the shade;
The same his table, and the same his bed;
No murder cloth'd him, and no murder fed.
In the same temple, the resounding wood,
All vocal beings hymned their equal God:
The shrine with gore unstain'd, with gold undrest,
Unbrib'd, unbloody, stood the blameless priest:
Heav'n's attribute was Universal Care,
And Man's prerogative to rule, but spare.

ALEXANDER POPE

Vegetarianism has long been associated with many diverse theological concepts. An examination of these various concepts shows that vegetarianism did not necessarily exist as an important issue in itself, but was rather part of a broad attitude relating to religious precepts such as asceticism, pollution, metempsychosis, and respect for ani-

161

mals. Consequently, many spiritual leaders who espoused vegetarianism never actually made strict adherence to the fleshless diet mandatory as a religious tenet. Indeed, proposals to make abstinence from flesh food obligatory have been the cause of serious controversy within various religions throughout history.

ASCETICISM

EGYPTIAN PRIESTS

The practice of abstaining from flesh food has widely been associated with pious asceticism. One of the more curious notions associated with ascetic vegetarianism is that the use of flesh food stimulates sexual lust. Certain ancient Egyptian priests, believing that flesh foods and wine engendered strong carnal desires, abstained from these products in order to maintain their vows of celibacy. These priests also abstained from the use of eggs and milk, characterizing the former as "liquid flesh" while the latter was regarded as "blood with the color of flesh."[1]

CHRISTIAN

Tertullian railed against gluttons: "For to you your belly is god, and your lungs a temple, and your paunch a sacrificial altar."[2] The simple purity of the true Christian lifestyle, noted Tertullian, is reflected in the prayers that Jesus had taught: ". . . in our ordinary prayers likewise commanding us to request 'bread' not the wealth of Attalus therewithal."[3] Tertullian converted to Montanism sometime between 208 and 213 and became a leading figure of the Montanist Church. Montanus, the founder of this Christian heterodoxy, espoused vegetarianism as part of a doctrine of ascetic "purification" of the soul.

Clement of Alexandria, like Tertullian, strongly condemned flesh eaters as gluttons:

> But those who bend around inflammatory tables, nourishing their own diseases, are ruled by a most lickerish demon, whom I shall not blush to call Belly-demon, and the worst and most abandoned of all demons.

It is far better to be happy than to have a demon dwelling with us, and happiness is found in the practice of virtue. Accordingly, the apostle Matthew partook of seeds, and nuts, and vegetables, without flesh.[4]

The association between flesh eating and animal sacrifice which had been part of the Jewish and pagan religions is condemned as hypocrisy: "But I believe sacrifices were invented by men to be a pretext for eating flesh."[5] Notwithstanding his strong criticism of flesh eating, Clement equivocated on the question of total abstinence. While he argued that vegetarianism is conducive to a virtuous life of temperance, he stated that flesh eating per se is not really sinful if there is "moderation."

In discussing the issue of vegetarianism, Origen felt compelled to distinguish clearly between Christian concepts of abstinence (e.g., pious asceticism, temperance) and the advocacy of vegetarianism as set forth in various pagan doctrines. However, while Origen argued against the concept of metempsychosis, he boldly asserted that all animals have souls: "Now that there are souls in all living things, even in those which live in the waters, is, I suppose, doubted by no one."[6] Origen, nonetheless, maintained the orthodox position that the pre-eminence of the human species is part of the deity's design for life on earth.

Jerome emphasized the importance of Christian temperance in his treatise "Against Jovinianus": "The preparation of vegetables, fruit, and pulse is easy, and does not require the skill of expensive cooks: our bodies are nourished by them with little trouble on our part; and, if taken in moderation, such food is easier to digest, and at less cost, because it does not stimulate the appetite, and therefore is not devoured with avidity."[7] He further notes: ". . . we cannot devote ourselves to wisdom if our thoughts are running on a well-laden table, the supply of which requires an excess of work and anxiety."

Abstinence from flesh was viewed as a commitment to pious asceticism within various Christian monastic orders. St. Benedict, who established the Benedictine Order in 529, stressed simplicity in diet: "For nothing is more contrary to the Christian spirit than gluttony."[8] However, the monks of the Benedictine Order were not actually required to be strict vegetarians. The thirty-ninth chapter of St. Benedict's rule stipulates that, while vegetable foods are to be the staple fare of this order, the only flesh food which is not generally permitted is that of "quadrupeds."[9] Benedictine monks were therefore permitted to eat poultry and fish. Other monastic orders generally prohibited all animal foods.

An 18th-century manuscript which describes the dietary habits of the Culdees of Ireland and Scotland notes: "Never did they eat flesh or fish, nor did they permit cheese or butter, except on Sundays and feast days . . ."[10] Fintan, an Irish saint who flourished in the later half of the 6th century, did not allow any type of animal food at the monastery of Cluain Eidnech where he was abbot. The monks there lived exclusively on plant foods and water. If perchance some visitor unwittingly brought milk into the grounds of the monastery, Fintan demanded that the vessel should be broken immediately.[11]

The question of abstinence from flesh foods had been a volatile issue within many monastic orders over the course of their history. The evolution of the Cistercian Order is a case in point. A few centuries after Benedict's death, observance of his rules had been relaxed within the Benedictine community. This relaxation of ascetic guidelines was opposed by a certain segment of the Benedictine community, who subsequently formed their own separate order in 1098. This order, which came to be known as the Cistercians of the Strict Observance, was established in Citeaux, France, by St. Robert of Molesme. However, in time the Cistercians abandoned the very principles on which their order was founded—a rededication to pious asceticism. In 1598, Octave Arnolphini, abbot of the monastery in Charmoye, France, reintroduced the long-abandoned custom of total abstinence from meat. When Abbot Denis Largentier of Clairvaux, France, did likewise in 1615, the issue of abstinence from flesh became the basis of a movement within the Cistercian Order. By the year 1660, sixty-nine monasteries (62 of men and 7 of women) had come under this reform. Resentment of the "abstainers" intensified, and in 1664 Pope Alexander VII invited representatives of the two factions to Rome in a vain effort to mediate this dispute. As a result of the failure to reconcile their differences, the Cistercian Order was divided into two observances: the "Strict," which required abstinence from meat, and the "Common," which did not.

Armand Jean de Rance, the abbot of the La Trappe monastery, who represented the "abstainers" in Rome, was highly regarded for his efforts within the reform movement. The "Strict Observance" came to be associated with his monastic reforms at La Trappe, and consequently, the abbeys of the "Strict" became popularly known as "Trappists." From the middle of the 17th century until as late as the 1960s, Trappists uniformly observed regulations forbidding the use of eggs as well as all flesh foods. Certain aspects of Trappist tradition were modified as a result of decisions made at the Second Vatican Council in the early 1960s. Despite the fact that abstinence from flesh is no longer a mandatory requirement for Trappist monks, most of them continue to observe the traditional standards of their order. Trappists had always been expected to work in order to support themselves. It is somewhat ironic that cattle raising has traditionally been a favorite occupation of the Trappist community. This, indeed, serves to underscore the fact that Trappists abstain from flesh food for reasons of asceticism, not compassion for animals.

William Booth, the founder of the Salvation Army, advocated vegetarianism in his manual entitled *Orders and Regulations for Field Officers*. Although Booth never actually condemned flesh eating as gluttony, he noted that abstinence from luxury is most helpful in advancing the cause of Christian charity: "If twenty thousand people abstain from animal, or other unnecessary kinds of food, and save thereby only two shillings a week each, and give a shilling of it to the Army, it would thereby reap an increased income of £52,000 per annum, and the self-denying band of Soldiers who handed over this amount, would be healthier, happier, and holier thereby into the bargain." General Booth, who was a vegetarian himself, never made abstinence from flesh food a requirement for members of his "army."

JUDAISM

A considerable number of Jews abstained from flesh foods after the Temple at Jerusalem was destroyed in A.D. 70. Practices such as offering the first of the flocks to the deity as well as other religious obligations involving sacrifice could not be properly fulfilled, since ritual sacrifice was discontinued as a result of the Temple's destruction and the continuing religious persecution. To eat a food that was regarded as a luxury without making flesh offerings to the deity was deemed to be sacrilegious—at best it was an act of gluttonous greed. Moreover, since flesh food was regarded as a symbol of joy, many Jews felt it would be highly improper to use it at a time when great calamity had befallen the entire Jewish nation. During this period, many rabbis admonished those who abstained from flesh foods and wine to abandon their ascetic practices: "Since the day of the destruction of the Temple we should by rights bind ourselves not to eat meat nor drink wine, only we do not lay a hardship on the community unless the majority can endure it."[12] This statement by Rabbi Ishmael ben Elisha is representative of the view held by many other rabbis at this time who opposed ascetic vegetarianism.

ABSTINENCE FROM FLESH FOOD
AS AN ACT OF PENITENCE

JUDAISM

Since animal flesh was regarded as a desirable food, abstinence was often practiced as an act of penance. It is related in "The Testament of the Twelve Patriarchs" that Reuben abstained from flesh food and wine for seven years as penance for his sin, euphemistically referred to in the Bible as "going up to his father's bed." Similarly, there is a tradition that Judah, whose carnal knowledge of his daughter-in-law resulted in a deep sense of remorse, sought to atone for his sin by abstaining from flesh food, wine, and other "pleasures" for a great many years.[13]

VEGETARIANISM ASSOCIATED WITH
VARIOUS MYSTICAL CONCEPTS

GNOSTICISM

The common element of various Gnostic sects was the dualistic concept that one's existence on earth was characterized by a continuous conflict between the forces of good and evil. The material world, including the corporeal human form itself, was essentially evil whereas one's spiritual nature (the soul) was good. Curiously, different attitudes on ethics developed over the basic Gnostic concept that the human being is essentially a spirit that is good, held captive in an alien body which is part of the material world and therefore evil. By the end of the third century A.D. there was a proliferation of Gnostic sects, whose ethics ranged from asceticism to libertinism. Many of the ascetic Gnostic sects espoused vegetarianism.

We must exercise caution in ascribing specific motives to the practice of vegetarianism within these sects. There is a paucity of genuine Gnostic documents available to us. Unfortunately, much of the information on Gnosticism written during the era when this religious movement flourished is derived from hostile patristic sources. For instance, Irenaeus referred to the practice of vegetarianism advocated by Saturnilus as an "affectation of asceticism." This dissimulation, asserts Irenaeus, is designed to "make many their dupes."[14] Similarly, the author of the first epistle to Timothy (formerly thought to be Paul) impugns the sincerity of those who advocate vegetarianism and celibacy as part of their ascetic doctrines, characterizing them as "seducing spirits . . . speaking lies in hypocrisy."[15]

MANICHAEANISM

Manichaeanism was one of the more notable dualistic religious sects. Mani, the founder of this sect, taught that the soul is subject to the impure deeds of the body. Thus defiled, a person is condemned to a rebirth in a succession of bodies. Such things as procreation, possessions, and the use of wine or flesh foods were all considered contaminations. Mani, however, realized that relatively few people would be able to adhere to such rigorous asceticism. Consequently, he established two categories of membership in the Manichaean Church, the "elect" and the "hearers." Abstinence from flesh foods and other contaminations was mandatory for the elect. However, the hearers were not specifically enjoined from those things that were considered defilements. Nonetheless, the hearers were encouraged to emulate the elect, who were regarded as models of purity. By minimizing the extent of their contamination, they could then at least hope to lessen their number of reincarnations before attaining salvation. The elect would find paradise immediately after death. There was always the possibility, however, that hearers could be promoted to the order of the elect by strict compliance with Manichaean doctrine.

ALBIGENSIANISM

The Cathari, a medieval dualistic sect, is generally regarded as a neo-Manichaean religious movement. Albi, a county in southern

France, became the center of Cathari influence. Consequently, the sect eventually came to be known as the Albigensians. Like Manichaeanism, Albigensianism was comprised of two categories—the ordinary believers or "hearers" and members of the pious category, the "venerate," who strictly adhered to the ascetic lifestyle set forth in Albigensian doctrine. Members of the venerate abstained from all animal foods except fish, while the hearers were strongly encouraged to adopt this abstemious diet. A passage from a Catharist work written in the middle of the 13th century instructs members on dietary taboos: "Moreover, you will make this commitment to God: that you will never, knowingly or of your own will, eat cheese, milk, the flesh of birds, or creeping things, or of animals, prohibited by the Church of God."[16] Fish were believed to be mysteriously born of the water itself. Accordingly, the prohibition on the use of flesh foods did not apply to fish.

It appears that significant numbers of the Albigensians were resolute in their adherence to the injunction on killing animals for food. This is evidenced by the fact that a person's refusal to kill animals or eat their flesh was commonly used by ecclesiastical authorities of the Roman Church as a means to detect heresy. Many heretics chose death and even torture to apostasy. A group of heretics were hanged at Goslar in 1052 for their refusal to kill a chicken. Some, however, were persuaded to "convert" to Christianity under duress. In 1229, two Tuscan heretics who were brought before Gregory IX in a heresy case refused to eat flesh. Within two days, however, they were persuaded by ecclesiastical authorities of their error and proved the sincerity of their conversion by eating flesh in the presence of several prelates and a notary, who officially recorded this act.[17]

JUDAISM

Samson Raphael Hirsch, a prominent 19th-century German rabbi, subscribed to the metaphysical notion that one's character is affected by the type of food one consumes:

Anything which gives the body too much independence or makes it too active in a carnal direction brings it nearer to the animal sphere, thereby robbing it of its primary function, to be the intermediary between the soul of man and the world outside. Bearing in mind this function of the body and also the fact that the physical structure of man is largely influenced by the kind of food he consumes, one might come to the conclusion that the vegetable food is the most preferable, as plants are the most passive substance; and indeed we find that in Jewish law all vegetables are permitted for food without discrimination.[18]

Hirsch, who associated flesh eating with violence and carnality, viewed the use of flesh food as an impediment to one's spiritual development.

HINDUISM

The Hindu doctrines of karma and metempsychosis are allied with the concept of unity in all life. Metempsychosis is the belief that, after death, the soul passes into another body, either human or animal. Karma, an extension of the metempsychosis concept, is the belief that people will be rewarded or punished in future incarnations based on the good and bad deeds of their present life. Virtuous individuals will be born into a higher caste in their next incarnation, whereas those who are evil will be reincarnated in the form of some undesirable person or animal. Accordingly, it is noted in the *Manu-smriti* that persons who actually delight in harming others will become some type of carnivorous animal in their next incarnation. Similarly, it is recorded in the *Institutes of Vishnu* that people who steal meat will be reincarnated as vultures. The attitudes on flesh eating that are held by those who believe in the concepts of karma and metempsychosis are curiously dissimilar. Some consider the slaughter of animals for food as just punishment, since the soul's incarnation in this wretched form was the result of evil deeds committed in a previous incarnation. Some, however, feel that perpetuating this cycle of evil is an impediment to their own salvation and, therefore, they eschew all flesh foods.

RESPECT FOR ALL ANIMALS

HINDUISM

The doctrine of *ahimsā* (non-injury to sentient beings) is found in Hinduism, Buddhism, and Jainism. The references to *ahimsā* in

Hindu literature are ambiguous in terms of its application to Hindu *dhrama* (duty based on social and religious obligations). The doctine of *ahimsā* has been represented as a means of purifying one's soul,[19] as a religious duty,[20] and as an ideal that one should strive to attain.[21]

The view that vegetarianism should be regarded as part of the *ahimsā* doctrine is reflected in various passages of the *Manusmriti:*

> Meat can never be obtained without injury to living creatures, and injury to sentient beings is detrimental to [the attainment of] heavenly bliss; let him therefore shun [the use of] meat.

> Having well considered the [disgusting] origin of flesh and the [cruelty of] fettering and slaying corporeal beings, let him entirely abstain from eating flesh.

> He who permits [the slaughter of an animal], he who cuts it up, he who kills it, he who buys or sells [meat], he who cooks it, he who serves it up, and he who eats it, [must all be considered as] slayers [of the animal].[22]

Notwithstanding such passages, which link vegetarianism with *ahimsā,* other passages in the *Manusmriti* refer to the practice of eating flesh as "the natural way of created beings."[23]

Vasishtha, while acknowledging the principle of *ahimsā,* declares that meat which is obtained as a by-product of sacrifice is not actually considered to be the product of slaughter:

> Meat can never be obtained without injuring living beings, and to injure living beings does not procure heavenly bliss; therefore the [sages declare] the slaughter [of beasts] at a sacrifice not to be slaughter [in the ordinary sense of the word].[24]

Similarly, there are various passages in the *Manusmriti* which sanction flesh eating when it is done in conjunction with religious ceremonies involving animal sacrifice but otherwise discourage the use of flesh foods:

> There is no greater sinner than that [man] who, though not worshipping the gods or the manes, seeks to increase [the bulk of] his own flesh by the flesh of other [beings].[25]

The consumption of meat [is befitting] for sacrifices, that is declared to be a rule made by the gods; but to persist [in using it] on other [occasions] is said to be a proceeding worthy of Râkshasas.*26

There is another passage which refers to the practice of shaping clarified butter or flour into the image of an animal. This device enabled vegetarians to participate in sacrificial rituals while, at the same time, strictly adhering to the doctrine of *ahimsā:*

> If he has a strong desire [for meat] he may make an animal of clarified butter or one of flour, [and eat that]; but let him never seek to destroy an animal without a [lawful] reason.27

There are deities such as the mother goddess in the form of Devi who thrive on blood. Vegetarian devotees simply use red flowers to represent blood in their ceremonial worship of Devi.28 Other deities are vegetarians and, as such, never receive blood sacrifices. They are worshiped instead with "pure" offerings consisting of flowers, and/or vegetarian foods.

The Buddhist and Jain religions, which are essentially Hindu heterodoxies, emerged as viable religious movements in the 6th century B.C. Unlike Hinduism, both Buddhism and Jainism place a particularly strong emphasis on observance of the *ahimsā* principle. In fact, it is widely believed that vegetarianism was adopted as a religious precept by certain Hindu sects largely as a result of Buddhist and Jain influences. These influences developed imperceptibly over an extended period of time. The Buddhists and Jains were sternly opposed to the Hindu practice of animal sacrifice. In fact, the Jains even disapproved of making animal models from flour to be offered as a sacrifice since this was construed to involve the intention of taking life.

BUDDHISM

Although Buddha espoused vegetarianism, citing the relationship between this diet and observance of the *ahimsā* principle, strict abstinence from flesh foods was not actually a tenet of the Buddhist religion. A section of the *Sutta-Nipâta* asserts that the practice of

* Demons.

meat eating per se is not sinful: "Destroying living beings, killing, cutting, binding, stealing, speaking falsehood, fraud and deception, worthless reading, intercourse with another's wife;—this is Amagandha, but not the eating of flesh."[29] How then can one avoid the sinful act of destroying sentient beings if one eats flesh, a practice that is not, in itself, considered sinful? The Buddha formulated a most curious rationale on this paradox. Pious members of the Buddhist religion were expected to abstain from all flesh of animals slaughtered expressly for their benefit. They could, however, eat flesh food that was *pavattamamsa* (already existing). Accordingly, they disavowed their culpability in the animal's death. Equally significant is the fact that this rule precluded devout Buddhists from becoming slaves to their desire for flesh since this food could not be obtained at will. Indeed, according to Buddhist doctrine the cause of suffering is "ignorant craving" *(trsnā)*. Various passages found in Buddhist texts suggest that Buddha himself occasionally ate *pavattamamsa* flesh food.

The question of complete abstinence from flesh food has long been a matter of controversy within the Buddhist religion. The first schism to occur within the Buddhist religion resulted from the Buddha's rejection of a petition that called for the imposition of stricter rules on the clergy. Among the five propositions that Buddha rejected was one to require all members of the clergy to abstain completely from eating flesh foods, including fish. Devadatta, Buddha's cousin, was the leader of this schism. The Buddhist scriptures characterize Devadatta's strict posture on this issue as dissimulation: the sentiment to adopt stricter guidelines on diet as well as other matters was supported by a substantial number of Buddhist monks, and this situation was seized upon by Devadatta, whose agitation on behalf of this position was actually a devious ploy to wrest control of the order from Buddha. Despite his initial success, most of the schismatics left Devadatta's movement to rejoin the orthodox clergy within a short period after their break with the Buddha.

The schisms that occurred in the Buddhist religion after its founder's death were inevitable. While some factions of the Buddhist community believed that standards should be more relaxed, other factions adopted standards that were even more stringent than those prescribed by the Buddha. Vegetarianism was among the various reforms adopted by those sects which regarded flesh eating as a serious violation of *ahimsā*. This view was given additional impetus by prominent

Buddhist political leaders like Aśoka and Harsha, who actively promoted vegetarianism out of their pious devotion to the doctrine of *ahimsā.*

JAINISM

The Jain religion outlines different categories of harmful acts which are antagonistic to the *ahimsā* doctrine, including: (1) accidental injury, (2) occupational injury, (3) protective injury, and (4) premeditated injury or killing. Although the first three categories of violence are considered antagonistic to *ahimsā,* these acts are, to some extent, tolerated in the lay community. The impracticality of avoiding these particular types of violence is regarded as a mitigating factor. A sincere commitment to the avoidance of any form of violence is nonetheless evidenced by the extent to which the *ahimsā* doctrine is observed by the lay community at large. Any act of premeditated injury or killing is regarded as a serious infraction of this doctrine and is therefore not allowed for any reason. Since Jains respect the right of all innocent beings to live in peace, they do not distinguish between the willful murder of innocent humans and the willful killing of harmless creatures. Consequently, such activities as hunting and flesh eating are strictly taboo. While only a certain portion of Hindus and Buddhists are vegetarians, all members of the Jain religion are expected to abstain from eating flesh.

The Jains have established hospitals as well as sanctuaries for animals in various parts of India. They have also established universities and other educational institutions. Although these schools are secular in nature, the Jains maintain their prerogative as patrons, to prohibit any activities that would violate the Jainist concept of *ahimsā.* Consequently, biology studies which involve animal experimentation are not included in the curriculum, and flesh eating is not allowed on campus.

MOSLEM HETERODOXIES

Many of the Moslem heterodoxies espoused vegetarianism on the grounds that it was wrong to destroy harmless animals. One 8th-century Moslem historian relates that two Zindigis (Moslem heretics) who had seen an ostrich swallow some jewels suffered themselves to be severely beaten by men who accused them of stealing the precious gems rather than allowing the ostrich to be killed.[30]

The biographers of the poet Abu L-Ala have speculated that he had been greatly influenced by the Indian concept of *ahimsā* in the course of his many travels. Views associated with the principles of *ahimsā* are particularly evident in various passages from Abu L-Ala's collection of poems entitled *Luzumiyyat (Double Rhymes)*.

CHRISTIAN

Notwithstanding the fact that respect for animals was not a feature of Christian doctrine, there were several leading figures of the Christian Church who espoused the belief that kindness to animals should be regarded as a Christian duty. Some advocated abstinence from flesh food out of respect for innocent animals that are slaughtered for food. St. John Chrysostom implored people to avoid degrading themselves by eating flesh—a practice which he considered both unnatural and cruel: ". . . we imitate but the ways of wolves, but the ways of leopards, or rather we are even worse than these. For to them nature has assigned that they should be thus fed, but us God hath honored with speech and a sense of equity, and we are become worse than the wild beasts."[31] While St. Hilarion seems to have adopted the vegetarian diet primarily out of ascetic zeal, he showed much compassion for animals, which he believed unjustly suffered for the sins of humans.[32] Although St. Francis is celebrated as the patron saint of animals, it appears that he was not a consistent vegetarian. The Irish saint Molua MacOcha, who founded the monastery of Cluain Ferta Molua, was known for his kindness to animals as well as people. In fact, his tenderness to animals is legendary. It is reported that when Molua died a certain little bird was found lamenting his passing: "Molua MacOcha has died, and therefore all living creatures bewail him, for never has he killed any animal, little or big; so not more do human beings bewail him than the other animals, and the little bird which thou seest."[33]

VEGETARIANISM AS A UTOPIAN CONCEPT

JUDAISM

Several of the major Hebrew prophets, in their apocalyptic visions of the Messianic Era, refer to a world where all species will dwell together in peace. Hosea, the 8th-century B.C. prophet, envisions this period as a time when wars will cease and the human population will become reconciled with all other species. These events will be set in action by the deity: "And in that day will I make a covenant for them with the beasts of the field, and with the fowls of heaven, and with the creeping things of the ground: and I will break the bow and the sword and the battle out of the earth, and will make them to lie down safely."[34] Like his older contemporary, Hosea, the prophet referred to as the first Isaiah, declares that peace will prevail in the Messianic Era. He prophesies that even the animals that normally eat flesh will no longer kill for food but shall dwell in peaceful coexistence with species which had formerly been their prey:

> The wolf also shall dwell with the lamb, and the leopard shall lie down with the kid; and the calf and the young lion and the fatling together; and a little child shall lead them.
>
> And the cow and the bear shall feed; their young ones shall lie down together: and the lion shall eat straw like the ox.
>
> And the sucking child shall play on the hole of the asp, and the weaned child shall put his hand on the cockatrice' den.
>
> They shall not hurt nor destroy in all my holy mountain: for the earth shall be full of the knowledge of the LORD, as the waters cover the sea.[35]

This extraordinary prophecy is quoted in Book III of the *Sibylline Oracles*. It is also quoted by the 6th-century B.C. prophet who is referred to as Trito-Isaiah.

In the passage where Trito-Isaiah foretells an era when lions will feed on straw he states that "dust shall be the serpent's meat,"[36] an obvious allusion to the Hebrew creation myth. According to that myth, God had originally intended all species to sustain themselves exclusively on plant foods:

> And God said, Behold, I have given you every herb bearing seed, which is upon the face of all the earth, and every tree, in that which is the fruit of a tree yielding seed; to you it shall be for meat.
>
> And to every beast of the earth, and to every fowl of the air, and to every thing that creepeth upon the earth, wherein there is life, I have given every green herb for meat: and it was so.[37]

There are distinct similarities between the Hebrew creation narratives and the Sumerian and Babylonian creation myths. The Sumerian story of Enki and Damkina, who are placed in the paradise of Dilmun by two deities, bears a strong resemblance to the Hebrew story of Adam and Eve, who were placed in Paradise by the creator deity. In Dilmun, as in the garden of Eden, animals that would be classified as carnivores do not kill for their food.[38]

FLESH EATING AS POLLUTION

CHRISTIAN HETERODOXIES AND HINDUISM

The association of flesh eating with pollution (both spiritual and physical) is found in many of the dualistic Christian heterodoxies as well as Hinduism. Ebionites believed that the demons' insatiable lust for meat prompted them to enter the bodies of people who ate flesh foods. Similarly, demons are represented in Hindu scriptures as favoring flesh foods. While some Hindus totally eschewed meat because of its association with pollution, others abstained from flesh food only on specified occasions as part of purificatory rites.

CHRISTIAN

Hippolytus, in his exegetical commentary on the story of Daniel, characterizes this Biblical hero and his three companions as pious ascetics. Alluding to the Biblical passage that tells how these four young men did not wish to "defile" themselves with the king's meat, Hippolytus symbolically equates the purity of their vegetarian diet with the purity of their thoughts: "These, though captives in a strange land, were not seduced by delicate meats, nor were they slaves to the pleasures of wine, nor were they caught by the bait of princely glory. But they kept their mouth holy and pure, that pure speech might proceed from pure mouths, and praise with such [mouths] the heavenly Father."[39]

Hygiene is an important part of the Seventh-Day Adventist Church's doctrine. Members of this Christian fundamentalist sect believe that abstinence from products that are known to be injurious to one's health (e.g., coffee, tobacco, meat) is a religious duty, since the "spirit of God" dwells in each individual. However, while vegetarianism is strongly advocated by the Seventh-Day Adventist Church, abstinence from flesh food was never made a requirement for membership in this sect. Some of the church's members felt that any toleration of flesh eating compromised Seventh-Day Adventist doctrine. This controversy over the question of abstinence from flesh foods was a major factor contributing to the schism within the church which originated in 1914. This schism culminated in the establishment of the Seventh-Day Adventist Reform Movement. This group, which was formally organized in 1925, officially adopted the position that all its members must be vegetarians.

CIRCUMSTANTIAL VEGETARIANISM

JUDAISM

Strict adherence to Jewish dietary laws (kashrut) has always been an important part of the Jewish faith. There are several restrictions on the use of flesh foods which Jews are expected to follow. Observance of Jewish rituals involving the slaughter of animals and the preparation of their meat became difficult during periods when Jews were subjected to harassment, especially during times when they were expressly forbidden to practice their religion. Under such circumstances many pious Jews found that vegetarianism was a practical means of avoiding the difficulties encountered in adhering to kashrut. Some had no choice except to abstain from flesh foods in circumstances where the only meat that was available possessed one or more characteristics which did not conform to the criteria set down in Jewish dietary law. Josephus refers to certain Jewish priests on trial in Rome who restricted themselves to figs and nuts in order to avoid eating flesh which had been offered to heathen idols.[40] Adherence to kashrut was particularly difficult during the first part of the Maccabean Era. The Syrian ruler Antiochus Epiphanes IV sought to impose Hellenistic culture on the Jews of Judaea. His edict, which forbade Jews to practice their religion, created a serious threat to the observance of kashrut. Moreover, as part of his campaign to promote Hellenization in Judaea, this Syrian king instructed his soldiers to compel Jews to eat swine's flesh or to eat the flesh of animals sacrificed in pagan rituals. There are several references to such repressive measures in the first and second books of Maccabees. It is noted in one section of II Maccabees that Judas Maccabaeus escaped to the mountains with nine others, where they subsisted exclusively on plant foods "in order that they might not be polluted like the rest."[41]

CHRISTIAN

The question of observing *kashrut* was a matter of great controversy within the nascent Christian Church. Many Jews who accepted Jesus as the promised Messiah were most unwilling to abandon their Jewish customs, including *kashrut.* Contrasted with the beliefs of these Judaized Christians was the view that strict adherence to Jewish dietary law was superfluous since the "new covenant" of Jesus superseded the covenants referred to in the Hebrew Bible. Therefore, the early Christians were divided on the question of whether or not it was permissible to eat the flesh of animals that had been sacrificed to pagan idols.

Significantly, much of the meat sold at the public markets in cities such as Rome and Corinth came from animals that had been sacrificed in pagan rituals. Consequently, a considerable segment of the early Christian community in these cities ate very little meat or abstained from flesh foods altogether. Paul deals with this issue at length in his letters to the Christian community in Rome and Corinth. Paul maintains that, in theory, Christians are free to eat any type of flesh food, since neither Mosaic dietary law nor pagan belief in the supernatural powers of idols was recognized as valid within the framework of the Christian Church. Accordingly, Paul refers to Christians who do not subscribe to his own liberal views on this matter as "the weak," i.e., their faith is weak. Notwithstanding his characterization of these people as unenlightened Christians, Paul pleads with members of both factions in this dispute to tolerate each others' views. Paul's epistle addressed to the Church in Rome states: "For one believeth that he may eat all things: another, who is weak, eateth herbs. Let not him that eateth despise him that eateth not; and let not him which eateth not judge him that eateth: for God hath received him."[42] This same spirit of reconciliation is found in Paul's epistle to the Corinthians: "But meat commendeth us not to God: for neither, if we eat, are we the better; neither, if we eat not, are we the worse."[43] It is particularly curious to note that while Paul himself is antagonistic to the position of those Christians he refers to as "weak" he, nonetheless, implores enlightened members of the church to refrain from eating flesh of pagan origin in the presence of their "weak" coreligionists. Paul forthrightly states that this request is based purely on pragmatic considerations. While Paul repudiates the position of the "weak," it is this very weakness that prompts him to call on the liberal-minded members of the church to exercise such restraint. Thus, in his epistle to the Christian community in Rome, Paul writes:

> Let us not therefore judge one another any more: but judge this rather, that no man put a stumblingblock or an occasion to fall in his brother's way. I know, and am persuaded by the Lord Jesus, that there is nothing unclean of itself:* but to him that esteemeth any thing to be unclean, to him it is unclean. But if thy brother be grieved with thy meat, now walkest thou not charitably. Destroy not him with thy meat, for whom Christ died. . . .
>
> For meat destroy not the work of God. All things indeed are pure; but it is evil for that man who eateth with offence. It is good neither to eat flesh, nor to drink wine,† nor any thing whereby thy brother stumbleth, or is offended, or is made weak.[44]

Likewise, Paul writes in his epistle to Christians in Corinth: "But when ye sin so against the brethren, and wound their weak conscience, ye sin against Christ. Wherefore, if meat make my brother to offend, I will eat no flesh while the world standeth, lest I make my brother to offend."[45] Paul's remark that he would become a strict vegetarian for the sake of his "weak" brethren should be regarded as hyperbole.

---

* See Mark 7:15–23.

† Wine as well as meat was often the product of pagan ritual and was, therefore, avoided by "weak" Christians.

12

A History of Meat as a Status Symbol

They make their pride in making their dinner cost much; I make my pride in making my dinner cost little.

HENRY DAVID THOREAU

Custom will reconcile people to any atrocity; and fashion will drive them to acquire any custom.

GEORGE BERNARD SHAW

THE PREHISTORIC ERA

Flesh food was, indeed, a necessity for pre-historic hominids living on the open savannas and nomadic tribes who were constantly moving. The development of settled, agricultural communities (in about 9,000 B.C.), eliminated the need to use animals as a source of food. Instead of being eliminated, however, the use of animals as food became an integral part of a more sophisticated agricultural system, presently referred to by the amusing term "animal husbandry." The systematic raising of livestock gradually replaced hunting as the human population increased and the number of wild animals that were used for food diminished. The people in the early agricultural communities continued to enjoy meat even though animal flesh became more of a luxury than a necessity.

The number of agricultural communities increased, creating more leisure time and food surpluses. A strong communal spirit developed within these primitive agricultural societies, including a division of labor. Food preparation became an art, and cuisine could be counted among the various qualities that distinguished the people of the many different cultures emerging at this time.

THE MIDDLE EAST, ANCIENT GREECE, AND ROME

As class divisions became more pronounced, factors such as the quality of one's diet and the quantity of livestock owned distinguished the rich from the poor. King Solomon extended the luxuries of lavish meat dinners to the members of his court. The provisions for one day were said to consist of 30 beeves, 100 sheep, assorted poultry and wild game.[1] However, Solomon, who was known for his wisdom and sense of justice, reflected on the fate of his livestock and seems to have acknowledged that meat was not necessary: "Better is a dinner of herbs where love is, than a stalled ox and hatred therewith."[2] The wealth and status of the Biblical patriarchs was determined by the number of cattle, sheep, and goats they possessed. We find that in ancient Hebrew manuscripts words translated as "cattle" are used interchangeably with the words "substance" and "possessions" in other passages.[3] In many of the early primitive societies only the patriarchal leaders were lawfully entitled to slaughter cattle or to use them for barter. Adam Smith notes that cattle were used as "the common instrument of commerce" in early historical times, and "things were frequently valued according to the number of cattle which had been given in exchange for them."[4] Homer refers to this practice in *The Iliad,* noting that the armor of Diomede cost only 9 oxen while that of Glaucus was valued at 100 oxen. Similarly, in ancient Rome, wealth was often reflected in the number of cattle a person owned. The head count of cattle was expressed by the Latin word *"capita,"* the origin of our contemporary term "capital." Cato, in his treatise on farming, refers to the fact that cattle are a measurement of wealth: "Doubtless the art of breeding and of feeding cattle consists in getting the maximum profit out of those things from which the very name of money is derived, for our word for money (pecunia) comes from pecus (cattle), which is the foundation of all wealth."[5] In fact, the etymology of the word "fee" can be traced back to the Latin word for cattle, "pecus," and to the Indo-European base, "pek," which represents the possession of sheep, and/or cattle.

The wealthy citizens of Rome were by no means content with the standard domesticated breeds of animals to supply their meat. The flesh of all manner of exotic creatures was highly favored by aristocratic gourmets. Philo, in his essay "The Contemplative Life," speaks disdainfully of lavish banquets that characterized the lifestyle of so many of his rich contemporaries: "Some perhaps may approve the method banqueting now prevalent everywhere through hankering for the Italian expensiveness and luxury emulated both by Greek and non-Greeks who make their arrangements for ostentation rather than festivity." Continuing, he describes the scene at a typical banquet: "Seven tables at the least and even more are brought in covered with the flesh of every creature that land, sea and rivers or air produce, beast, fish or bird, all choice and in fine condition, each table differing in the dishes served and the method of seasoning."[6] These banquets featured such items as specially fattened dormice, snails fattened on a special diet of milk and cornmeal, pâté de foie gras, flamingo tongues, and thrushes' tongues in wild honey.[7] Guinea hens were brought all the way from North Africa, peacocks from Media, and pheasants from the Caspian Sea area. The flesh of peacocks and pheasants may have proved interesting but the favored part of these birds was actually their brains. Sows' stomachs were stuffed with live thrushes while the udder of this animal might be filled with fried baby mice.[8] It was not sufficient simply to satiate one's appetite at these opulent gatherings. It was desirable to partake of the full magnificent variety of food the host was offering. This was accomplished by forced regurgitation, which appears to have been a common practice. "People eat to vomit and vomit to eat," quipped Seneca, who cited the irony of eating expensive food that was not even digested.

Throughout the course of history, the poor and working classes were rarely afforded the opportunity to compete with the rich for the ultimate luxury of eating fresh meat at every meal. The inability to afford meat became a stigma for the proletariat from earliest times and was one of many characteristics that distinguished them from the rich. There is ample evidence in the historical literature of various cultures to support the view that people who relied on pulse and grains as their primary, if not exclusive, source of nourishment, were sometimes looked upon with disdain. The lowest classes in ancient Egypt lived almost exclusively on bread.[9] Barley, to Homer's Greeks, was not a food for sustenance, but, when roasted, was used as a condiment to be sprinkled on their beef. They were particularly contemptuous of the Scythians, who ate oats, which the Greeks considered suitable for horses but not human beings. The ancient Greeks may have enjoyed their pea soup, which was freshly prepared and served hot by street vendors, but the stigma was still there. Referring to a nouveau riche, a character in a play by Aristophanes remarks: "Now he doesn't like lentils any more." The line, however, was hardly original. It seems to have been a proverb that was used in ancient Greece to describe wealthy people who had formerly been poor.[10]

Onions and pulse were commonly eaten by the poor in Mesopotamia. These foods were accordingly regarded as peasants' fare. Dishes made with chickpeas, beans, lentils, and cereals are all very much a part of an ancient tradition in Middle Eastern cuisine. Despite their great popularity, however, these items have always been considered food of the poor and are represented as such in the literature of this region.[11]

There are numerous references in Roman literature to the fact that while varieties of pulse were extensively cultivated they were considered more as a food for the proletariat. Pompey, whose principal political support came from the patricians, had very definite opinions on food. At one time during his military campaign against Julius Caesar (who drew his support from the plebeians), Pompey discovered a cache of food that was being used by Caesar's army. Finding bread that was made with herbs, he commented to an aide that they were now fighting "beasts" and ordered the food to be hidden lest their men should know that Caesar's army remained resolute in their struggle despite the adversity of having to subsist on such fare.[12]

CHINA

Peasants in China have traditionally subsisted largely, if not exclusively, on simple vegetarian fare. Historically, such items as bean curd soup or a bowl of rice have been represented in Chinese literature as symbols of poverty. However, such fare has also been used in the Chinese literary tradition as representing the embodiment of an unpretentious and virtuous lifestyle. The lavish dinners enjoyed by members of the royal court were a sharp contrast to the simple meals of the peasants. The extravagant taste of Empress Yong Kweifei culminated in the demise of the Tang dynasty in the 8th century. The empress, who was particularly fond of elaborately prepared meats, has been duly memorialized by her fellow gluttons, when they order "Kweifei chicken." A manuscript considered to have been written during the Sung dynasty (960–1279) contains several references to the meals prepared for Chinese royalty. Included are such items as quail sautéed with bamboo shoots, fried snake relish, sautéed frogs' legs, toasted minced kidney, crab legs with venison, pigs' knuckles with wine and vinegar, and brains doused in vinegar sauce.[13] As many as forty different meat dishes were served at grand banquets in 13th-century China and might include the following concoctions: deer tail with clams and duck, chicken testicles, deer heart garnished with plums, sparrow's tongues, and whole roasted raccoon.[14]

EUROPE FROM MEDIEVAL TIMES THROUGH THE 18TH CENTURY

The notion that meatless meals were undesirable was well reinforced in medieval Europe when the Church recommended the use of legumes as a suitable substitute for meat during the Lenten season. The implication was that substituting legumes for meat was an act of penitence. This same notion is represented in the Church's edict designating one day of the week (Friday) to forgo the use of flesh foods. Voltaire sarcastically referred to the farcical nature of Lent:

> Idiotic and cruel priests! On whom do you impose Lent? Is it on the rich? They take good care not to observe it. Is it on the poor? They keep Lent the whole year. The wretched farmer hardly eats meat and has no money to buy fish.[15]

The benevolent ruler Henri IV of France noted the equation of poverty with lack of meat when he stated his concern that even the poorest of his subjects should be able to put a chicken in their pot every Sunday.

The prevailing attitude in the 18th century was that grains and legumes were food for livestock and horses but not for people. The illustrious glutton Samuel Johnson used what he felt was the ultimate insult to express his contempt for the Scottish people. In his famous dictionary, published in 1775, Johnson's definition for the word "oats" reads: "A grain, which in England is generally given to horses, but in Scotland supports the people." Discussing the relative value of flesh foods and vegetarian fare, the Scottish economist Adam Smith deals forthrightly with the issue of necessity versus luxury. In *The Wealth of Nations,* published in 1776, he referred to the fact that bread was taxed in Great Britain, Holland, Italy, and France. While Smith was very much opposed to the practice of taxing such "necessaries of life," he did concede that flesh food, which was also taxed, is not a necessity but is rather an extravagance:

> Taxes upon butchers meat are still more common than those upon bread. It may indeed be doubted whether butchers meat is any where a necessary of life. Grain and other vegetables, with the help of milk, cheese, and butter, or oil, where butter is not to be had, it is known from experience, can, without any butchers meat, afford the most plentiful, the most wholesome, the most nourishing, and the most invigorating diet. Decency no where requires that any man should eat butchers meat, as it in most places requires that he should wear a linen shirt or a pair of leather shoes.[16]

THE UNITED STATES FROM THE 18TH THROUGH THE 20TH CENTURY

Emigrants from Europe came to "the land of plenty" hoping to find a better way of life. There was a vast western frontier to be settled, a wilderness with an abundance of game. When animals were plentiful, even the poor found extravagant uses for them. Many buffalo were killed for their hides alone. Even the hunters who killed them for meat took only select portions. The celebrated Buffalo Bill, who provided the railroad crews with buffalo meat, is noted to have taken only the hindquarters and hump. Many buffalo were killed for the hump section alone, while thousands more were slain solely for their tongues. These practices are referred to by Sergeant John Ordway of the Lewis and Clark expedition. The entry in his journal for July 3, 1805, reports that two hunters from his party killed six buffalo. They took only the tongues to be used as food, while the brains were used to dress animal skins.[17]

At the end of the 18th century, bread was the principal staple of the American poor who lived in the cities. The large numbers of unskilled workers could afford to purchase fresh meat only once a week. This situation had not changed to any significant extent in the 19th century. The desire of the working class for meat is noted in a Democratic satire on Whig politics in 1842:

> And then your wages we'll raise high,
> Two dollars and roast beef.

Many of the homesteaders who settled in the Midwest were crop farmers who did not actually raise livestock. Their lifestyle was characterized by inventive frugality. One Nebraska newspaper featured a list of thirty-three different ways to prepare meals using corn.

Americans, like the early Greeks and Romans, realized that meat was not necessary to life. This was evident in the fact that, for the most part, they lived without it. Meat on the menu, however, was part of a way of life they sought to attain. Eating meat, especially quality meats, was one way in which the poor could emulate their wealthy counterparts. A New York City butcher in the early 19th century noted that poor people with large families would often purchase choice porterhouse steak despite the extravagant cost.[18] When a butcher in Boston asked a poor seamstress why she did not take less expensive meat (other than tenderloin), she indignantly replied: "Do you suppose because I don't come here in my carriage I don't want just as good meat as rich folks have?"[19]

Herbert Hoover was elected President of the United States in 1928 on his pledge of continued prosperity. Echoing the words of King Henri IV, he promised the American public "a chicken in every pot." However, few people ate much chicken or any other kind of meat during Hoover's term in office. Those were the years of the great depression. The most popular food during that era seemed to be apples that were sold by unemployed laborers who pushed their small carts through the city streets.

THE PRESENT SITUATION

The attitude that meat is more desirable than vegetable fare persists in most parts of the world. In a report on Italian consumption patterns, it was noted that after the economy of that country had improved following World War II, there was a significant reduction in the use of legumes. This study, published in 1959, noted that legumes have traditionally been referred to as "meat for the poor" and that Italians had wished to avoid this "psychological" stigma.[20] Another study, published in 1958, on trends in French eating habits, reported a similar pattern—there was a decline in the consumption of legumes as a result of an improved economy and the stigma attached to eating food that is considered a meat substitute.[21] One writer recalls attending a Rotary Club luncheon in England where corn on the cob was included for the benefit of American guests. Inquiring on the reason why most of the English hosts avoided this item, several of them replied that corn was primarily animal food.[22] Americans have similar feelings about the soybean. Soybeans, despite their value as an inexpensive source of protein, are used primarily as livestock feed. A recent article on soybeans notes that less than 4 percent of the annual American harvest is used for human consumption and that most of this is in the form of extenders (used with meat) and additives. The author of this article observes that "few Americans have ever seen a soybean." He adds, "only food faddists eat them plain."[23]

Soybeans are used as a principal ingredient in the production of meat analogues. These "vegetable meats" are specifically designed to imitate their real counterparts in every respect, including appearance, taste, and texture. The leading manufacturers of these products have made vegetable imitations of virtually every conceivable type of meat: bacon, ham, steak, chicken, turkey, roast beef, sausage, "hot dogs," and other such items. These products are available to the general public in most areas of the United States, Canada, England, and West Germany. The advantages of meat analogues are that they cost less than real meat, there is no fat or waste, they are lower in calories, contain no antibiotics or chemical preservatives, and, because they are vegetable products, contain no cholesterol or saturated fats.

Meat analogues have become increasingly popular since they were first produced in 1957, but they are still not totally accepted by the vast majority of people in Europe and America, where they are sold. What is the cause of the public's reluctance to use such products? Perhaps the answer lies in a story that was related to me by a friend. This woman had become a vegetarian because of her concern for animals. Her husband, despite his involvement in animal-welfare work, had no intention of becoming a vegetarian like his wife. He had always expected a good meat dinner when he came home from work. During one period of time, his wife prepared a different kind of "vegetable meat" for dinner on four consecutive days. He assumed it was real meat and found the meals to be no better or worse than the fare he was normally accustomed to eating. On the fourth day, however, he happened to look in the cupboard. Finding the containers of vegetable imitation meats, he realized the deception and was quite annoyed. "Don't you think I make enough to be able to afford real meat?" he protested to his wife.

Many people have become accustomed to the taste of meat and eat it despite the fact that flesh eating has been linked to heart disease and cancer, despite the fact that livestock production is ecologically unsound, and despite the fact that innocent animals are killed to provide them with food. Why then do people eat it? The meat analogue would seem to be an ideal substitute for real meat if people really ate flesh foods for their taste alone. However, the meat analogue is regarded as a travesty by people who feel it is absurd to purchase an imitation of an item which, traditionally, has been viewed as a status symbol.

13

From Necessity to Sin

Not so the Golden Age, who fed on fruit,
Nor durst with bloody meals their mouths pollute.
Then birds in airy space might safely move,
And timorous hares on heaths securely rove:
Nor needed fish the guileful hooks to fear,
For all was peaceful; and that peace sincere.
Whoever was the wretch (and curs'd be he)
That envied first our food's simplicity;
Th' essay of bloody feasts on brutes began,
And after forg'd the sword to murder man.
Had he the sharpen'd steel alone employ'd
On beasts of prey that other beasts destroy'd,
Or men invaded with their fangs and paws,
This had been justify'd by nature's laws,
And self-defence: but who did feasts begin
Of flesh, he stretch'd necessity to sin.

The Metamorphoses OF OVID,
TRANSLATION BY JOHN DRYDEN

Do we, as human beings, possess the "killer instinct," and if not, what have we done to compensate for this deficiency? There are numerous historical examples of peoples from a wide variety of cultures who actually sympathized with the animals that were killed for their food. Instead of forswearing the use of meat, however, various subterfuges were developed to assuage these feelings of guilt.

This practice of using subterfuge has taken various forms throughout history, including religious ritual, semantics, repression and rationalization.

RITUAL AS SUBTERFUGE

Animal sacrifice was an important aspect of ancient cultures, including that of the Greeks, Romans, Hebrews, and Hindus. Various animals were ritually killed as an oblation to propitiate a particular deity. In many instances, however, the people who made such oblations did not feel it was improper to partake of that which was being offered to their deity. Edible portions of the victim's flesh were often retained by the person making the sacrifice. The practice of sacrificing animals was, nonetheless, perceived as a meritorious act made on behalf of a particular deity—whatever benefit the sacrificer derived from this practice was considered to be incidental.

When an animal or human being was sacrificed as part of a primitive ritual, like a fertility rite, it was deemed necessary. This was simply considered the known and accepted way of insuring a good crop. Despite this "necessity," however, there was still a sense of guilt. People sought to dissociate themselves from the act of killing. One example of this point is found in ancient Greece. An ox representing the spirit of vegetation was sacrificed as part of the rites of Dionysus.

The weapons were then sharpened and handed to the butchers, one of whom felled the ox with the axe and another cut its throat with the knife. As soon as he had felled the ox, the farmer threw the axe from him and fled; and the man who cut the beast's throat apparently imitated his example. Meantime the ox was skinned and all present partook of its flesh. Then the hide was stuffed with straw and sewed up; next the stuffed animal was set on its feet and yoked to a plough as if it were ploughing. A trial then took place in an ancient law-court presided over by the King (as he was called) to determine who had murdered the ox. The maidens who had brought the water accused the men who had sharpened the axe and knife; the men who had sharpened the axe and knife blamed the men who had handed these implements to the butchers; the men who handed the implements to the butchers blamed the butchers;

and the butchers laid blame on the axe and knife, which were accordingly found guilty, condemned and caste into the sea.[1]

The axe and knife are certainly suitable scapegoats, since these implements were ultimately responsible for the ox's murder. The culpability of the butchers and others was not considered significant.

Frazer cites several cultures in which the consumption of an animal's blood was taboo. This injunction was observed by such diverse cultures as certain North American Indian tribes and the ancient Hebrews. The reason for this taboo in both these instances was the belief that the blood itself contained the animal's life and spirit.[2] Deuteronomy 12:23 states: "Only be sure that thou eat not the blood: for the blood is the life; and thou mayest not eat the life with the flesh."* The prophet Ezekiel equated the eating of animal blood with the sins of murder and idolatry.[3] Commenting on the nature of immolation and the taboo on the eating of animal blood, anthropologist Robert Eisler hypothesized that these ritualistic practices developed as a means of subterfuge: "Knowing that their ancestors were not carnivorous, men try to placate their resentment of the new ways by inviting the ancestral spirits of the tribe to take their share in the meat of the slaughtered victim, which becomes a 'sacrifice'; or they return the red blood which 'is life' to the earth before they allow themselves to eat the meat of the killed animal."[4]

Discussing the *trefah* taboo, Philo asserted that Jews are enjoined from eating the flesh of animals which have been maimed or killed by predators because it is unbefitting for one to become a "tablemate with savage beasts."[5] Carnivorous animals themselves are not to be eaten since one may thereby inherit their violent nature.[6] Philo comments that such food should not be eaten by "gentle-minded" people. Rabbi Abraham Isaac Kook, the first Ashkenazi Chief Rabbi of Israel, noted that the word *trefah* specifically means "torn or rent to pieces" although it is now used to describe all meat that is considered nonkosher for any variety of reasons. Rabbi Kook, like Philo, believed that the original purpose of the trefah taboo was to permit flesh-eating human beings to dissociate themselves from the predatory class of animals who savagely mangle their victims. Notwithstanding the fact that human beings are more humane than

* Cf. Gen. 9:4; Lev. 17:10–11.

the carnivores in this respect, carnivorous animals kill for food out of necessity—there is no such compelling reason for human beings to kill innocent creatures for food.

There are people in various cultures who have felt compelled to communicate with their intended victim or the victim's spirit (after its death), entreating the animal to forgive them. An 18th-century account is given of an Ottawa tribe that pleaded with their victim, a bear, to forgive them, stating: "Cherish us no grudge because we have killed you. You have sense; you see that our children are hungry."[7] The Ainos of Saghalien rear bear cubs only to kill them, but not without some feelings of remorse. A person from the village is designated to inform the bear that it will be shot by their best archer so its death will be as quick and painless as possible. It is also told that it will now go to the "god of the forest." The archer who is assigned to kill the bear first asks the animal to forgive him and then weeps.[8] One African tribe is somewhat less candid with its victims. Upon killing an elephant in a hunt, they make a practice of apologizing to the animal's spirit, pretending its death was quite accidental.[9] Certain North American Indian tribes wept in premeditated remorse for the buffalos they were about to kill.[10]

These are just a few illustrations which seem to indicate that even when animals were killed out of necessity, or what was deemed to be necessity, there was still an element of compassion—a certain respect for the animal and a genuine feeling of grief at its death. Frazer himself was impressed with this aspect of the primitive cultures he studied:

> The explanation of life by the theory of an indwelling and practically immortal soul is one which the savage does not confine to human beings but extends to the animate creation in general. In doing so he is more liberal and perhaps more logical than the civilized man, who commonly denies to animals that privilege of immortality which he claims for himself. The savage is not so proud; he commonly believes that animals are endowed with feelings and intelligence like those of men, and that, like men, they possess souls which survive the death of their bodies either to wander about as disembodied spirits or to be born again in animal form. Accordingly, he makes it a rule to spare the life of those animals which he has no pressing motive for killing.[11]

In cultures where killing animals for food ceased to be a necessity, more sophisticated methods of subterfuge were devised to mitigate feelings of guilt.

LANGUAGE AS SUBTERFUGE

Language has always been used to reinforce our concepts of those things we do not wish to change and to justify our actions by providing an efficient means of setting double standards for master and slave, men and women, and, most notably, *Homo sapiens* and other species. Thomas Hobbes cited the awesome power of words and the enforcement of their definitions. Comparing other animals to human beings, he commented on the prostitution of our linguistic abilities:

> . . . that these creatures though they have some use of voice in making known to one another their desires and other affections, yet they want that art of words by which some men can represent to others that which is good in the likeness of evil, and evil in the likeness of good, and augment or diminish the apparent greatness of good and evil, discontenting men and troubling their peace at their pleasure.[12]

Since language is used every day, the process of inculcation serves to reinforce the standards of morality that are part of our culture. The acceptance of these standards is automatic on our part. Most people do not consciously analyze this. In an address entitled "The Unity of the Human Being," John Dewey noted: "The words are so loaded with associations derived from a long past that instead of being tools for thought, our thoughts become subservient tools of words."[13] Let us take for example the word "civilized." In addition to the intellectual development of an individual or a society, the word also encompasses the whole nature—courteous, refined. To civilize is "to bring out of a condition of savagery or barbarism."[14] We, of course, do not consider ourselves savages. We protect our image by setting a double standard for defining our actions. Gandhi did not accept this semantic facade. When asked by a reporter what he thought of Western civilization, he replied: "I think it would be a good idea." To take another example, one cannot murder an animal since murder is used to define the killing of a human being. Some people, however, persist in defiling the English language by referring to the killing of animals as murder. One such person was George Bernard Shaw, who stated: "When a man wants to murder a tiger, he calls it sport; when a tiger wants to murder him he calls it ferocity."[15] Our treatment of animals can be compared to the ancient concept of slaves in certain cultures. Neither animals nor slaves can actually be murdered, since both are regarded merely as the property of their "owners" and can be dealt with in any manner the owner deems proper.

Vegetarians are in error to claim that killing animals for food is immoral. The definition of "immoral" is that which is "not in conformity with accepted principles of right and wrong behavior; contrary to the moral code of the community."[16] Society determines what is right and what is wrong. It is obvious that since killing animals and eating their flesh is part of our culture, this practice cannot be considered immoral. We may sanctimoniously proclaim that cannibalism is not moral if we are to judge this practice by the standards of our own society. However, cannibalism is moral to practicing cannibals, since it is justified by the mores of their own community. Certainly cannibals must think of "civilized" societies as immoral when their members kill one another in organized warfare without even bothering to eat the victims. They well might ask: Why kill people if you don't intend to eat them? The fact that a cannibal's logic is more practical and honest than that of "civilized" society is noted by Voltaire. In 1725 he had the opportunity to speak with four cannibals that had been captured. When Voltaire told the cannibals that he was "scandalized" by their dietary habits, one of them commented "it was better to eat one's dead enemy than to let him be devoured by beasts, and the victors deserved to have that preference."[17] Voltaire, convinced by this logic, cited the hypocrisy of civilized people who considered these cannibals immoral:

> We kill our neighbors in pitched and unpitched battle, and for the meanest rewards prepare meals for the crows and the worms. There is the horror, there is the crime. When one has been killed what does it matter whether one is eaten by a soldier or by a crow or a dog?
>
> We respect the dead more than the living. We ought to respect both.[18]

Shaw once noted that to be a moral individual one must acquiesce to the standards set down by one's society. Morality is acceptance of the status quo. Therefore, concluded Shaw, all progress is immoral.

The double standard we apply to the value of animal and human life is justified by a linguistic practice of relegating species other than our own to an inferior status. After all, we note, animals are dumb. Indeed, animals may not be as intelligent as human beings, but for the most part they are virtuous in their dealings with other animals and members of their own species. Even the carnivore kills only out of necessity to survive. As Bernard Mandeville notes: "Tis only Man, mischievous Man, that can make Death a Sport."[19] Realizing the flaws in the human character, we seek to bring the rest of creation down to our own level. This is done by equating the cruelest, most odious people with the entire animal kingdom at large. A terrible person is referred to as a "brute," a "beast," or simply an "animal." By equating such people with animals we justify our treatment of them, mitigating any sense of guilt we may possess.

In addition to this general view of animal life, there are numerous specific examples where different species are used to describe one's enemies or loathsome individuals. Petty criminals who take unfair advantage of an adverse situation are sometimes compared to the jackal who scavanges on the flesh of animals that were killed by other carnivores. The term "jackal" might be more appropriately applied to people who dine on the flesh of animals which have been killed for them by the slaughterer. However, flesh-eating human beings are more respectable than the wretched jackal, since they at least pay the victim's slayer for his trouble. Americans are quite fond of using "pig" as an invective when they find themselves engaged in verbal battles. "Pig" is also a popular colloquialism used in France *(cochon)*, Germany *(schwein)*, Italy *(porco miseria*—that is, "miserable pig"), and Spain *(cerdo)*. Americans, however, are not content to think of pigs as the epitome of filth—to further demean their nature they are now cruel (e.g., "fascist pigs") as well. In reality, no pig has ever come near to approaching the degree of cruelty perpetrated by human beings on other animals as well as their own species. Unlike human beings, pigs are not known to steal, rape, torture, or kill for greed or sport. Through our use of semantics as subterfuge we seek to distort reality, convincing ourselves that animals are not worthy of life and may as well be put to some practical use—food for human beings.

REPRESSION AS SUBTERFUGE

Ernest Crosby once perceptively noted that we are people who "see clearly the barbarity of all the ages except our own." Many people like to think of themselves as kind, compassionate, and just. Their philosophy is described with such mottos as "Do unto others as you would have them do unto you" or "Live and let live." It is difficult, however, to reconcile these sentiments with the reality that animals are subjected to miserable living conditions and are ultimately killed to provide "tasty" meals. It is simply best not to think of these disturbing matters. Such thoughts are therefore repressed, or to express it in terms of another cliché: "Out of sight, out of mind."

IN THE SHADOW OF THE BUTCHER

Costumes of doctors, nurses, sailors, and soldiers, in addition to erector sets, chemistry sets, miniature ovens, doll houses, and miniature farm sets are all made, encouraging children to imitate the adult occupations which impress them. Even games of mock violence such as "army," "cowboys and Indians," or "cops and robbers" are encouraged or at least condoned by many parents. One then must ask these parents why their children are not encouraged to imitate butchers. The child could mimic cutting the throat of some stuffed toy or bash it over the head. The child might even wear a butcher's costume—an apron which could be splattered with catsup to imitate blood. After all, isn't this an honorable profession—like being a doctor, a farmer, or a builder? Rather, it seems we wish to protect our children from those aspects of our own character that we find in our subconscious mind to be disturbing.

We do not think of ourselves as people who would kill animals for pleasure—that is, presuming we find the taste of meat pleasant or enjoyable as opposed to eating it simply because it is food. People would not think of themselves as butchers or killers because the animals they eat are killed for them by proxy. People who eat flesh repress the concept of themselves as killers because, even though they are aware of the fact that animals are killed for their food, they do not kill them—they simply eat them. They are not butchers or killers but merely consumers. They do not hold themselves to be accountable for the actions of butchers. Indeed, they are far removed from that house of death where the butchers ply their trade. In the restaurants they patronize, lovers in candlelit places think of little more than romance, executives discuss their business affairs and the state of the stock market. They know, of course, that animals were killed for their meal but that is hardly on their minds when eating their filet mignon—nor would they really ever want to think about such things while dining. Ralph Waldo Emerson took this question into account when he stated: "You have just dined, and however scrupulously the slaughter-house is concealed in a graceful distance of miles, there is complicity." Despite his evident compunction, however, Emerson continued to patronize the slaughterhouse that was separated from the dining area of his own home by a graceful distance of miles.

REPRESSION AND REALITY

Tolstoy referred to the use of repression as a defense mechanism when he observed that we "cannot believe that if we refuse to look at what we do not wish to see, it will not exist. This is especially the case when what we do not wish to see is what we wish to eat."[20] Alexandra Tolstoy, in *Tolstoy: A Life of My Father*, relates a story of how her aunt was exposed to the shocking reality of killing for food:

> Auntie was fond of food and when she was offered only a vegetarian diet she was indignant, said she could not eat any old filth and demanded that they give her meat, chicken. The next time she came to dinner she was astonished to find a live chicken tied to her chair and a large knife at her place.
> "What's this?" asked Auntie.
> "You wanted chicken," Tolstoy replied, scarcely restraining his laughter. "No one of us is willing to kill it. Therefore, we prepared everything so that you could do it yourself."[21]

People who would be appalled at the thought of killing the animals they wish to eat have no compunction about eating animals which have been killed for their benefit. After an animal has been slaughtered, the carcass dismembered and conveniently prepared, it ceases to be considered the remains of some creature: It is simply food.

What does one do when the reality of one's diet ceases to be repressed and comes to the conscious mind for full consideration? Some people simply cannot reconcile the thought of themselves as humane while at the same time eating innocent creatures that were killed for their food. Henry S. Salt in his book *Seventy Years Among Savages,* gives us an account of just such an experience:

> . . . and then I found myself realizing, with an amazement which time has not diminished, that the "meat" which formed the staple of our diet, and which I was accustomed to regard like bread or fruit, or vegetables—as a mere commodity of the table, was in truth dead flesh—the actual flesh and blood of oxen, sheep, and swine, and other animals that were slaughtered in vast numbers.[22]

After this dramatic revelation, Salt committed himself to the cause of animal rights. He wrote several books and pamphlets which deal with vegetarianism as an important ethical issue.

IF CALLED BY ANY OTHER NAME

Our practice of using euphemisms when referring to different types of meat has proved an effective means of repressing the unpleasant thought of devouring dead bodies. People refer to the dead pigs they eat as "pork," "bacon," or "ham." In restaurants people order "beef, well-done" or "filet mignon," not a part of a well-cooked dead steer. Even when people order a chicken or turkey dinner, their concession to reality is nonetheless incomplete. They refuse, somehow, to acknowledge the fact that these animals ever died. After all, when a person dies or is killed, that person is often referred to as "the deceased" by relatives, "the body" by homicide detectives, or simply "a corpse" by others. However, chickens and turkeys never really die. They just fade away to miraculously reappear as a "drumstick" on someone's dinner plate.

RATIONALIZATION AS SUBTERFUGE

Cruelty to animals as well as people is perpetuated by members of a society who rationalize that their behavior conforms to contemporary customs. Commenting on the fact that most people do not choose to transcend the standards of their society, Tolstoy contends that people thus "violate" their true feelings of sympathy and pity and in doing so become cruel.

FOLLOWING THE BANDWAGON

The moral justification for eating flesh is represented by statements like: "It can't really be wrong; everyone does it." There are even anthropological studies to support the notion that human beings are naturally predacious animals, and therefore, flesh eating should be regarded as natural for our species. Violence, whether directed at animals or even at other human beings, is believed by some to be part of human nature. Robert Ardrey even postulates that "our killing imperative" is responsible for the development of our civilization. Commenting on the popularity of such theories, M. F. Ashley Montagu notes: "The myth of the ferocity of 'wild animals' constitutes one of Western man's supreme rationalizations, for it not only has served to 'explain' to him the origins of his own aggressiveness, but also to relieve him of the responsibility for it—for since it is 'innate,' derived from his early apelike ancestors, he can hardly, so he rationalizes, he blamed for it!"[23]

The question is often raised as to the value of human life versus the value of animal life. This is an altogether specious issue. The premise that human life is of greater value than animal life would only be a valid argument when citing extraordinary cases such as the Eskimos, who must kill animals to survive. Therefore, the fact remains that, with the possible exception of self-defense or survival, the killing of animals or people cannot be justified except by rationalizations. Examples of such rationalizations are represented in Ovid's *Metamorphoses*. Ovid's Pythogoras believes it is justifiable to kill beasts of prey in self-defense but disputes the notion that we therefore have the "extended license to devour." Ovid states that by such acts we have "stretch'd necessity to sin," setting a dreadful precedent.[24]

RELIGIOUS RATIONALIZATION

Many Christians and Jews conceive of human beings as having been created in the image of their God. As such, human beings themselves are tacitly accorded the status of demigods. Pope, in *An Essay on Man*, comments on the folly of this anthropocentric notion:

> What would this Man? Now upward will he soar,
> And little less than Angel, would be more;
> Now looking downwards, just as griev'd appears
> To want the strength of bulls, the fur of bears.
> Made for his use all creatures if he call,
> Say what their use, had he the pow'rs of all?[25]

Christians of the medieval period were assured by Thomas Aquinas that killing animals is sanctioned by "divine providence." Aquinas asserts that animals "are intended for man's use according to the order of nature. Hence it is not wrong for man to make use of them, either by killing or in any other way whatever."[26] The Thomism doctrine that animals have no souls is ridiculed by Pope in *An Essay on Man.** Pope favors the "untutor'd mind" of the Indian, who believes that animals, like people, will be "admitted to that equal sky."[27]

MIGHT IS RIGHT

Like the religious concept of "holy wars," the secular idea of "survival of the fittest" has been used to justify killing. Superior strength in itself justifies the subjugation of any species, whether we attribute our power to "the will of God" or the "survival of

---

* The question of whether or not women possessed souls had previously been raised in the 6th century by prominent authorities within the Church. Despite the decision that women do in fact at least have souls, many influential figures within the Church, like Aquinas, continued to maintain that they were distinctly inferior to men—a grade below men but superior to the wretched beast that was not considered to possess a soul.

the fittest." The definition of justice, as Thrasymachus states in Plato's *Republic*, is "nothing else than the interest of the stronger."[28] Thrasymachus continues with a sarcastic analogy comparing shepherds to rulers: ". . . you fancy that the shepherd or neatherd fattens or tends the sheep or oxen with a view to their own good and not to the good of himself or his master; and you further imagine that the rulers of states, if they are true rulers, never think of their subjects as sheep, and that they are not studying their own advantage day and night."[29] People commonly rationalize the mistreatment of their fellow human beings as well as animals. The stronger are "better" and can, therefore, do whatever they deem best in the name of justice. Indeed, Thrasymachus's postulate can be and has been used to rationalize war and all forms of human discrimination as well as the killing of animals for food.

TWO WRONGS MAKE A RIGHT

Individuals with any degree of sensitivity could not eat animals simply because they possess the power to use them at their will. Such individuals must be more inventive in formulating rationalizations to justify their behavior. A truly classic example of rationalization is found in Benjamin Franklin's autobiography. Franklin actually became a vegetarian when he was about 16 years of age. Franklin states that he was originally motivated to adopt this diet for reasons of economy, but had later found several other advantages such as the time he saved in eating simple fare and "greater progress, from that greater clearness of head and quicker apprehension."[30] He was also convinced that flesh eating was unethical, referring to this practice as "unprovoked murder." When Franklin desired to eat flesh once again, it was necessary for him to rationalize his apostasy.

I believe I have omitted mentioning that, in my first voyage from Boston, being becalm'd off Block Island, our people set about catching cod, and hauled up a great many. Hitherto I had stuck to my resolution of not eating animal food, and on this occasion I consider'd with my master Tyron,* the taking every fish as a kind of unprovoked murder,

---

* Tyron was a 17th-century author who had written several books on vegetarian nutrition.

since none of them had, or ever could do us any injury that might justify the slaughter. All this seemed very reasonable. But I had formerly been a great lover of fish, and, when this came hot out of the frying-pan, it smelt admirably well. I balanc'd some time between principle and inclination, till I recollected that, when the fish were opened, I saw smaller fish taken out of their stomachs; then thought I, "If you eat one another, I don't see why we mayn't eat you." So I din'd upon cod very heartily, and continued to eat with other people, returning only now and then occasionally to a vegetable diet. So convenient a thing it is to be a reasonable creature, since it enables one to find or make a reason for every thing one has a mind to do.[31]

Franklin himself had once said: "What you are to be depends upon the character of your resolutions." Franklin, however, found that it was more "convenient" to be a "reasonable creature."

ANIMALS LOVE TO BE EATEN

The meat and fish industries are well aware of the nature of their business. It is most interesting to find that many of their advertisements insult the intelligence of their potential customers by suggesting rationalizations, instead of letting the consumers devise their own. These media ads tell us that animals actually desire to be eaten! This is their sole aspiration in life. The cartoon of a smiling bull winks at you in one newspaper ad. The caption reads: "Save money, buy a side of beef for your freezer today." There is a television commercial that features cartoon hens singing as they dance the can-can in chorus-line fashion. On the one-step they sing of how we will enjoy their legs—that is, eating them for dinner. Another television commercial features an all-American-type freckle-faced boy chomping into a hot dog and bun. A chorus of children are singing in the background:

> Oh I wish I was an Oscar Mayer wiener,
> for that is what I'd really like to be.
> For if I was an Oscar Mayer wiener,
> everyone would be in love with me.

Nellie Shriver of the American Vegetarians had intended to sue this company for false advertising.[32] "I hardly think the children singing this jingle really wish to be made into pigs, be kept in filthy pens, butchered and transformed into wieners—not Oscar Mayer's or any other brand," asserted Ms. Shriver. In each episode of the continuing commercial saga of "Charlie the Tuna," Charlie is shown devising different ways to be caught so he can be used as a Star-Kist tuna fish by some appreciative patron of that particular brand. However, each of these episodes ends in tragedy as the man who does the voice-over for the Star-Kist people regretfully informs Charlie of his rejection. "Star-Kist," the man tells us, "only uses the best." Again Ms. Shriver contemplated a false-advertising challenge. However, as she would be the plaintiff in such an action, the burden of proof would be on her, and no one has ever really proved conclusively that tuna fish are not, in fact, masochists. One is mistaken to think of such commercials as simply entertainment to induce you to buy a particular product. There is, indeed, a common theme to their subliminal message: The animals desire to be eaten. Don't disappoint them.

Young children, who have not been exposed to the complexities and deceptions that are so much a part of adult life, have neither the ability nor the desire to develop rationalizations to the same degree as adults. Some people feel it is best to shield children from the horrible realities of life. One of the largest hamburger companies obviously concurs with this notion. McDonald's has a television commercial that is used to sponsor children's programming. It features a lovable clown, "Ronald McDonald," who informs his young audiences that hamburgers grow in little hamburger patches. The old maxim that honesty is the best policy does not apply if you expect children to eat meat without compunction. Some of them have not yet "learned" that the value of an animal should be determined by its ability to satisfy human desires and that some animals, such as cattle, are only able to give us pleasure after they are dead.

As sophisticated adults, many people reject the notion that children sometimes have a better understanding of certain matters than we do. However, some adults are willing to concede there is much that can be learned from the peculiar wisdom of a child. One such person is Harvard philosophy professor Robert Nozick. Despite his sympathy for the issue of animal rights, Professor Nozick and his wife finally abandoned their practice of eating meat only after their ethics were challenged by their two-year-old daughter. While eating a turkey that was prepared for a Thanksgiving dinner, the girl exclaimed: "That turkey wanted to live. Why was it killed?"[33] How does one explain to a child the logic of killing for food and at the same time maintain one's integrity?

Appendix:
The Vegetarian Movement

ENGLAND

The subject of vegetarianism had attracted considerable attention in England long before a vegetarian society was formally established there in 1847. The health aspects of vegetarianism were dealt with in John Frank Newton's *Return to Nature* (1811) and various writings of Thomas Tryon, including his *Way to Health, Long Life and Happiness, or a Discourse of Temperance* (1691). George Cheyne, an English physician who converted John Wesley to vegetarianism, had written several essays on the relationship between diet and health. William Lambe, another English physician, discussed the relationship between flesh eating and cancer in his writings.* Vegetarianism had been espoused in the writings of Mandeville, Pope, Thomson, Goldsmith, Cowper, Paley, Ritson, and Shelley. Other writers satirized the vegetarian lifestyle.

Aside from the many references to vegetarianism in 18th- and early 19th-century English literature, there are reports of English vegetarians banding together before there were formally organized vegetarian societies. A considerable number of Shelley's circle of friends at Bracknell were vegetarians. Much to the dismay of Shelley's friend Thomas Jefferson Hogg, the subject of vegetarianism was frequently discussed by this set.[1] Furthermore, Hogg relates that small vegetarian communes existed in various rural areas of the country.[2] Edward Fitzgerald, in a letter dated November 19, 1833, notes that

---

* Dr. Lambe had prescribed a vegetarian diet for Keats. The ailing poet reluctantly followed this regimen for a short period of time.

he had attended a lecture on the subject of vegetarianism. The term "vegetarianism" originated in 1842, five years before the first English vegetarian society was formally established. Prior to 1842, the vegetarian diet was referred to by various terms, including "Pythagorean diet," "vegetable diet," and "fleshless dietary."

Although vegetarianism had apparently enjoyed a certain degree of popularity for some time before the middle of the 19th century, there was no viable movement as such prior to the establishment of the vegetarian society in Manchester in 1847. The precursor of this society was a peculiar Christian sect known as the Bible Christian Church. This sect, which included vegetarianism among its doctrines, was founded by the Reverend William Cowherd in 1809. Cowherd's advocacy of vegetarianism was based on his belief that compassion and proper hygiene should be regarded as a Christian duty. Moreover, the story of the world's creation in Genesis was viewed as proof that God had not designed human beings as flesh eaters. While members of the Bible Christian Church looked upon vegetarianism as a religious doctrine, some of them wished to promote vegetarianism within the general population. Having concluded that the most effective way to go about this task would be to establish a secular vegetarian society, a conference was held at Ramsgate, Kent, on September 30, 1847, to form such an organization. The objects of the society as outlined in the society's charter read:

> To induce habits of abstinence from the flesh of animals as food, by the dissemination of information on the subject, by means of tracts, essays, and lectures, proving the many advantages of a physical, intellectual, and moral character resulting from vegetable habits of diet: and thus to secure, through the association, example, and efforts of its members, and adopting of a principle which will tend essentially to true civilization, to universal brotherhood, and to the increase of human happiness generally.[3]

The vegetarian society started publishing a periodical called *The Vegetarian Messenger* in September, 1849. This monthly contained reports on the society's meetings and lectures, essays, reviews, and letters from its readers. It was sold to the general public for a penny and had a monthly circulation of over 21,000 by the year 1854.

Many of the more active members of the nascent vegetarian society might well be characterized as puritanical idealists. Having been actively involved in the temperance movement, they stressed a link between vegetarianism and their campaign against the use of tobacco and alcohol. Some members also sought to impose their own peculiar dietary habits on the group as a whole. These individuals inveighed against the use of items such as coffee, tea, cocoa, salt, milk, and eggs. Some even advocated a strictly fruitarian regimen. Professor Francis W. Newman, who became president of the vegetarian society in 1873, felt that the society should not be associated with specific dietary programs nor should it take any position on other matters, such as the use of tobacco or alcohol. Newman did not allow the views of the radical minority within the society to go unchallenged, proclaiming: ". . . the number of dogmatic prohibitions against everything that makes food palatable will soon ruin our Society, if not firmly resisted."[4]

A leading member of the vegetarian society who was obviously impressed with Gustav Schlickeysen's "Obst und Brod" ("Fruit and Bread"), purchased copies of an English translation of this treatise and mailed them to members of the society. Newman countered by writing a critical review of this treatise in the society's magazine. Newman attacked Schlickeysen's whole approach, stating that he "seems quite unacquainted with the first principles needed for practical persuasion." Similarly, Newman did not mince words when he criticized Schlickeysen's notion that people should abstain from beans, lentils, sugar, honey, tea, coffee, and all cooked food in addition to meat. Characterizing the author of "Fruit and Bread" as a "pernicious foe to our Society," Newman commented that Schlickeysen's views could only serve to weaken the society in its efforts to promote vegetarianism by "caricaturing our excellent arguments and running into doctrine which ninety-nine out of every hundred will pronounce fanatical."[5] Another controversy arose when Newman proposed that nonvegetarians should be admitted to the society as associate members. A year after this resolution was passed, there were more than twice as many associate members as there were regular members enrolled in the vegetarian society.

Many local vegetarian societies were formed in various parts of the United Kingdom, beginning in 1853. These groups existed as branches of the vegetarian society in Manchester. The Dietetic Reform Society, formed in London in 1875, existed as a totally separate organization. This group, which became known as the National Food

Reform Society, included abstinence from alcohol and tobacco among its doctrines. In July, 1881, it started its own publication, called the *Food Reform Magazine*. The National Food Reform Society amalgamated with the vegetarian society in Manchester in 1885. However, the two organizations were not able to overcome their differences. Leaders of the National Food Reform Society, having been left out of the decision-making process of the new organization, felt slighted. The amalgamation of these two societies was finally dissolved in March, 1888. After establishing itself as a separate organization once again, the London group became known as the London Vegetarian Society and published its own journal, *Vegetarian News*. In 1958, the two principal British vegetarian societies (in Manchester and London) agreed to issue jointly a single publication, which was called *The British Vegetarian*. However, these two groups continued to exist as separate societies up until October, 1969, when they amalgamated under the name the Vegetarian Society of the United Kingdom, Ltd. This organization currently publishes a bimonthly magazine called *Alive*.

In view of the fact that vegetarianism as a secular movement had originated in England, it is hardly surprising to find that the Vegetarian Society of the United Kingdom is generally considered to be the most successful and best organized of all the vegetarian organizations in existence today.

UNITED STATES

The secular vegetarian movement in the United States, as in England, evolved from religious vegetarianism. William Metcalfe, pastor of the Bible Christian Church in Manchester, England, along with forty other members of this sect, emigrated to the United States in 1817. Metcalfe and members of his congregation settled in Philadelphia, where they established a U.S. branch of the Bible Christian Church. Metcalfe's treatise *Abstinence from Flesh of Animals,* written in 1823, is the first book on vegetarianism published in the United States. Just three years after members of the Bible Christian Church started a secular vegetarian society in England, Metcalfe founded an American vegetarian society. The first meeting of this new group was held in New York City in 1850.

Sylvester Graham, a Presbyterian minister who became a well-known leader in the health reform movement, was converted to vegetarianism by a member of the Bible Christian Church. Graham lectured extensively throughout the New England states and New York, drawing as many as 2,000 people to his talks. He established vegetarian boardinghouses (known as "Graham Houses") in New York, Boston, and other cities. Graham is best remembered for popularizing the use of unsifted whole-wheat flour in making bread and crackers—the so-called "graham bread" and "graham crackers."

William Alcott, a Boston physician, was one of the more notable people who was influenced by Graham's teachings. Vegetarianism was championed in the *Moral Reformer* and the *Library of Health,* two of the journals which Alcott edited. William Alcott's cousin, Bronson Alcott, was also a staunch vegetarian. Bronson Alcott, who became a vegetarian in 1835, viewed his commitment to this diet as an animal-rights issue; his journal contains several references to vegetarianism as an ethical issue. He and his friend Charles Lane conceived the idea of establishing a self-sufficient vegetarian commune. They purchased farmland in Harvard, Massachusetts, to develop this project in 1843. The so-called Fruitlands experiment failed after only seven months. Louisa May Alcott later wrote about her father's ill-fated vegetarian commune experiment in her work *Transcendental Wild Oats.* Louisa May herself was raised as a vegetarian but abandoned this diet after she left her parents to work as a nurse for the Union Army during the Civil War.

From the time of its humble beginnings in the mid-19th century up through the present era, the Seventh-Day Adventist Church has always been in the vanguard of the health reform movement. In 1866 the church established a naturopathy institute on seven acres of Michigan farmland. The institute, headed by a naturopathic doctor, specialized in hydrotherapy. However, this did not prove to be a commercially successful venture. The church eventually turned its attention to other methods of promoting its views on proper hygiene. Ellen White and her husband, James, encouraged Seventh-Day Adventist members to enter the medical profession. They even sponsored the medical training of worthy members like Merritt G. Kellogg and his younger half-brother, John Harvey Kellogg.

John H. Kellogg studied at the University of Michigan Medical School and later transferred to Bellevue Hospital Medical College, where he graduated in 1875. He allocated various periods of time over the next three decades to furthering his medical studies in Europe, despite his already crowded schedule of duties. Kellogg was installed as director of the Seventh-Day Adventist Battle Creek Sanitarium in 1876. Under his able guidance the sanitarium became a highly successful enterprise. In fact, this institute quickly developed a reputation as the leading health resort in the world. By 1901 it had a regular staff of 70 physicians and the capacity to treat as many as 7,000 people at any given time. Among those who sought treatment there was a motley assortment of personages, including Susan B. Anthony, Upton Sinclair, Admiral Byrd, John D. Rockefeller, Jr., John Burroughs, Henry Ford, Percy Grainger, Eddie Cantor, and Amelia Earhart. Along with success, however, there were problems. Disputes arose between Kellogg and the church elders in regard to issues of sanitarium policy. Through a bit of crafty maneuvering, Kellogg finally wrested control of the sanitarium from the church. Using the pretext that the sectarian nature of the Battle Creek institution jeopardized its tax-exempt status, Kellogg succeeded in changing the by-laws under which it operated. It was, hence, noted in the new by-laws that the sanitarium was officially undenominational and nonsectarian. One of the ramifications of this move was that the Seventh-Day Adventist Church was now precluded from using the sanitarium's funds to subsidize its other numerous and varied health reform programs.

The few established vegetarian organizations which have existed in this country, being somewhat staid and conservative in nature, have never really attracted significant numbers of young people. Moreover, none of the American vegetarian organizations have been able to build a broad-based constituency of different types of vegetarians, e.g., health, ethical, religious. We can assume that ethical vegetarians were hardly overwhelmed with enthusiasm when John Maxwell, an 84-year-old naturopathic doctor from Chicago, ran for President of the United States in the 1948 election. The American Vegetarian party, which Maxwell represented, advocated the mass extermination of cattle to appropriate their grazing land for food production.[6]

The great increase in the number of Americans turning to vegetarianism within the past two decades is attributable to several factors:

1. There is increasing evidence on the correlation between flesh eating and heart disease.

2. Many Americans are outraged that the meat industry continues to use chemicals which are known to cause cancer.

3. There is a growing interest in the ecology movement.

4. There is a growing resistance to the high cost of meat, particularly since meat is no longer regarded by many people as a necessary food.

5. There has been a great deal of adverse publicity on the tremendous wastefulness of feeding grains to livestock, as a result of the growing concern over the world hunger issue.

6. There is a growing interest in the issue of animal rights. The advocacy of ethical vegetarianism, once viewed as a somewhat radical position within the animal-welfare movement, is now generally looked upon with approval. Indeed, several major animal-welfare organizations have gone on record as endorsing vegetarianism, despite the fact that most of their directors are not vegetarians themselves.

The growing interest in vegetarianism as evidenced by the items outlined above seems to have been a significant factor in the proliferation of vegetarian organizations which has occurred in recent years.

While most vegetarian societies cover a broad range of issues associated with vegetarianism in their literature, many such groups do have a particular orientation to their promotion of this diet. Indeed, the differences that exist between health-oriented vegetarian organizations and ethical-oriented vegetarian groups are quite significant. Many people who belong to health-oriented vegetarian groups look askance at ethical vegetarians who smoke or drink alcohol or coffee. Most ethical vegetarians are hostile toward health vegetarians who wear fur coats or even leather. The U.S. vegetarian community is also divided on the issue of vivisection. Many ethical vegetarians are actively involved in the antivivisection cause. Conversely, there are many health vegetarians who condone the practice of using animals for medical research. In fact, there are vegetarians in the medical profession who do various types of research which involve painful experiments with innocent animals.

Because of major differences in attitudes on issues such as health and animal rights which exist among the various American groups, there has never been a truly unified vegetarian movement in the

United States. Yet, despite this lack of unity within the U.S. vegetarian community at large, the number of Americans turning to a vegetarian diet continues to grow. There has been a great proliferation of vegetarian restaurants and vegetarian cooperative food stores within recent years. Also, many colleges have established special vegetarian meal programs, as a result of the growing numbers of college students who have adopted a vegetarian diet.

GERMANY

The first major German vegetarian society was organized in 1866 by Eduard Baltzer. Actually, the groundwork for Baltzer's society was set much earlier by the interest in vegetarianism that had been generated from various books written on this subject by people such as Gustav von Struve and Dr. Heinrich Lahmann.

Estimates on the number of vegetarians living in West Germany at the present time range as high as 100,000, while the number of vegetarians in East Germany is thought to be only about 800. There are several vegetarian organizations in West Germany. The largest of these is the Bund für Lebenserneuerung (Association for Life-renewing) which has about 3,000 members and publishes a bimonthly magazine called *Der Vegetarier (The Vegetarian)*.

ARBEITSGEMEINSCHAFT DDR-VEGETARIERFREUNDE (GERMAN DEMOCRATIC REPUBLIC WORK UNION OF VEGETARIAN FRIENDS)

The Work Union of DDR Friends was started in 1956 to establish a liaison between vegetarians living in West Germany and the East German vegetarian community. The Communist government in East Germany does not allow vegetarians living there to establish a formal organization. In fact, the Work Union of DDR Friends is not even permitted to send printed material on vegetarianism to their East German counterparts. They are, however, allowed to exchange information on vegetarianism in personal correspondence. The West German–based group has, therefore, established an organized network of "pen pals" to maintain a semi-formal relationship with their

East German friends. The West Germans also send foodstuffs, such as nuts, dried fruits and citrus fruits to their East German counterparts, since these types of foods are not widely available in East Germany.

There are twenty active members who organize the activities of the Work Union of DDR Friends. The general membership numbers about 120 people. About 60 percent of this group's membership are ethical vegetarians, 20 percent are vegetarians for religious reasons, and 20 percent are vegetarians primarily for health reasons. There are about 300 vegetarian "friends" in East Germany.

DEUTSCHE REFORM-JUGEND (GERMAN REFORM YOUTH)

The German Reform Youth organizes camping and hiking trips. This is an educational as well as a recreational organization. While vegetarianism is not a mandatory requirement for membership in German Reform Youth, approximately three-quarters of this group's 1,000 members are vegetarians. Almost all of these are vegetarians for ethical reasons.

NETHERLANDS

Felix Ortt, an engineer who quit his job to work full time for the vegetarian cause, founded the Vegetarian Society of the Netherlands in 1894. The original group, which consisted of Ortt and seven of his friends, promoted vegetarianism by selling vegetarian cookbooks and distributing free vegetarian literature. The Dutch society, as originally constituted, was dedicated to the principles of nonviolence. Many of the society's members were imprisoned during World War I because, as pacifists, they refused military service. Ortt and one of his friends established a special school in 1920 which emphasized vegetarianism and pacifism. The children were taught how to grow vegetable and flower gardens. Ortt's school had an enrollment of 30 students at the time of its founding, and there were as many as 100 students enrolled in later years. The school was discontinued in 1935.

At present, the Nederlandse Vegetariërsbond has about 2,500 mem-

bers in its 6 local chapters. This society publishes a bimonthly magazine called *Leven & Laten Leven (Live and Let Live)* which is sent
to various libraries throughout the country in addition to the society's
own members. The Dutch vegetarian society has established a vegetarian home for elderly people. Members of the youth section of
the Dutch Vegetarian Society set up booths in various towns, where
they distribute literature and sell food, as well as organizing a wide
range of social activities including camping trips.

The Dutch government cooperated with the Nederlandse Vegetariërsbond when a controversy arose over a law which required all
Dutch cheese manufacturers to use rennet (a meat by-product) in
their cheese processing operations.* The government ultimately
agreed to permit the manufacture of rennet-free cheese in quantities
sufficient to meet the needs of the Dutch vegetarian community.
Vegetarianism has won a great degree of acceptance in the Netherlands in recent times. A considerable number of health-food stores
and vegetarian restaurants have been established there. Vegetarian
meals are available on request to members of the armed forces, prison-
ers, and hospital patients. There are estimated to be about 12,000
vegetarians in the Netherlands at the present time.

ITALY

Società Vegetariana Italiana, a private vegetarian group founded
in 1952, was reorganized as a national society in 1967. In 1970
the group was renamed Associazione Vegetariana Italiana, and has
1,500 members at the present time, with regional sections in Pied-
mont, Lombardy, Venezia, Giulia, Emilia, Tuscany, and Latium.
This society is comprised of both ethical and health vegetarians.
In addition to their quarterly magazine *L'Idea Vegetariana (The
Vegetarian Idea),* the Associazione Vegetariana Italiana publishes
various pamphlets on vegetarianism, including one on vegetarian
nutrition. They also have printed a pamphlet which lists various
vegetarian restaurants and hotels located in different parts of the

---

* The Dutch government strictly regulates the cheese industry since cheese is an
important export commodity for the Netherlands. The Dutch government had conducted a 3-year study which showed that cheese processed with rennet had better
keeping qualities than cheese made with non-animal Noury.

country for the benefit of vegetarian tourists as well as the society's own members.

SPAIN

According to Spanish government statistics, there are between 3,000 and 4,000 people in Spain who are members of vegetarian organizations. However, the actual number of vegetarians in Spain is believed to be considerably higher. Unfortunately, there are no accurate figures available on the number of Spanish vegetarians who are not officially listed as members of a vegetarian society. Articles on the topic of vegetarianism have appeared in various Spanish newspapers with some frequency in recent years.

ASOCIACIÓN VEGETARIANA ANTROPONOMICA DE ZARAGOZA (ANTHROPONOMIC VEGETARIAN ASSOCIATION OF ZARAGOZA)

The vegetarian society in Zaragoza has 150 members, most of whom are vegetarians for health reasons.

SOCIEDAD VEGETARIANA NATURISTA DE VALENCIA (NATURALIST VEGETARIAN SOCIETY OF VALENCIA)

The Sociedad Vegetariana Naturista de Valencia emphasizes the hygenic and "naturalistic" aspects of the vegetarian diet, and most of its members are vegetarians for health reasons: health (318), ethical (31), religious (27), economic (22). This society organizes conferences on natural medicines, nutrition, yoga, and the "morality of naturalism." Their meetings include discussions and demonstrations on hydrotherapy and vegetarian cooking. Many of the people in this group are actively involved in the Esperanto movement (universal language). News of the society's activities is published in the local press. The principal goals of the Sociedad Vegetariana Naturista de Valencia as expressed by its president, Vincent Michael, are:

> . . . the establishment of a mountain retreat for young people, where, by growing with nature, they will become the foremost proponents of nature, the creation of vegetarian colonies where our new generations

may thrive in love and health, and a home where retired people may continue a happy life for many years.

SOCIEDAD VEGETARIANA DE ALCOY
(VEGETARIAN SOCIETY OF ALCOY)

The Sociedad Vegetariana de Alcoy has 135 members. Most of them (85 percent) are vegetarians for health reasons, 15 percent are ethical vegetarians, and one person is a vegetarian for religious reasons. The secretary of the Alcoy Vegetarian Society notes that the local newspapers and radio stations have been most cooperative in publicizing various activities scheduled by the society.

SOUTH AFRICA

There were about 30,000 vegetarians in South Africa in the mid-1960s according to a survey taken at that time. It is believed there has been a substantial increase in the number over the past decade. A representative of the South African Vegetarian Union estimates the South African vegetarian population as follows: 25,000 Caucasians, from 5 to 10 percent of the 250,000 Indian population, approximately 1 percent of the native Bantu population. There is great diversity in the types of vegetarians found among these various population groups, including ethical, health, religious, and economic.

The South African Vegetarian Union has about 500 members. There are two vegetarian groups in the city of Johannesburg: the Jewish Vegetarian Association and the Johannesburg Vegetarian Society. There are two vegetarian restaurants in Johannesburg and one in Cape Town. There are more than 100 health-food stores in various parts of the country. The frequent appearance of articles on vegetarianism in the past few years reflects an increased interest in this subject there.

NIGERIA

Owing to problems encountered in reorganizing the Nigerian Vegetarian Society immediately following the civil war there (1966–1970), the Aba affiliate of this group decided upon establishing itself as a new national organization. This group, known as the Soul Vegetarian Society, was established in 1970. A large segment of this society is comprised of ethical vegetarians. A strong concern for the rights of animals is evidenced by the fact that many Soul members avoid using toiletries manufactured with animal products. Apropos of the Soul Vegetarian Society's emphasis on the ethical aspect of vegetarianism, J. O. M. Okpe, the secretary for this organization, closes his letters with the phrase, "Yours in defense of life."

Aside from disseminating vegetarian literature, members of the Soul Vegetarian Society encourage proprietors of food markets to stock a greater variety of wholesome fruits and vegetables. They also make visits to restaurants and hotels to make sure that vegetarian meals will be available for vegetarian customers. The society is presently making arrangements to establish its own vegetarian restaurant in Aba, as well as a health-food store and a Beauty Without Cruelty boutique.*

INDIA

Aside from the many people in India who rarely, if ever, eat meat simply because they cannot afford to buy it, about 18 percent of this country's population are strict vegetarians by choice. Many of them follow this diet as a matter of religious tradition, having been brought up in families that belong to any of the various Hindu sects which strictly observe the ahimsā doctrine. The Jains are all vegetarians, but the number of Jains in India is relatively small.

There were no formal vegetarian societies in India prior to 1957, although various animal-welfare organizations, such as the Bombay Humanitarian League, espoused vegetarianism as part of its work. The decision to organize a national society in India was prompted in large part by the considerable number of Indians who were abandoning their traditional vegetarian diet as a result of Western influences. Many Indians, especially those studying abroad, came to regard flesh eating as a status symbol.

---

* Beauty Without Cruelty is a British-based organization which manufactures a line of toiletries that are not made with by-products of the meat industry (e.g., tallow) or any sort of product which involves cruelty to animals, e.g., perfume derived from civet cats.

When the charter for the Indian Vegetarian Union was being drawn up in 1957, a controversy arose over the definition of the word "vegetarian." Most Indian vegetarians do not eat eggs. Many of the lacto vegetarians were strongly opposed to what they viewed as condoning the use of eggs by allowing persons who used this food to be classified as vegetarians in their charter. Those who argued for a broader definition of vegetarianism prevailed.

It is not particularly surprising to find that the vegetarian movement in India is largely dominated by leaders in the animal-welfare field. The eminent dancer and former member of Parliament Rukmini Devi Arundale and Morarji Desai, the Prime Minister of India, are among the prominent advocates of vegetarianism presently associated with the Indian Vegetarian Union.

SRI LANKA (CEYLON)

The Sri Kapila Humanitarian Society was founded in 1962. The vast majority of this society's 5,000 members are vegetarians for ethical and/or religious reasons. A considerable number of Buddhists belong to this organization. The emphasis on vegetarianism as an ethical issue is reflected in the society's motto: "Live and let live." The Sri Kapila Humanitarian Society is, in fact, actively involved in various aspects of animal-welfare work other than vegetarianism. The educational program of this group includes the scheduling of lectures, debates, and question-and-answer sessions. The society publishes vegetarian literature in both English and Sinhalese. A free library has been established at the president's home.

IRAN

The Iran Vegetarian Society was established by J. Ermian in 1964. In addition to its own material, the Iran Vegetarian Society has printed Persian translations of literature originally published by the London Vegetarian Society. Most of the individuals who belong to this relatively small society are vegetarians for ethical reasons, with approximately 10 percent for health reasons. Mr. Ermian notes that since there is not a large variety of fresh fruits and vegetables in

Iran, vegetarians in that country experience some difficulties in obtaining nutritious foods. There are no so-called health-food stores there. Mr. Ermian estimates there are approximately 2,000 vegetarians in Iran.

CANADA

TORONTO VEGETARIAN SOCIETY

The Toronto Vegetarian Society, formed in 1945, has about 300 members at the present time. Most of the members of this society are vegetarians for ethical reasons. The aims and objects of this society, as stated in their charter, strongly emphasize the ethical aspect of vegetarianism.

OTTAWA VEGETARIAN GROUP

Formed in 1973, the Ottawa Vegetarian Group is a small organization. Five of this group's ten members are vegetarians primarily for health reasons; the other five are ethical vegetarians. They have organized vegetarian dinners, which are usually attended by about 150 people. Peter Hyde, the president of this group, is also active in the Animal Defense League of Canada and serves as secretary to the International League for Animal Rights.

JEWISH VEGETARIAN SOCIETIES

Some Jewish vegetarians are simply Jews who are vegetarians or vegetarians who are Jews. While maintaining that vegetarianism is by no means antagonistic to Judaism, they do not actually feel that vegetarianism has a strong connection with Jewish tradition. However, some Jewish vegetarians do, in fact, make a connection between vegetarianism and Judaism. While they do not regard vegetarianism as essential to Judaism, they nonetheless feel that following a vegetarian diet is conducive to adherence to Jewish principles. Noting that many of the Jewish dietary laws (kashrut) are seemingly designed to mitigate the suffering of animals used for food, many Jewish vege-

tarians regard total abstinence from flesh foods as particularly meritorious, since the killing of animals is thereby eliminated altogether.
Abraham Isaac Kook, the first Ashkenazi Chief Rabbi of Israel,
wrote extensively on vegetarianism as a moral issue. Shlomo Goren,
the present Ashkenazi Chief Rabbi of Israel as well as Shear-Yashuv
Cohen, the Chief Rabbi of Haifa, are both vegetarians.

INTERNATIONAL VEGETARIAN UNION

The International Vegetarian Union, formed in 1908, organizes
international vegetarian congresses, where vegetarians from different
countries can become acquainted with one another and exchange
information on the work they are doing to promote vegetarianism
in their respective countries. Controversies that arise at these congresses serve to point up the differences that exist in the international
vegetarian community. Many Indians who attended the twenty-third
congress in Orono, Maine (U.S.A.), complained that the food was
too bland. This view was politely expressed in private conversations.
However, much to the chagrin of the Indian delegation, one American
at a public forum sternly denounced the Indian penchant for heavily
spiced foods. During another public session, a British woman dogmatically characterized the vegan diet as the only true vegetarian diet.
At another public session, an American speaker made a disparaging
and altogether gratuitous remark about "hippies," which he was
later compelled to retract. The person who organized this congress,
a conscientious health reformer, did not permit coffee to be served
in the cafeteria. The coffee drinkers who protested this decision were
told that the coordinator of this convention did not want to be responsible for "poisoning" them.

The vegetarians who attend international vegetarian congresses
generally tend to band together on the basis of their orientation to
vegetarianism, e.g., health, ethics, religion. However, there are a substantial number of vegetarian eclectics who enjoy the great diversity
in the activities scheduled. The programs of past congresses have
included yoga classes, cooking demonstrations, tennis, folk dancing,
reports from representatives on the status of vegetarianism in their
respective countries, as well as talks on a wide range of topics, including eye care, food combining, conducting media campaigns, feeding

vegetarian pets, and much discussion on various aspects of animal rights.

A special scientific research council was formed at the eighteenth International Vegetarian Congress (1965). The Scientific Council of the I.V.U. (S.C.I.V.U.) consists of scientists and economists who abstract articles from various scientific periodicals. Items covered in the bulletin they produce include ecology and economics as well as nutrition and epidemiological studies.

Notes

CHAPTER 1. THE THREE BASIC VEGETARIAN DIETS

1. Dr. Jean Mayer, "Egg vs. Cholesterol Battle," New York *Daily News,* October 9, 1974, p. 48.
2. "Orders a Stop on Egg Claims," New York *Daily News,* December 12, 1975, p. 62.
3. Statement by Sheila Harty before the Subcommittee on Domestic Marketing, Consumer Relations and Nutrition of the House Agriculture Committee, September 28, 1977. *Nutrition Education,* U.S. Government Printing Office, 1977, p. 237.
4. Walton W. Shreeve, M.D., *Physiological Chemistry in Mammals,* W. B. Saunders, 1974, p. 48.
5. Harty, supra note 3, p. 237.
6. Norman Sapeika, "Meat and Dairy Products," from *Toxic Constituents of Animal Foodstuffs,* ed. Irvin E. Liener, Academic Press, 1974, p. 18.
7. Dr. Robert Angelotti, Administrator, Food Safety and Quality Service, USDA, "Consumer Concerns About Additives and Residues in Food and Fiber," *1978 Food and Agricultural Outlook,* prepared for the Committee on Agriculture, Nutrition, and Forestry, U.S. Senate, December 19, 1977, p. 99.
8. Mervyn G. Hardinge, M.D., Hulda Crooks, Fredrick J. Stare, M.D., "Nutritional Studies of Vegetarians: Part IV, Dietary Fatty Acids and Serum Cholesterol," *American Journal of Clinical Nutrition,* vol. 10, no. 6 (June, 1962), p. 522.
9. Statement of Glenn Lake, President, National Milk Producers Federation, hearing before the Subcommittee on Agricultural Research and General Legislation of the Committee on Agriculture and Forestry, U.S. Senate, April 14, 1975. *Beef Research and Consumer Information Act,* U.S. Government Printing Office, 1975, p. 65.
10. Statement by Alfred Franklin before the Subcommittee on Dairy and Poultry of the Committee on Agriculture, U.S. House of Representatives, on The Dairy Herd Reduction Act of 1978 (H.R. 10768), April 6, 1978.
11. Fergus Clydesdale and Frederick Francis, *Food, Nutrition and You,* Prentice-Hall, 1977, p. 168.
12. *Handbook on the Care and Management of Farm Animals,* ed. University Federation of Animal Welfare, Churchill & Livingstone, 1971.
13. Jon A. Jackson, "The Life and Death of an American Chicken," *Saturday Review,* September 2, 1972, p. 12.
14. Peter Singer, *Animal Liberation,* New York Review Book, 1975, p. 116.
15. C. E. Ostrander and R. J. Young, "Effects of Density on Caged Layers," *New York Food and Life Sciences,* vol. 3, no. 3 (July–September, 1970), pp. 5–6.

16. Michael Pousner, "Of the Narrow Cell and the Thinning Shell," New York *Daily News,* September 1, 1971, p. 54.

17. Singer, supra note 14, pp. 111–12.

18. Pousner, supra note 16, p. 54.

19. Mary Rita Kiereck, "Which Comes First?," *Upstate,* August 5, 1973, p. 8.

20. D. M. Hegsted, "Calcium Requirements," *Nutrition Reviews,* vol. 15, no. 9 (September, 1957), p. 257.

21. Ibid., p. 258.

22. Bernard L. Oser, Ph.D., ed., *Hawk's Physiological Chemistry,* 14th ed., McGraw-Hill, 1965, p. 712.

23. Ibid., p. 714.

24. *Recommended Dietary Allowances,* 8th ed., National Academy of Sciences, 1974, p. 55.

25. Robert Goodhart, M.D., and Maurice Shils, M.D., *Modern Nutrition in Health and Disease,* Lea & Febiger, 5th ed., 1973; reprint, 1978, p. 273.

26. Ibid., p. 273.

27. E. Lester Smith, "Vitamin B_{12}," *Plant Foods in Human Nutrition,* Pergamon Press (N. Ireland), vol. 2, 1970, p. 69.

28. U. D. Register, Ph.D., "Are Nonflesh Proteins Adequate?," *Review and Herald,* August 7, 1958.

29. Frey R. Ellis, M.D., and V. M. E. Montegriffo, "The Health of Vegans," *Plant Foods in Human Nutrition,* Pergamon Press (N. Ireland), vol. 2, no. 2 (1971), p. 95.

30. Frey R. Ellis, M.D., and V. M. E. Montegriffo, "Veganism, Clinical Findings and Investigations," *American Journal of Clinical Nutrition,* vol. 23, no. 3 (March, 1970), p. 253.

31. Smith, supra note 27, p. 70.

32. Mervyn G. Hardinge, M.D., and Fredrick J. Stare, M.D., "Nutritional Studies of Vegetarians: Part I, Nutritional, Physical, and Laboratory Studies," *Journal of Clinical Nutrition,* vol. 2, no. 2 (March–April, 1954), p. 76.

CHAPTER 2. THE PROTEIN MYTH

1. Mervyn G. Hardinge, M.D., Hulda Crooks, and Fredrick J. Stare, M.D., "Nutritional Studies of Vegetarians: Part V, Proteins and Their Essential Amino Acids," *Journal of the American Dietetic Association,* vol. 48, no. 1 (January, 1966), p. 27.

2. Committee on Nutritional Misinformation, National Academy of Sciences, "Can a Vegetarian Be Well Nourished," *Journal of the American Medical Association,* vol. 233, no. 8 (August 25, 1975), p. 898.

3. J. B. Orr and J. L. Gilks, "Studies in Nutrition: The Physique and Health of Two African Tribes," *Medical Research Council, Special Report Series,* no. 135, London, H.M. Stationery Office, 1931.

4. Albert Sanchez, M.S., J. A. Scharffenberg, M.D., and U. D. Register, Ph.D., "Nutritive Value of Selected Proteins and Protein Combinations," *American Journal of Clinical Nutrition,* vol. 13, no. 4 (October, 1963), p. 247.

5. Ibid., p. 247.

6. Hardinge, M.D., et al., supra note 1, p. 27.

7. Mervyn G. Hardinge, M.D., and Fredrick J. Stare, M.D., "Nutritional Studies of Vegetarians: Part I, Nutritional, Physical, and Laboratory Studies," *Journal of Clinical Nutrition,* vol. 2, no. 2 (March–April, 1954), p. 81.

8. "Spun Vegetable Protein with Texture that Stands Up to Anything You Can Dish Out," *National Provisioner,* October 2, 1971, pp. 18–19.

CHAPTER 3. ANATOMY, DIET, AND DISEASE

1. Plutarch, "On Eating of Flesh," *Plutarch's Moralia,* vol. 12, tr. Harold Cherniss and William Helmbold, Loeb Classical Library, Harvard University Press, 1957, pp. 551, 553.

2. Percy Bysshe Shelley, "A Vindication of Natural Diet," *Shelley's Prose or the Trumpet of a Prophecy,* ed. David Lee Clark, University of New Mexico Press, 1954, p. 83.

3. Ibid., p. 84.

4. "Western Civilization, Diet, and Disease," *Drug Therapy,* January, 1974, pp. 54, 59.

5. Mervyn G. Hardinge, M.D., et al., "Nutritional Studies of Vegetarians: III. Dietary Levels of Fiber," *American Journal of Clinical Nutrition,* vol. 6, no. 5 (September–October, 1958), pp. 523–24.

6. John Harvey Kellogg, M.D., *The New Dietetics,* Modern Medicine Publishing Co., 1927, p. 870.

7. Pamela Howard and Sandy Treadwell, "Dr. Atkins Says He's Sorry," *New York Magazine,* vol. 6, March 26, 1973, p. 57.

8. (a) Michael J. Hill, M.D., "Metabolic Epidemiology of Dietary Factors in Large Bowel Cancer," *Cancer Research,* vol. 35, no. 11, part 2 (November, 1975), pp. 3398–3402.

    (b) W. E. C. More and L. V. Holdeman, "Discussion of Current Bacteriological Investigations of the Relationships between Intestinal Flora, Diet, and Colon Cancer," *Cancer Research,* vol. 35, no. 11, part 2 (November, 1975), pp. 3418–20.

    (c) Michael J. Hill, M.D., et al., "Bacteria and Etiology of Cancer of Large Bowel," *Lancet,* January 16, 1971, pp. 95–100.

    (d) Bandaru S. Reddy, Ph.D., and Ernest L. Wynder, M.D., "Large-Bowel Carcinogenesis: Fecal Constituents of Populations with Diverse Incidence Rates of Colon Cancer," *Journal of National Cancer Institute,* vol. 50, 1973, pp. 1437–1441.

9. Hill, et al., supra note 8 (c).

10. Reddy and Wynder, supra note 8 (d).

11. "Diet Changes Alter Stomach Flora," *Journal of American Medical Association,* vol. 230, no. 1 (October 7, 1974), p. 23.

12. (a) Hill, et al., supra note 8 (a).

    (b) More and Holdeman, supra note 8 (b).

(c) Hill et al., supra note 8 (c).

(d) Reddy and Wynder, supra note 8 (d).

(e) *Drug Therapy*, supra note 4, p. 59.

(f) *JAMA*, supra note 11.

13. (a) "Roughage in the Diet," *Medical World News*, September 6, 1974, p. 41.

(b) *Drug Therapy*, supra note 4, p. 55.

14. *Drug Therapy*, supra note 4, p. 54.

15. William S. Collens, M.D., "Atherosclerotic Disease: An Anthropologic Theory," *Medical Counterpoint*, December, 1969, pp. 54, 56.

16. William E. Connor, M.D., and Sonja L. Connor, "The Role of Nutritional Factors in the Prevention of Coronary Heart Disease," *Preventive Medicine*, vol. 1, Academic Press, 1972, p. 60.

17. Edward J. Masoro, Ph.D., *Physiological Chemistry of Lipids in Mammals*, W. B. Saunders, 1968, p. 122.

18. Connor and Connor, supra note 16, p. 60.

19. R. J. Rossiter and K. P. Strickland, "The Metabolism and Function of Phosphatides" from *Lipide Metabolism*, ed. Konrad Block, John Wiley & Sons, 1960, p. 113.

20. Samuel A. Levinson, M.D., "The Effect of a Relief Vegetable Protein Diet on 'Normal' Human Subjects," *Journal of American Dietetic Association*, vol. 22, November, 1946, pp. 992–93.

21. Folke Henschen, "Geographic and Historical Pathology of Arteriosclerosis," *Journal of Gerontology*, vol. 8, 1953, pp. 1–5.

22. Alex Strom, M.D., and R. Adelsten Jensen, M.D., "Mortality from Circulatory Diseases in Norway 1940–1945," *Lancet*, vol. 260, January 20, 1951, pp. 126–29.

23. Kyu Taik Lee, M.D., et al., "Chemicopathologic Studies in Geographic Pathology," *Archives of Internal Medicine*, vol. 109, 1962, pp. 426–27.

24. Connor and Connor, supra note 16, p. 52.

25. "Diet and Coronary Heart Disease," a statement developed by the Committee on Nutrition and authorized for release by the central committee for medical and community program of the American Heart Association. American Heart Association, 1973.

26. "Diet and Coronary Heart Disease," *Journal of the American Medical Association*, vol. 222, no. 13, (December 25, 1972), p. 1647.

27. Ancel Keys, Ph.D., "Diet and the Epidemiology of Coronary Heart Disease," *Journal of American Medical Association*, vol. 164, no. 17 (August 24, 1957), p. 1916.

28. B. Bronte-Stewart, M.D., et al., "Serum-Cholesterol, Diet, and Coronary Heart-Disease," *Lancet*, November 26, 1955, p. 1105.

29. (a) *Medical World News*, supra note 13 (a), pp. 36–37.

(b) Knut Kirkeby, "Plasma Lipids on a Moderately Low-Fat, High-Carbohydrate Diet, Rich in Polyunsaturated Fatty Acids," *Acta Medica Scandinavica*, vol. 180, 1966, pp. 772, 775.

(c) *Drug Therapy*, supra note 4, pp. 55, 59.

(d) Hugh Trowell, "Ischemic Heart Disease and Dietary Fiber," *American Journal of Clinical Nutrition*, vol. 25, September, 1972, pp. 928–29, 932.

30. Trowell, supra note 29d, p. 928.

31. Sherman M. Mellinkoff, M.D., et al., "The Effect of a Fat-free Diet in Causing Low Serum Cholesterol," *American Journal of Medical Sciences,* vol. 220, 1950, p. 220.

32. Frank Richman, M.D., et al., "Changes in Serum Cholesterol During the Stillman Diet," *Journal of American Medical Association,* vol. 228, no. 1 (April 1, 1974), p. 57.

33. (a) Bernard L. Oser, Ph.D., ed., *Hawk's Physiological Chemistry,* McGraw-Hill, 14th ed., 1965, p. 787.

    (b) Keys, supra note 27, p. 1916.

    (c) Jane E. Brody, "Chemical Carriers of Cholesterol Puts Light on Heart-Attack Puzzle," *New York Times,* January 18, 1977, p. 13.

    (d) B. Bronte-Stewart, supra note 28, pp. 1103–107.

34. Knut Kirkeby, "Blood Lipids, Lipoproteins, and Proteins in Vegetarians," *Acta Medica Scandinavica,* vol. 149, 1966, supplement 443, pp. 52–55.

35. J. Gordon Barrow, M.D., et al., "Studies in Atherosclerosis: III. An Epidemiologic Study of Atherosclerosis in Trappist and Benedictine Monks: A Preliminary Report," *Annals of Internal Medicine,* vol. 52, no. 2 (February, 1960), pp. 372–75.

36. Report of Inner-Society Commission for Heart Disease Resources, *Circulation,* vol. 42, December, 1970, p. A-84.

37. (a) Kyu Taik Lee, M.D., et al., "Geographic Studies of Atherosclerosis: the Effect of a Strict Vegetarian Diet on Serum Lipid and Electrocardiographic Patterns," *Archives of Environmental Health,* vol. 4, no. 1 (January, 1962), pp. 14–15.

    (b) Richard T. Walden, M.D., et al., "Effect of Environment on the Serum Cholesterol-Triglyceride Distribution Among Seventh-Day Adventists," *American Journal of Medicine,* vol. 36, February, 1964, p. 271.

    (c) Mervyn G. Hardinge, M.D., et al., "Nutritional Studies of Vegetarians: IV. Dietary Fatty Acids and Serum Cholesterol Levels," *American Journal of Clinical Nutrition,* vol. 10, no. 6 (June, 1962), pp. 522–23.

    (d) Kirkeby, supra note 29(b), p. 771.

    (e) Barrow et al., supra note 35, p. 372.

    (f) Kirkeby, supra note 34, pp. 58–59.

38. Hardinge et al., supra note 37c, p. 522.

39. (a) Mervyn G. Hardinge, M.D., and Fredrick J. Stare, M.D., "Nutritional Studies of Vegetarians: II. Dietary and Serum Levels of Cholesterol," *Journal of Clinical Nutrition,* vol. 2, no. 2 (March–April, 1954), p. 86.

    (b) Lee et al., supra note 37(a) pp. 14–15.

    (c) Walden et al., supra note 37(b), pp. 272–74.

    (d) Kirkeby, supra note 37(d), p. 769.

    (e) Barrow et al., supra note 35, p. 372.

    (f) Kirkeby, supra note 34, p. 46.

40. (a) Frey Ellis, M.D., and V. M. E. Montegriffo, "Veganism, Clinical Findings and Investigations," *American Journal of Clinical Nutrition,* vol. 23, no. 3 (March, 1970), p. 252.

    (b) Lee et al., supra note 37(a), pp. 14–15.

    (c) Hardinge and Stare, supra note 39(a), p. 86.

41. Amnon Wachman, M.D., and Daniel S. Bernstein, M.D., "Diet and Osteoporosis," *Lancet,* May 4, 1968, p. 958.

42. Frey R. Ellis, M.D., and John W. Ellis, B. S., "Incidence of Osteoporosis in Vegetarians and Omnivores," *American Journal of Clinical Nutrition,* vol. 25, June, 1972, p. 555.

43. Oser, supra note 33(a), p. 1193.

44. Ellis, supra note 42, p. 557.

CHAPTER 4. THE MEAT INDUSTRY, THE CONSUMER, AND THE LAW

1. (a) "A Close Look at Hamburger," *Consumer Reports,* August, 1971, pp. 478, 479, 482.

    (b) "Frankfurters," *Consumer Reports,* February, 1972, pp. 74–66.

    (c) "Sausages for Breakfast," *Consumer Reports,* August, 1968, pp. 410–11.

2. Statement by Dr. Richard Novick, Chief, Department of Plasmid Biology, Public Health Research Institute, New York, N.Y., hearings before the Subcommittee on Agricultural Research and General Legislation of the Committee on Agriculture, Nutrition, and Forestry, U.S. Senate, September 21, 1977. *Food Safety and Quality: Use of Antibiotics in Animal Feed,* U.S. Government Printing Office, 1977, p. 24.

3. Harrison Wellford, *Sowing the Wind,* (orig. pub. 1972), Bantam, 1973, p. 46.

4. *Second Report of the Joint FAO/WHO Committee on Meat Hygiene,* 1962, p. 30.

5. Ibid., p. 31.

6. Michael Clark, "It's Time to Stamp Out Trichinosis!" *Prevention,* January, 1975, p. 137.

7. Robert H. Moser, M.D., "Trichinosis: From Bismarck to Polar Bears," *Journal of the American Medical Association,* vol. 228, no. 6 (May 6, 1974), p. 737.

8. *An Evaluation of the Salmonella Problem,* a report of the USDA and FDA, prepared by the Committee on Salmonella, National Research Council, National Academy of Sciences, 1969, p. 6.

9. "Salmonellae in Slaughter Cattle," *Journal of American Veterinary Medical Association,* vol. 160, no. 6 (March 10, 1972), p. 884.

10. "Salmonella Contamination in a Commercial Poultry (Broiler) Processing Operation," *Poultry Science,* vol. 53, 1974, pp. 814–21.

11. Wellford, supra note 3, pp. 133–34.

12. Committee on Salmonella, National Research Council, supra note 8, p. 10.

13. Ibid., p. 129.

14. Ibid., p. 125.

15. (a) "Oral Beefs Only," New York *Daily News,* April 21, 1973.

    (b) John J. O'Connor, "TV: the Agribusiness," *New York Times,* December 21, 1973.

    (c) Peter Schuck, "The Curious Case of the Indicted Meat Inspectors," *Harper's Magazine,* September, 1977, pp. 81–88.

    (d) Wellford, supra note 3, pp. 47–48.

16. Schuck, supra note 15(c), p. 82.

17. Jean Snyder, "What You'd Better Know About the Meat You Eat," *Today's Health,* vol. 49, December, 1971, pp. 38–39.

18. Statement by Donald Kennedy, Commissioner, FDA, June 7, 1977, submitted to Subcommittee on Agricultural Research and General Legislation of the Committee on Agriculture, Nutrition, and Forestry, U.S. Senate. *Food Safety and Quality: Regulation of Chemicals in Food and Agriculture,* U.S. Government Printing Office, 1977, pp. 101–104.

19. Statement of David A. Phillipson, D.V.M., President, Animal Health Institute, and Vice President, Upjohn Co., hearings before the Subcommittee on Agricultural Research and General Legislation of the Committee on Agriculture, Nutrition, and Forestry, U.S. Senate, September 22, 1977. *Food Safety and Quality: Use of Antibiotics in Animal Feed,* U.S. Government Printing Office, 1977, p. 36.

20. William Lijinsky and Samuel S. Epstein, "Nitrosamines as Environmental Carcinogens," *Nature,* vol. 225, January 3, 1970, pp. 22, 23.

21. O'Connor, supra note 15(b).

22. "Arsenic in Chicken Liver to Be Reviewed by Agency," *Wall Street Journal,* January, 13, 1972.

23. Snyder, supra note 17, p. 67.

24. William Proxmire, "The Great Debate: DES in Meat," *Environmental Quality,* August, 1972, p. 52.

25. "Livestock Drug Freed from Ban," *New York Times,* January 26, 1974.

26. Hearing before Subcommittee on Health and the Environment of the Committee on Interstate and Foreign Commerce, House of Representatives, on Title I of S. 963, December 16, 1975. *Diethylstilbestrol (DES),* U.S. Government Printing Office, 1976, p. 30.

27. Phillipson, supra note 19, p. 36.

28. Novick, supra note 2, p. 27.

29. Ibid., p. 27.

30. "Drogen im Futter, Gift auf den Tisch," *Der Spiegel,* June 21, 1971, p. 52.

31. Novick, supra note 2, pp. 17, 27.

32. Ibid., p. 17.

33. Phillipson, supra note 19, p. 36.

34. Statement of Mary T. Goodwin, Chairperson, Consumer Liaison Panel, Food and Nutrition Board, National Academy of Sciences, hearings before the Subcommittee on Agricultural Research and General Legislation of the Committee on Agriculture, Nutrition, and Forestry, U.S. Senate, September 22, 1977. *Food Safety and Quality: Use of Antibiotics in Animal Feed,* U.S. Government Printing Office, 1977, p. 119.

35. Murray Kempton, "The Wrong End," *The Progressive,* August, 1974, p. 38.

36. "Mart Is Beefed Up," New York *Daily News,* July 11, 1974, p. 52.

37. *Environmental Quality,* the Sixth Annual Report of the Council on Environmental Quality, U.S. Government Printing Office, December, 1975, p. 212.

38. (a) Ibid., pp. 212–20.
    (b) "Eco Notes," *The Audubon,* May, 1975.

39. Alice M. Rivlin, Director, Congressional Budget Office, letter of December 5, 1977, to Morris K. Udall, Chairperson, Committee on Interior and Insular Affairs,

U.S. House of Representatives. *Report No. 95–859, 95th Congress, 2nd Session on Grazing Fee Moratorium of 1977 (H.R. 9757)*, p. 5.

40. Richard Madden, "Senate Seniority Wins Chicken Battle," *New York Times*, April 24, 1974. See also B. Drummond Ayres, Jr., "Swift Killing of Tainted Chicken Pushed in South," *New York Times*, March 28, 1974, p. 40.

41. *Disaster Assistance for Farmers*, U.S. Government Printing Office, January 18, 1978, p. 46.

42. David T. Cook, "Gloom Thick in Beef Industry," *Christian Science Monitor*, July 18, 1974, financial section, p. 7.

43. "Cattlemen's Beef," *New York Times* editorial, June 30, 1974.

44. Dick Seim, "Producer Promotion Can Help Meat Sales," *Farm Journal*, February, 1970, p. 35.

45. Statement of George W. Strathearn, Manager, California Beef Council, hearing before the Subcommittee on Agricultural Research and General Legislation of the Committee on Agriculture and Forestry, U.S. Senate, on S. 772, April 14, 1975. *Beef Research and Consumer Information Act*, U.S. Government Printing Office, 1975, p. 54.

46. Statement of Robert Choat, President, Council on Children, Media and Merchandising (Washington, D.C.), before the Subcommittee on Domestic Marketing, Consumer Relations, and Nutrition of the Committee on Agriculture, House of Representatives, September 27, 1977. *Nutrition Education*, U.S. Government Printing Office, 1977, p. 65.

47. Strathearn, supra note 45, pp. 51–52.

CHAPTER 5. FISH AND OTHER MARINE ANIMALS

1. Bernard Gui, *Practice of the Inquisition into Heretical Perversity* (1325), quoted in G. G. Coulton, *Inquisition and Liberty*, (orig. pub., 1938), Peter Smith, 1969, p. 74.

2. Benjamin Franklin, *Benjamin Franklin's Autobiographical Writings*, ed. Carl Van Doren, Viking Press, 1945, p. 226.

3. William Paley, *The Principles of Moral and Political Philosophy* (1785), Harper & Brothers, 1849, pp. 283–84.

4. William Paley, *Natural Theology* (1802), *Works of William Paley*, vol. 4, George Cowie & Co., 1837, p. 322.

5. James Thomson, "Spring," from *The Seasons*, 1746 edition, line 425.

6. Ibid., line 396.

7. Ibid., line 392.

8. Ibid., lines 384–89.

9. Brigid Brophy, *Don't Never Forget*, Holt, Rinehart and Winston, 1966, p. 15.

10. Ibid., p. 21.

11. Peter Singer, *Animal Liberation*, New York Review Book, 1975, p. 186.

12. Ibid., p. 188.

13. Ibid., p. 188.

14. Jacques-Yves Cousteau, "Butchery at Sea," *Saturday Review*, July 10, 1976, p. 43.

15. Lester R. Brown, *In the Human Interest*, W. W. Norton, 1974, p. 46.

16. Lester R. Brown, *Man and His Environment: Food,* Harper & Row, 1972, p. 92.

17. *Environmental Quality,* sixth annual report of the Council on Environmental Quality, U.S. Government Printing Office, December, 1975, p. 80.

18. Harold R. Jones, *Pollution Control in Meat, Poultry, and Seafood Processing,* Noyes Data Corp., 1974, pp. 229–36.

19. Ibid., p. 229.

20. Ibid., p. 237.

21. Ibid., p. 238.

22. Seth Lipsky, "Come to the Fish Fry at Dow and Find Out How Bad Fish Can Be," *Wall Street Journal,* January 9, 1973.

23. *Environmental Quality,* supra note 17, p. 387.

24. Richard Severo,, "Environment at Issue: Slow Response of New York State Agency on PCBs and Mirex Raises Key Questions," *New York Times,* September 14, 1976, p. 36.

25. Rachel Carson, *Silent Spring,* Houghton Mifflin, 1962, pp. 26–27.

26. Jack Lucas, *Our Polluted Food,* John Wiley & Sons, 1974, p. 167.

27. Barry Commoner, *The Closing Circle: Nature, Man and Technology,* Alfred A. Knopf, 1971, p. 166.

28. Richard Halloran, "Japanese Decide Pollution Case," *New York Times,* March 21, 1973.

29. "Tuna Cans Recalled in Woman's Death," New York *Daily News,* May 4, 1973.

30. "FDA Warning on Swordfish," New York *Post,* May 6, 1971.

31. "Frozen Fish Sticks," *Consumer Reports,* September, 1970, p. 546.

32. *An Evaluation of the Salmonella Problem,* a report of the USDA and FDA, prepared by the Committee on Salmonella, National Research Council, National Academy of Sciences, 1969, p. 31.

33. Eugene J. Gangarosa, M.D., et al., "Epidemic of Febrile Gastroenteritis Due to Salmonella Java Traced to Smoked Whitefish," *American Journal of Public Health,* vol. 58, no. 1 (January, 1968), pp. 114–21.

34. "Government Official Says Some Frozen Fish Inedible," *Health Bulletin,* May 8, 1965, p. 1.

35. "Frozen Breaded Fish Portions," *Consumer Reports,* May, 1965, p. 235.

36. N. P. Sen, "Nitrosamines," from *Toxic Constituents of Animal Foodstuffs,* ed. Irvin E. Liener, Academic Press, 1974, p. 133.

37. Caryl Rivers, "After the Red Tide," *Saturday Review,* November 25, 1972, pp. 13–16.

38. Arthur F. Novak, "Microbiological Considerations in the Handling and Processing of Crustacean Shellfish," from *Microbial Safety of Fishery Products,* ed. C. O. Chichester and H. D. Graham, Academic Press, 1973, p. 60.

CHAPTER 6. DIET AND ECONOMY

1. "Drogen im Futter, Gift auf den Tisch," *Der Spiegel,* June 21, 1972, p. 49; also Judith Randal, "Down on the Farm, Medicated Feed Breeds a New Brand of 'Bugs,' " New York *Daily News,* January 9, 1976, p. 46.

2. Georg Borgstrom, *The Hungry Planet,* Collier, 1967, p. 311.

3. Richard Oliver, "Packers' Profit: Often Lean, Rarely Juicy," New York *Daily News,* April 4, 1972, pp. 3, 69.

4. Everett Groseclose, "Hoof to Hamburger: Follow Cattle Herd to Market Helps Show Why Meat's So Costly," *Wall Street Journal,* May 24, 1973, p. 29.

5. Ibid.

6. N. W. Pirie, *Food Resources, Conventional and Novel,* Pelican Books, 1969, p. 130.

7. Zbigniew Duda, *Vegetable Protein Meat Extenders and Analogues,* FAO of the UN, Rome, 1974, p. 5, figure 1.

8. Alan Berg and Robert J. Muscat, *The Nutrition Factor, Its Role in National Development,* a study sponsored jointly by the foundation for child development and the Brookings Institution, published in *National Nutritional Policy: Selected Papers on Technology, Agriculture Advances and Production,* prepared for the Select Committee on Nutrition and Human Needs, U.S. Senate, U.S. Government Printing Office, June, 1974, p. 23.

9. Borgstrom, supra note 2, p. 407.

10. Aaron M. Altschul, *Proteins, Their Chemistry and Politics,* Basic Books, 1965, p. 264.

11. *Energy and Protein Requirements,* report by joint FAO/WHO Ad Hoc Expert Committee, FAO Nutrition Series, no. 52, WHO Technical Report Series, no. 522, FAO of the UN, Rome, 1973, p. 19.

12. Ibid.

13. Boyce Rensberger, "Curb on U.S. Waste Urged to Help World's Hungry," *New York Times,* October 25, 1974, p. 20.

14. Ibid.

15. H. J. Maidenburg, "The Livestock Population Explosion," *New York Times,* July 1, 1973, p. 1, business and finance section.

16. Jane E. Brody, "The Quest for Protein," from *Give Us This Day . . . ,* Arno Press, 1975, p. 222.

17. Mary Bralove, "The Food Crisis: the Shortages May Pit the 'Have Nots' Against the 'Haves,' " *Wall Street Journal,* October 3, 1974, p. 20.

18. L. Dudley Stamp, *Land for Tomorrow: Our Developing World,* Indiana University Press, revised 1969, p. 121.

19. Lester Brown and Gail W. Finsterbusch, *Man and His Environment: Food,* Harper & Row, 1972, p. 26.

20. F. Wokes, "Proteins," *Plant Foods in Human Nutrition,* vol. 1, Pergamon Press (N. Ireland), 1968, p. 28.

21. James P. Sterba, "Direct Use of Soy Protein Cut by Taste for Meat," *New York Times,* August 17, 1974, p. 19.

22. Boyce Rensberger, "World Food Crisis: Basic Ways of Life Face Upheaval from Chronic Shortages," *New York Times,* November 5, 1974, p. 14.

23. Alastair I. MacKay, *Farming and Gardening in the Bible,* (orig. pub. 1950), Spire, 1970, p. 18.

24. I Kings 4:23.

25. Richard Lewinsohn, *Animals, Men and Myths,* tr. from German, Harper & Brothers, 1954, p. 370.

26. Ibid.

27. Rensberger, supra note 13, p. 20.
28. Lester R. Brown with Erik P. Eckholm, *By Bread Alone*, Praeger, 1974, pp. 106–107.
29. Rensberger, supra note 13, p. 20.
30. "For Beef: Less Grain, More Roughage," *Farm Journal*, October, 1975, p. 72.
31. James L. Breeling, "How Does Animal Feed Influence Meat Flavor," *Journal of American Medical Association*, vol. 227, no. 9 (March 4, 1974), p. 1067.
32. *Farm Journal*, supra note 30, p. 72.
33. Vance Bourjaily, "Eight Months on Full Feed," *Harper's*, March, 1972, p. 78.
34. Maidenburg, supra note 15, p. 1.
35. Borgstrom, supra note 2, p. 327.
36. Ibid., p. 380.
37. Maidenburg, supra note 15, p. 1.
38. "Here's What Grazing Land Costs—By Regions," *Successful Farming*, March, 1976, p. B12.
39. Colin Clark, *Starvation or Plenty*, Taplinger, 1970, p. 97.
40. Ibid.
41. Maidenburg, supra note 15, p. 1.
42. *Environmental Quality:* the sixth annual report of the Council on Environmental Quality, U.S. Government Printing Office, December, 1975, p. 109.
43. James E. Roper, "Why Food Prices Keep Rising," *Reader's Digest*, January, 1973, p. 64.
44. Ibid.
45. Ibid.
46. William Robbins, "Smaller Crops in U.S. Dims Prospects for Large World Food Assistance," *New York Times*, September 22, 1974, p. 31.
47. Rensberger, supra note 13, p. 20.
48. Ibid., p. 44.
49. "Nibbling at Food Prices," *Time*, July 10, 1972, p. 76.
50. Maidenburg, supra note 15, p. 3, business and finance section.
51. Theodore Shabad, "Basic Soviet Grain Policy Change Seen," *New York Times*, August 2, 1975, pp. 27, 31, business and finance section.
52. "Soviet Union: Meatless Thursdays," *Newsweek*, vol. 87, May 31, 1976, p. 34.
53. "Are Some Counties Disaster-Prone?" *Farm Journal*, June–July, 1975, p. 6.
54. Harold M. Schmeck, "Changing Climates Threaten Food Supplies," from *Give Us This Day . . .* , Arno Press, 1975, p. 174.
55. "Fertilize Pasture? Sometimes Yes; Sometimes No," *Successful Farming*, March, 1976, p. 34.
56. Clyde H. Farnsworth, "U.S. Urges a Curb on Fertilizer Use Except for Crops," *New York Times*, November 10, 1974, p. 35.
57. "Farmcast," *Farm Journal*, June–July, 1976, p. 2.
58. Brown and Finsterbusch, supra note 19, p. 171.
59. Barry Commoner, *The Closing Circle: Nature, Man and Technology*, Alfred A. Knopf, 1971, p. 150.

60. Ibid., p. 149.
61. Harold Farber, "Farms in State Declined 32% Over 10-Year Period," *New York Times*, February 7, 1972, p. 22.
62. *Report to the President and to the Council on Environmental Quality* by the Citizens' Advisory Committee on Environmental Quality, submitted December 31, 1974, U.S. Government Printing Office, April, 1975, p. 24.
63. Ibid., p. 23.
64. *Environmental Quality*, supra note 42, p. 179.
65. Ibid.
66. Ibid., p. 180.
67. *Report to Pres., Environmental Quality*, supra note 62, p. 24.
68. Borgstrom, supra note 2, p. 40.
69. Declaration of an emergency by the executive board of UNICEF issued May 24, 1974.
70. *Reference Material to Part I, Food Price Changes, 1973–74*, prepared by the staff of the Select Committee on Nutrition and Human Needs, U.S. Senate, U.S. Government Printing Office, February, 1974, p. 181.
71. "Meatless Menus Urged by Bishop," *New York Times*, November 3, 1974, p. 29B.
72. William Reel, "Offer Meaty Proposal to Help the Starving," New York *Daily News*, June 9, 1974, p. 63.
73. "Food Supply of the World" from table 2, *Encyclopaedia Britannica*, vol. 7, p. 500.
74. Borgstrom, supra note 2, p. 332.
75. Brown and Finsterbusch, supra note 19, p. 87.
76. W. R. Aykroyd and Joyce Doughty, *Legumes in Human Nutrition*, FAO of the UN, FAO Nutritional Studies no. 19, 1964, pp. 81–82.
77. *Manual of Nutrition*, Ministry of Agriculture, Fisheries and Food, Her Majesty's Stationery Office, London, 1970, p. 46.
78. Berg and Muscat, supra note 8, p. 62.
79. Ibid., p. 59.
80. Harold M. Schmeck, Jr., "Malnutrition, the Global Scourge," from *Give Us This Day . . .* , Arno Press, 1975, pp. 85–86.
81. *Food Price Changes, 1973–74*, supra note 70, p. 163.
82. Ibid., p. 199.
83. "A Close Look at Hamburger," *Consumer Reports*, August, 1971, p. 480.
84. "Frankfurters," *Consumer Reports*, February, 1972, p. 75.
85. MacKay, supra note 23, p. 224.
86. Genesis 13:5–7.
87. Numbers 31:32–33.
88. Plato, *The Republic*, Book II, tr. B. Jowett.
89. Ibid.
90. Henry Weinstein, "CIA Report Says Worsening World Grain Shortages Could Give U.S. Great Power," *New York Times*, March 17, 1975, p. 13. Quotes used in article are taken from CIA report of August, 1974, entitled "Potential Implications of Food, Population and Climate."
91. Ibid.

CHAPTER 7. ECOLOGY AND VEGETARIANISM

1. Boyce Rensberger, "Can Eating Less Meat Here Relieve Starvation in the World," *New York Times,* November 28, 1974, p. 44.
2. Raymond C. Loehr, *Pollution Implications of Animal Wastes—A Forward Oriented Review,* prepared for Office of Research and Monitoring, Environmental Protection Agency, July, 1968, reprinted June, 1973, p. 48.
3. Ibid., p. 127.
4. Bruce Myles, "U.S. Antipollution Laws May Boost Cattle-Feeders' Cost—and Meat Prices," *Christian Science Monitor,* March 11, 1974, p. 3A.
5. Ibid.
6. Ibid.
7. James P. Sterba, "Cattle Fed from Own Waste to Cut Protein Shortage," *New York Times,* September 9, 1973, p. 40B.
8. Myles, supra note 4.
9. Loehr, supra note 2, p. 5.
10. Ibid., p. 77.
11. Lester R. Brown, *In the Human Interest,* W. W. Norton, 1974, p. 31.
12. Lester R. Brown and Gail W. Finsterbusch, *Man and His Environment: Food,* Harper & Row, 1972, p. 69.
13. Paul R. Ehrlich and Anne H. Ehrlich, *Population, Resources, Environment,* W. H. Freeman, 1972, p. 75.
14. John Hollis and James McEvoy III, "Demographic Effects of Water Development," from *Environmental Quality and Water,* ed. Charles R. Goldman, James McEvoy III, et al., W. H. Freeman, 1973, p. 220.
15. Ehrlich, supra note 13, pp. 75–76.
16. Sylvia Porter, "Food Price Rises," New York *Post,* July 27, 1973.
17. *Pollution Control Costs and Research Priorities in the Animal Slaughtering and Processing Industries,* Sub-Council Report, National Industrial Pollution Control Council, June, 1973, p. 19.
18. A. J. Steffen, "Waste Disposal in the Meat Industry: A Comprehensive Review of Practice in the U.S.," *Pure and Applied Chemistry,* vol. 29, 1972, pp. 173–74.
19. Ron Litton, *Terracide,* Little, Brown, 1970, pp. 291–92.
20. Jean Dorst, *Before Nature Dies,* Pelican Books, 1971, p. 147.
21. C. D. Darlington, "The Silent Millennia in the Origin of Agriculture," from *The Domestication and Exploitation of Plants and Animals,* ed. Peter J. Ucko and G. W. Dimbleby, Aldine Atherton, 1969, pp. 68–69.
22. Russell Lord, *The Care of the Earth,* Mentor Books, 1962, p. 102.
23. *Environmental Quality,* sixth annual report of the Council on Environmental Quality, U.S. Government Printing Office, December, 1975, p. 212.
24. Ibid., p. 213.
25. Ibid., p. 213.
26. Ibid., p. 580.
27. Georg Borgstrom, *The Hungry Planet,* Collier, 1967, p. 190.
28. This statistic is cited by the National Parks and Conservation Association, Washington, D.C.

29. Frank Graham, Jr., *Man's Dominion: The Story of Conservation in America,* M. Evans & Co., 1971, p. 211.
30. "Cape Cod's Shellfish Industry Periled by Scarcity and Prices," *New York Times,* October 21, 1974, p. 28.
31. *Environmental Quality,* supra note 23, p. 404.
32. Ibid., p. 404.
33. "The Mustang Hunters," *Newsweek,* April 22, 1974, p. 78.
34. Mike Goodman, "Wild Horses," Los Angeles *Times,* March 3, 1974.
35. *Environmental Quality,* supra note 23, p. 220.
36. Ibid., p. 219.
37. "Eco Notes," *The Audubon,* May, 1975.
38. *Environmental Quality,* supra note 23, p. 219.
39. Ibid., p. 219.

CHAPTER 8. KILLING FOR FOOD

1. Leonard S. Mercia, *Raising Poultry the Modern Way,* Garden Way, 1975, p. 98.
2. Ibid., p. 150.
3. Ruth Harrison, *Animal Machines,* Ballantine Books, 1966, p. 46.
4. D. F. Stevens, "Beef Cattle Management," from *Introduction to Livestock Production,* 2d ed., ed. H. H. Cole, W. H. Freeman & Co., 1966, p. 570.
5. "Livestock Safety," pamphlet published by Livestock Conservation, Inc., Omaha, Neb.
6. "Winter Hints," Livestock Conservation, Inc.
7. "Animals into Meat: A Report on the Pre-Slaughter Handling of Livestock," Argus Archives Report Series, vol. 2, no. 1, New York, N.Y., 1971, p. 4.
8. Ibid., p. 10.
9. Ibid., p. 16.
10. Ibid., p. 17.
11. Ibid., p. 17.

CHAPTER 9. SENSE PERCEPTION AND REALITY

1. Percy Bysshe Shelley, "Essay on the Vegetable System of Diet," *Shelley's Prose or the Trumpet of a Prophecy,* ed. David Lee Clark, University of New Mexico Press, 1954, p. 96.
2. Henry David Thoreau, "Higher Laws," from *Walden,* 1854.
3. Upton Sinclair, *The Jungle,* 1906.
4. Ovid, *Metamorphoses,* Book 15, lines 686–90, tr. John Dryden.
5. Isaac Bashevis Singer, "The Slaughterer," from *The Séance,* Avon Books, 1969, p. 24.
6. *Stories from a Ming Collection,* tr. Cyril Birch, Grove Press, 1958, pp. 10–11.
7. François Voltaire, "Viands," *Philosophical Dictionary* (1764), E. R. DuMont, 1901, vol. 10, p. 160.

8. Plutarch, *The Lives of the Noble Grecians and Romans,* tr. John Dryden, Modern Library, p. 416.

9. Porphyry, *De Abstinentia,* II.57.

10. Plutarch, "De Esu Carnium" ("On the Eating of Flesh"), *Plutarch's Moralia,* vol. XII, tr. Harold Cherniss and William Helmbold, Loeb Classical Library, Harvard University Press, 1957, p. 541.

11. Mohandas K. Gandhi, *An Autobiography, the Story of My Experiments with Truth,* tr. Mahadev Desai (orig. pub. 2 vols., 1927–1929), Beacon Press ed., 1957, p. 22.

CHAPTER 10. VEGETARIANISM IN LITERATURE

1. Porphyry, *De Abstinentia,* I.47. tr. Thomas Taylor.

2. Ibid., II.20.

3. Ibid., II.58.

4. Kenneth Clark, *Leonardo da Vinci, an Account of his Development as an Artist,* Macmillan Co., 1939, p. 4.

5. Leonardo da Vinci, quotations from his notebooks as presented in: *Fantastic Tales, Strange Animals, Riddles, Jests, and Prophecies of Leonardo da Vinci,* ed. and annotated by Emery Kelen, Thomas Nelson, 1971, pp. 117, 119, 120.

6. Leonardo da Vinci, *The Notebooks of Leonardo da Vinci,* ed. and tr. Edward MacCurdy, Jonathan Cape (London), 1938, vol. 2, p. 506.

7. Leonardo da Vinci, quotations from his notebooks as presented in *Leonardo da Vinci, Philosophical Diary,* tr. Wade Baskin, Philosophical Library, 1959, pp. 31–32.

8. Aylmer Maude, *The Life of Tolstoy, Later Years,* 7th ed., Dodd, Mead, 1917, vol. 2, pp. 215–16.

9. Ibid., p. 215.

10. Ilya Tolstoy, *Tolstoy, My Father: Reminiscences,* tr. Ann Dunnigan, Cowles Book Co., 1971, p. 269.

11. Maude, supra note 8, vol. 2, p. 213.

12. Leo Tolstoy, "The First Step" (1892), tr. Aylmer Maude, *Leo Tolstoy, Selected Essays,* Modern Library, Random House, 1964, p. 240.

13. Ibid., p. 234.

14. Ibid., p. 233.

15. Ibid., p. 240.

16. Ibid., p. 241.

17. Alexandra Tolstoy, *Tolstoy, A Life of My Father,* tr. Elizabeth Reynolds Hapgood, Harper & Brothers, 1953, p. 298.

18. Maude, supra note 8, vol. 2, p. 507.

19. George Bernard Shaw, *Sixteen Self Sketches,* Constable & Co., 1949, p. 53.

20. Ibid., p. 53.

21. George Bernard Shaw, *Shaw: An Autobiography, 1856–1898,* selected from his writings by Stanley Weintraub, Weybright and Talley, 1969, p. 92.

22. George Bernard Shaw, letter to Mrs. Pakenham Beatty, August 5, 1886, *Bernard Shaw, Collected Letters, 1874–1897,* ed. Dan Laurence, Dodd, Mead, 1965, p. 157.

23. *The Academy,* October 15, 1898.

24. George Bernard Shaw, *Shaw: An Autobiography, 1898–1950,* selected from his writings by Stanley Weintraub, Weybright and Talley, 1970, p. 7.

25. George Bernard Shaw, *Shaw—"The Chucker Out," A Biographical Exposition and Critique,* ed. Allen Chappelow, George Allen & Unwin, 1962, pp. 15–16.

26. George Bernard Shaw, letter to Joseph Teleki, November 22, 1910, *Bernard Shaw: Collected Letters 1898–1910,* ed. Dan Laurence, Dodd, Mead, 1972, p. 954.

27. Letter to H. G. Wells, August 14, 1907, ibid., p. 711.

28. Shaw, supra note 25, p. 15.

29. Ibid., p. 16.

30. Ibid.

31. Mohandas K. Gandhi, *An Autobiography, the Story of My Experiments with Truth,* tr. Mahadev Desai (orig. pub. 2 vols., 1927–1929), Beacon Press, 1957, pp. 22, 23.

32. Ibid., p. 48.

33. Mohandas K. Gandhi, *The Moral Basis of Vegetarianism,* compiled from Gandhi's writings by R. K. Prabhu, Navajivan Publishing House, 1959, p. 18.

34. Ibid., p. 18.

35. Ibid., p. 20.

36. Ibid., p. 21.

37. Mr. Singer's comments that are presented throughout this section are taken from an interview I had with him in June, 1975.

38. Edward John Trelawny, *Recollections of the Last Days of Shelley and Byron,* 1858.

39. Marguerite Blessington, *Lady Blessington's Conversations of Lord Byron,* ed. Ernest J. Lovell, Jr., Princeton University Press, 1969, p. 36.

40. Ibid., p. 14.

41. Ibid., pp. 86, 35, 36.

42. George Gordon Byron, letter to Thomas Moore, January 28, 1817, *Letters and Journals of Lord Byron,* compiled by Thomas Moore, J. J. Harper, 1830, vol. 1, p. 50.

43. Thomas Moore, letter to Mr. Murray, August 29, 1819, ibid., vol. 1, p. 178. Cf. Blessington, supra note 39, p. 86.

44. Trelawny, supra note 38.

45. Thomas Jefferson Hogg, *The Life of Percy Bysshe Shelley* (1858), J. M. Dent & Sons, 1933, vol. 1, p. 86.

46. Ibid., vol. 1, p. 86.

47. Harriet Shelley, letter to Elizabeth Hitchner, March 14, 1812, *Letters of Percy Bysshe Shelley,* ed. Fredrick L. Jones, Oxford, Clarendon Press, 1964, vol. 1, pp. 274–75.

48. Percy Bysshe Shelley, letter to Leigh and Marianne Hunt, June 29, 1817, supra note 47, vol. 1, p. 543.

49. Thomas Love Peacock, *Memoirs of Shelley.*

50. Ibid.

51. Ibid.

52. Percy Bysshe Shelley, *Alastor or the Spirit of Solitude,* 1815, lines 13–17.

53. Ralph Waldo Emerson, "Thoreau," *Atlantic Monthly,* August, 1862, p. 240.

54. Henry David Thoreau, "Economy," from *Walden*, 1854.
55. "Higher Laws," ibid.
56. "Brute Neighbors," ibid.
57. "Higher Laws," ibid.
58. Ibid.
59. Ibid.
60. Seneca, "On the Approaches to Philosophy," Epistle 108, *Ad Lucilim Morales*, tr. Richard M. Gummere, Harvard University Press, vol. 3, p. 239.
61. Ibid., p. 241.
62. Ibid., p. 243.
63. Plutarch, "Advice on Keeping Well," *Moralia*, tr. Frank Cole Babbitt, Harvard University Press, 1928, reprint 1962, vol. 2, p. 265.
64. Alphonse Lamartine, *Les Confidences (Confidential Disclosures)*, tr. Eugene Plunkett, D. Appleton, 1849, p. 60.
65. Ibid., p. 61.
66. H. Remsen Whitehouse, *The Life of Lamartine*, Houghton Mifflin, 1918, vol. 2, p. 469.
67. Gustav Mahler, letter to Emil Freund, November 1, 1880, quoted in Henry Raynor, *Mahler*, Macmillan, London, 1975, p. 23.
68. Alma Mahler, *Gustav Mahler, Memoires and Letters*, tr. Basil Creighton, (orig. pub. Viking Press, 1946), University of Washington Press, 1968, p. 19.
69. Alexander Pope, *An Essay on Man*, 1733, Epistle I, Part 3, line 84.
70. William Cowper, "The Winter Walk at Noon," *The Task*, 1785, lines 384, 388.
71. Bernard de Mandeville, "Remark (P)," *Fable of the Bees*, (1714), Oxford, Clarendon Press, 1924, vol. 1, p. 173.
72. François Voltaire, "Viands," *Philosophical Dictionary* (1764), E. R. DuMont, 1901, vol. 10, p. 160.
73. Richard Wagner, "An Open Letter to Herr Ernst von Weber, author of the work: 'the Torture-Chambers of Science,' " *Richard Wagner's Prose Works*, tr. William Ashton Ellis (orig. pub. 1897), Scholarly Press, 1972, vol. 6, pp. 196–97.
74. Oliver Goldsmith, "Letter 15," *Citizen of the World*, 1762.
75. Gilbert K. Chesterton, *All Things Considered*, Sheed & Ward, 1956, p. 7.
76. Ovid, *Metamorphoses*, tr. John Dryden, Book 15, lines 137–42.
77. James Thomson, "Spring," *The Seasons*, 1746 edition, lines 234–241.
78. Percy Bysshe Shelley, *Queen Mab*, 1813, VIII, lines 209–229.
79. H. G. Wells, *A Modern Utopia*, Chapman & Hall, 1905, p. 286.
80. H. G. Wells, "Days of Things to Come," *Twenty-Eight Science Fiction Stories* (orig. pub. 1932), Dover, 1952, p. 734.
81. Thomas More, *Utopia* (orig. pub. 1518 in Latin), tr. Robert M. Adams, W. W. Norton, 1975, p. 46.
82. Ibid., p. 46.

CHAPTER 11. VEGETARIANISM AND RELIGION

The following abbreviations are used for the series cited below:

* ANF: *Ante-Nicene Fathers*, ed. Alexander Roberts and James Donaldson, American reprint of Edinburgh edition, Wm. B. Eerdmans (Grand Rapids).

* N&PNF, ser. 1: *Nicene and Post-Nicene Fathers,* series 1, ed. Philip Schaft, Wm. B. Eerdmans (Grand Rapids).

* N&PNF, ser. 2: *Nicene and Post-Nicene Fathers,* series 2, ed. Philip Schaft and Henry Wace, Wm. B. Eerdmans (Grand Rapids).

* SBE: *Sacred Books of the East,* (originally pub. Oxford, Clarendon Press, 1910), Motilal Banarsidass (Delhi).

1. Jerome, "Against Jovinianus," Book II, N&PNF, ser. 2, vol. 6. p. 397. Jerome is quoting here from a treatise by Chaeremon (fl. 1st cent. A.D.).

2. Tertullian, "De Jejuniis: Adversus Psychosis" ("On Fasting in Opposition to the Psychics"), tr. S. Thelwall, ANF, vol. 4, 1965, p. 113.

3. Ibid., p. 112.

4. Titus Flavius Clemens, *Paidagogos* (the Instructor), Book II, ANF, vol. 2, 1967, p. 241.

5. Titus Flavius Clemens, *Stromata (Miscellanies),* ANF, vol. 2, 1967, p. 531.

6. Origen, "De Principiis," ANF, vol. 4, 1965, p. 286.

7. Jerome, supra note 1, p. 396.

8. *The Rule of Saint Benedict,* ch. 39, tr. Cardinal Gasquet, Cooper Square Pub., 1966, p. 73.

9. Ibid., p. 73.

10. George Boas, *Essays on Primitivism and Related Ideas in the Middle Ages,* Johns Hopkins Press, 1948, pp. 115–16.

11. John Ryan, *Irish Monasticism, Origins and Early Developments,* Cornell University Press, 2nd ed., 1972, p. 127.

12. Baba Bathra, sec. 60b, tr. Maurice Simon, *Babylonian Talmud,* Soncino Press (London), 1935, p. 246.

13. *Encyclopaedia Judaica,* vol. 3, Macmillan Co., 1971, p. 697.

14. Hippolytus, *The Refutation of All Heresies,* Book VII, ANF, vol. 5, 1965, p. 110.

15. I Timothy 4:1–2.

16. *Heresies of the High Middle Ages,* ed. and tr. Walter L. Wakefield and Austin P. Evans, Columbia University Press, 1969, p. 480.

17. G. G. Coulton, *Inquisition and Liberty* (orig. pub. William Heinemann, 1938), Peter Smith, 1969, p. 74.

18. Samson Raphael Hirsch, *Hoeb: A Philosophy of Jewish Laws and Obligations,* vol. 2, tr. I. Grunfeld, Soncino Press (London), 1962, p. 328.

19. Baudhayana, ch. 3, part 1, sec. 26, tr. Georg Bühler, *The Sacred Laws of the Āryas,* SBE, vol. 14, 1965, p. 287.

20. *Laws of Manu,* ch. 10, sec. 63, tr. Georg Bühler, SBE, vol. 25, 1965, p. 416.

21. Anugita, ch. 28, 35, tr. Kāshināth Trimbak Telang, *Bhagavadgītā,* SBE, vol. 8, 1965, pp. 348, 378.

22. *Manu,* supra note 20, ch. 5, sec. 48, 49, 51, p. 176.

23. Ibid., ch. 5, sec. 56, p. 177.

24. Vasishtha, ch. 4, sec. 7, tr. Georg Bühler, *The Sacred Laws of the Āryas,* SBE, vol. 14, 1965, p. 27.

25. *Manu,* supra note 20, ch. 5, sec. 52, p. 176.

26. Ibid., ch. 5, sec. 31, p. 174.
27. Ibid., ch. 5, sec. 37, p. 174.
28. Lawrence A. Babb, *The Divine Hierarchy, Popular Hinduism in Central India,* Columbia University Press, 1975, p. 225.
29. Âmagandhasutta of the Kûlavagga from the *Sutta-Nipâta,* tr. V. Fausböll, SBE, vol. 10, 1965, p. 40.
30. D. S. Margoliouth, "Atheism (Muhammadan)," *Encyclopedia of Religion and Ethics,* vol. 2, Scribners, p. 189.
31. St. John Chrysostom, Homily 69 (On Matthew 22:1–4), tr. George Prevost, N&PNF, ser. 1, vol. 10, 1956, p. 425.
32. *A Dictionary of Christian Biography: Literature, Sects and Doctrines During the First Eight Centuries,* vol. 3, ed. William Smith and Henry Wace, AMS Press, 1967, p. 53.
33. Ryan, supra note 11, p. 129.
34. Hosea 2:18.
35. Isaiah 11:6–9.
36. Ibid. 65:25.
37. Genesis 1:29–30.
38. Steven Herbert Langdon, *The Mythology of All Races,* vol. 5, *Semitic Mythology,* Cooper Square Pub., 1964, p. 164.
39. Hippolytus, "On Daniel," ANF, vol. 5, p. 185.
40. Josephus, *The Life,* sec. 3, tr. H. St. J. Thackeray, in *Josephus,* vol. 1, Loeb Classical Library, Harvard University Press, 1926, p. 7.
41. II Maccabees 5:27.
42. Romans 14:2–3.
43. I Corinthians 8:8.
44. Romans 14:13–15, 20–21.
45. I Corinthians 8:12–13.

CHAPTER 12. A HISTORY OF MEAT AS A STATUS SYMBOL

1. I Kings 4:23.
2. Proverbs 15:17.
3. Alastair Mackay, *Farming and Gardening in the Bible* (orig. pub. 1950), Spire, 1970, p. 220.
4. Adam Smith, *Wealth of Nations,* 1776, Modern Library Series, Random House, p. 23.
5. Cato and Varro, *Roman Farm Management,* collected treatises of Cato and Varro on Farming, Macmillan Co., 1913, p. 188.
6. Philo, "De Vita Contemplativa" ("On the Contemplative Life"), *Philo,* vol. IX, tr. F. H. Colson, Loeb Classical Library series, Harvard University Press, 1941, reprinted 1967, pp. 141, 143.
7. Reay Tannahill, *Food in History,* Stein & Day, 1973, p. 94; Cato, supra note 5, p. 318.
8. Ibid., p. 93.

9. H. E. Jacob, *Six Thousand Years of Bread,* tr. Richard and Clara Winston, Greenwood Press, 1970, p. 31.

10. W. R. Aykroyd and Joyce Doughty, *Legumes in Human Nutrition,* FAO of the UN, FAO Nutritional Studies, no. 19, 1964, p. 9.

11. Claudia Roden, *A Book of Middle Eastern Food,* Alfred A. Knopf, 1972, p. 261.

12. C. Suetonius Tranquillus, *The Lives of the Twelve Caesars,* tr. Alexander Thomson, George Bell & Sons, 1909, p. 421.

13. Hsiang Ju Lin and Tsuigeng Lin, *Chinese Gastronomy,* Pyramid, 1972, p. 36.

14. Ibid., pp. 43–44.

15. François Voltaire, *Philosophical Dictionary,* (1764), tr. Theodore Besterman, Penguin Books, 1971, p. 78.

16. Smith, supra note 4, p. 827.

17. *Journals of Captain Meriwether Lewis and Sergeant Ordway,* kept on the expedition of western exploration, 1803–1806, ed. Milo M. Quaite, the State Historical Society of Wis., 1916, reprinted 1965, p. 242.

18. Richard Osborn Cummings, *A History of Food Habits in the United States,* University of Chicago Press, revised ed., 1941, p. 80.

19. Ibid.

20. Aykroyd and Doughty, supra note 10, p. 34.

21. Ibid.

22. Frederick J. Stare and Martha F. Trulson, "The Implantation of Preference," from Seymour M. Farber, M.D., et al., *Food and Civilization: A Symposium,* Charles C. Thomas, 1966, p. 226.

23. Richard Rhodes, "A Bean to Feed the World," *Atlantic Monthly,* January, 1975, p. 38.

CHAPTER 13. FROM NECESSITY TO SIN

1. James Frazer, *The New Golden Bough,* revision of the original *Golden Bough* published 1890, ed. T. Gaster, Mentor, 1959, p. 524.

2. Ibid., p. 224.

3. Ezekiel 33:25.

4. Robert Eisler, *Man into Wolf,* Greenwood Press, 1951, p. 40.

5. Philo, "De Specialibus Legibus" ("The Special Laws"), Part IV, tr. F. A. Colson, *Philo,* vol. 8, Loeb Classical Library, Harvard University Press, 1939, p. 81.

6. Ibid., pp. 79, 81.

7. Frazer, supra note 1, p. 551.

8. Ibid., p. 546.

9. Ibid., p. 552.

10. Ibid., p. 553.

11. Ibid., p. 549.

12. Thomas Hobbes, "Of the Causes, Generation and Definition of a Commonwealth," from *Leviathan,* 1651.

13. John Dewey, "The Unity of the Human Being," an address before the College

of Physicians, St. Louis, April 21, 1937, *John Dewey's Philosophy,* ed. J. Ratner, Modern Library series, Random House, 1939, p. 817.

14. *Webster's New World Dictionary of the American Language,* World Publishing Co., 1964.

15. George Bernard Shaw, "Maxims for Revolutionists," from *Man and Superman,* 1903.

16. Webster, supra note 14.

17. François Voltaire, *Philosophical Dictionary* (1764), tr. Theodore Besterman, Penguin Books, 1971, p. 38.

18. Ibid.

19. Bernard de Mandeville, "Remark (P)," *Fable of the Bees,* (1714), Oxford, Clarendon Press, 1924, vol. 1, p. 178.

20. Leo Tolstoy, "The First Step," (1892), *Leo Tolstoy, Selected Essays,* tr. Alymer Maude, Modern Library series, Random House, 1964, p. 239.

21. Alexandra Tolstoy, *Tolstoy: A Life of My Father,* tr. Elisabeth Reynolds Hapgood, Harper & Brothers, 1953, p. 328.

22. Henry S. Salt, *Seventy Years Among Savages,* George Allen & Unwin, London, 1921, p. 9.

23. M. F. Ashley Montagu, "The New Litany of 'Innate Depravity,' or Original Sin Revisited," from *Man and Aggression,* ed. M. F. Ashley Montagu, Oxford University Press, 1968, pp. 4–5.

24. Ovid, *Metamorphoses,* Book 15, lines 151–154 tr. John Dryden.

25. Alexander Pope, *An Essay on Man,* 1733, Epistle I, Part 6, lines 173–178.

26. Thomas Aquinas, *Summa Contra Gentiles,* Book III, ch. 112, *Basic Writings of Saint Thomas Aquinas,* Random House, vol. 2, p. 222.

27. Pope, supra note 25, Epistle I, Part 3, lines 99–112.

28. Plato, *The Republic,* Book I, tr. B. Jowett.

29. Ibid.

30. Benjamin Franklin, *Benjamin Franklin's Autobiographical Writings,* ed. Carl Van Doren, Viking Press, 1945, p. 226.

31. Ibid., p. 240.

32. Judith Martin, "In Defense of Piggies," Washington *Post,* December 29, 1972, p. B4; Ms. Shriver's quote from personal interview with author.

33. Arlene Pianko Groner, "The Greening of Kashrut," *National Jewish Monthly,* April, 1976, p. 14.

APPENDIX: THE VEGETARIAN MOVEMENT

1. Thomas Jefferson Hogg, *The Life of Percy Bysshe Shelley,* (1858), J. M. Dent & Sons, 1933, vol. 2, p. 84.

2. Ibid., vol. 2, p. 87.

3. Charles W. Forward, *Fifty Years of Food Reform, A History of the Vegetarian Movement in England, 1847–1897,* Ideal Publishing Union, 1898, p. 22.

4. Ibid., p. 76.

5. Ibid.

6. *Time,* September 6, 1948, p. 17.

Index